The Day
Jesus the Christ Died

The Biblical Truth About His
Passion, Crucifixion and Resurrection

by Fred R. Coulter

York Publishing Company
Post Office Box 1038
Hollister, California 95024-1038

All New Testament Scriptures used in
this book are quoted from:
The New Testament In Its
Original Order—A Faithful
Version With Commentary
ISBN 0-9675479-3-8

ISBN 0-9675479-4-6
Copyright 2004 ©
York Publishing Company
Post Office Box 1038
Hollister, California 95024-1038

Table of Contents

Who is Jesus the Christ?

"In *the* beginning was the Word, and the Word was with God, and the Word was God. He was in *the* beginning with God. All things came into being through Him, and not even one *thing* that was created came into being without Him." John 1:1-3

"And undeniably, great is the mystery of godliness: God was manifested in *the* flesh, was justified in *the* Spirit, was seen by angels, was proclaimed among *the* Gentiles, was believed on in *the* world, was received up in glory." I Tim. 3:16

"Christ Jesus, Who, although He existed in *the* form of God, did not consider it robbery to be equal with God, but emptied Himself, *and* was made in *the* likeness of men, *and* took the form of a servant." Phil. 2:5-7

"And the angel answered *and* said to [Mary], '*The* Holy Spirit shall come upon you, and *the* power of *the* Highest shall overshadow you; and for this reason, the Holy One being begotten in you shall be called *the* Son of God.' " Luke 1:35

"And the Word became flesh, and tabernacled among us (and we ourselves beheld His glory, *the* glory as of *the* only begotten with *the* Father), full of grace and truth." John 1:14

"And being found in *the* manner of man, He humbled Himself, *and* became obedient unto death, even *the* death of *the* cross." Phil. 2:8

"Behold the Lamb of God, Who takes away the sin of the world." John 1:29

"We know that this is truly the Christ, the Savior of the world." John 4:42

"I am the bread of life; the one who comes to Me shall never hunger; and the one who believes in Me shall never thirst at any time." John 6:35

"I am the light of the world; the one who follows Me shall never walk in darkness, but shall have the light of life." John 8:12

"Truly, truly ... before Abraham was born, I AM." John 8:58

"I am the door of the sheep ... I am the good Shepherd." John 10:7, 11

"I am the resurrection and the life." John 11:25

"I am the way, and the truth, and the life; no one comes to the Father except through Me." John 14:6

"I am the true vine, and My Father is the husbandman. I am the vine ... you *are* the branches." John 15:1, 6

"I am the Alpha and the Omega, *the* Beginning and *the* Ending, says the Lord, Who is, and Who was, and Who *is* to come—the Almighty ... I am the Alpha and the Omega, the First and the Last ... even the one Who is living; for I was dead, and behold, I am alive into the ages of eternity. Amen." Rev. 1:8, 11, 18

Forward

From eternity past, before the foundation of the world, God the Father and God the Son planned for and predetermined the day that Jesus the Christ would die. In the history of the universe, no other day can be compared with it. So profound was this day that it will always be remembered even into the ages of eternity to come.

This day of destiny was the ultimate culmination of the spiritual battle for the lives of men; a battle waged between Jesus the Christ, Son of God and Savior of mankind, and Satan the devil, adversary of God and destroyer of mankind. This fierce battle was centered in Jerusalem, but its outcome would determine the destiny of the world. It was the power of God versus the power of Satan, the Advocate vs. the adversary, love vs. hatred, good vs. evil, humility vs. pride, compassion vs. brutality, righteousness vs. sin and forgiveness vs. condemnation.

All the evil forces and powers of the world were gathered together against one man, Jesus the Christ—the Son of God. Who would be victorious? Would good finally triumph over evil?

For healing the sick, raising the dead and teaching the love of God, Jesus Christ was condemned, beaten, scourged, reviled, ridiculed and crucified. Yet, He was faithful to the end—giving His life as a perfect sacrifice for the sins of the world.

Even Jesus' own disciples, whom He had taught for three and one-half years, did not understand the significance of this day. As they watched Jesus die and His body being placed into the tomb, they were bewildered. To them it appeared that evil had won—the political and religious establishments that held them in bondage were victorious. All they felt was a dark and foreboding despair because Jesus, the Anointed Messiah of God, was dead and buried. It was beyond their wildest imaginations that Jesus would come back to life after three days and nights in the tomb. But He was raised from the dead by the power of God the Father.

When Jesus showed Himself to them after He was raised from the dead, He personally revealed to them from the Scriptures that His death and resurrection were foreordained: "And He said to them, 'These *are* the words that I spoke to you when I was yet with you, that all *the* things which were written concerning Me in the Law of Moses and *in the* Prophets and *in the* Psalms must be fulfilled.' **Then He opened their minds to understand the Scriptures**, and said to them, 'According as it is written, **it was necessary for the Christ to suffer, and to rise from *the* dead the third day**'" (Luke 24:44-46).

In the world today, many people do not understand the significance of the death of Jesus the Christ and the specific day that He died. This book was especially written to help them understand the Scriptures concerning Him. The inspired Word of God reveals the full story.

Mel Gibson's movie confronted the viewer with a powerful emotional presentation of *The Passion of the Christ*. However, because of time constraints and artistic license, the movie did not bring the full biblical truth. This book is a composite of the Scriptures from the New Testament that chronicle the events of the crucifixion day to Jesus' resurrection and final ascension into heaven. Special commentaries tie together the prophecies of the Old Testament with the events of the New Testament to expound upon the meaning of this Day of Destiny—*The Day Jesus the Christ Died*.

Other Works by the Author

The New Testament In Its Original Order—A Faithful Version With Commentary is a new translation and is the only English New Testament that has the books arranged in their original order. It retains the grace and grandeur of the King James Version while clarifying many of its problematic Scriptures. Some commentaries answer the questions: What is the New Testament? Who wrote it? When was it written? When was it canonized? Who canonized it? Other commentaries show the history and preservation of the Bible. Appendices contain many detailed studies of controversial New Testament teachings. This 928-page book is an absolute must for all Christians.

The Christian Passover is a book of over 500 pages that details the scriptural and historical truths of the Passover in both the Old and New Testaments, leading the reader step-by-step through every aspect of one of the most vital and fundamental teachings revealed in the Bible. It fully explains the meaning of the Christian Passover—a remembrance of the sacrifice of Jesus Christ the Passover Lamb of God—in a most compelling and inspiring manner. The full meaning of the body and blood of Jesus Christ is revealed, showing the magnitude of God's love for every person, and His awesome plan and purpose for mankind.

A Harmony of the Gospels In Modern English brings to life the message and purpose of the true Jesus, portraying His life and ministry in their true historical setting. This easy-to-understand, step-by-step account of the life of Jesus Christ is an indispensable study aid for every serious Bible student.

The Seven General Epistles is designed for an in-depth verse-by-verse study of the epistles of James; I and II Peter; I, II and III John and Jude. As part of the living Word of God, these epistles are as meaningful today for personal Christian growth as when they were written.

Lord, What Should I Do? is a book for Christians who are confused and bewildered by the escalating spiritual and doctrinal chaos in Christian churches today, which is undermining the true faith of the Bible. Any religious organization that teaches truths from the Word of God is a target for the forces of evil behind this chaos. This book clarifies the problem and offers the solution.

On-Line Studies: For the serious Bible student, more written information and in-depth Bible studies in audio format can be obtained at **www.cbcg.org**.

These publications can be ordered directly from York Publishing Company, P.O. Box 1038 Hollister, CA 95024-1038 or from Amazon.com

About the Author

Fred R. Coulter attended the University of San Francisco and graduated from San Mateo State College before graduating from Ambassador University, Pasadena, California, with a BA in Theology in 1964. He was ordained a minister of Jesus Christ in 1965 and pastored churches of God in the Pacific Northwest, the Mountain States, the greater Los Angeles area and Monterey, including the central coast area in California. Mr. Coulter completed advanced biblical and ministerial studies in 1972-75 under the Ambassador University Master's program. While completing these studies, he was encouraged by his professor in Koiné Greek to consider translating the books of the New Testament.

After completing his formal instruction in Koiné Greek, Mr. Coulter continued to expand his knowledge by undertaking a verse-by-verse study of the books of the New Testament, using the Byzantine Text. In the course of his study, he was moved to translate the Gospel accounts into clearer, more understandable English for contemporary readers. The early fruit of his labor, *A Harmony of the Gospels in Modern English*, is now in its third edition.

Mr. Coulter's next publication was a major work regarding the observance of the Christian Passover. The Gospels record that Jesus and His disciples observed the Passover on the night of Nisan 14, between sunset and midnight. At that time, Jesus commanded His disciples to annually commemorate His death by partaking of the symbols of unleavened bread and wine on that night. This ordinance was observed by the New Testament churches in Judea and was delivered by the apostle Paul to the Gentile churches (I Cor. 11:23-25). In the following centuries, however, the churches departed from the apostolic practice and began to take the symbols of Christ's body and blood at other times in the year, calling their observance the Lord's Supper or the Eucharist. The original ordinances of the Christian Passover as delivered to the apostles were forgotten in the apostate Christian-professing world. To restore understanding of the scriptural time and manner for partaking of the bread and the wine, Mr. Coulter published the first edition of *The Christian Passover* in the winter of 1993. A greatly expanded edition, 482 pages in length, was published six years later in the fall of 1999.

In both *A Harmony of the Gospels in Modern English* and *The Christian Passover*, Mr. Coulter describes and expounds on the historical events of Jesus' last Passover and His subsequent crucifixion and resurrection. Unlike mainstream Christianity, Mr. Coulter defends the scriptural teaching that Jesus was in the grave for three full days and three full nights—a total of 72 hours. The scriptural facts as recorded in the Gospel accounts are clearly set forth in his translation of the Greek text of the New Testament, *The New Testament In Its Original Order: A Faithful Version With Commentary*, published in March, 2004.

Continuing his active ministry spanning almost 40 years, Mr. Coulter has again been moved to take up the sword of God's Word and publish yet another book regarding Christ, His life and His death. In view of the impact of Mel Gibson's new movie *The Passion of the Christ*, Mr. Coulter has felt compelled to set the record straight concerning the actual events of the crucifixion and resurrection of Jesus Christ. Most Christians consider the movie an accurate, unbiased and faithful presentation of the events leading to and including the crucifixion of Jesus Christ. However, as Mr. Coulter demonstrates in his new book *The Day Jesus the Christ Died*, the scriptural records of these events differ markedly from the mystical events depicted in the movie. The movie promotes a distorted view of the events, focusing on bloodshed and brutality while missing the real meaning of the shed blood of Jesus Christ. In contrast, Mr. Coulter explains the full meaning of the body and blood of Christ, and how His blood can bring forgiveness and reconciliation with the Father to those who repent of their sins and seek to live in newness of life. If you believe that Mel Gibson's portrayal of the suffering and crucifixion of Christ accurately represents the Scriptures, you need to read *The Day Jesus the Christ Died*.

Carl D. Franklin
Spring 2004

Acknowledgments

We first acknowledge God the Father and Jesus Christ and thank them for preserving the Holy Bible in spite of mankind's tumultuous history so that today the truth is available for everyone. It is the Word of God that gives us the true understanding about Jesus the Christ and why He died for the sins of the world. Jesus said, "Your Word is truth...and you shall know the truth and the truth shall set you free" (John 17:17, 8:31). It would not be possible to write this book without the true Word of God.

Many people have helped and shared in producing this book. Their diligent work and support made it possible. First, I give my heartfelt gratitude and appreciation to my lovely, dear wife, Dolores, for her personal encouragement. Special acknowledgments go to Carl and Jean Franklin, who for over thirty years have helped in editing all of the author's publications and books. Special thanks go to Marcia Ritke Momose for her diligent editing of the text and appendices. John and Hiedi Vogele are to be commended for the final formatting and proof reading of the entire text for publication of this book.

Fred R. Coulter
May 2004

Preface

Destined to be viewed and experienced by millions around the world, the movie *The Passion of the Christ* by Mel Gibson has confronted this generation, as never before in modern history, with these burning questions: "Who was Jesus Christ? Who killed Him? Why did He have to die? Why did He die such a horrific, humiliating, cruel and gruesome death by beating, scourging and crucifixion?"

Attempting to graphically portray the last twelve hours of Jesus' life, the movie has shocked its viewers with stark realism and gross brutality. On the one hand, it has been enthusiastically praised as the greatest religious film ever made. On the other hand, pundits have decried it as being filled with hatred and gruesome violence. Many church leaders have praised it for its love and forgiveness. Some Jews have denounced it as being just another rendition of the medieval Catholic anti-Semitic passion plays, which historically led to the killing of Jews.

From all the controversy and public discussion, it is evident that no movie about Jesus Christ has ever evoked such contradictory, polarized emotional reactions—belief and scorn, love and hate, praise and condemnation. There is little doubt that the controversy over this film will continue for years to come.

Gibson claims that he followed the Gospel accounts of Matthew, Mark, Luke and John as closely as possible. However, that is not quite correct. "To tell his story, Gibson has amalgamated the four Gospel accounts and was reportedly inspired by the visions of two nuns: Mary of Agreda (1602-1665) of Spain and Anne Catherine Emmerich (1774-1824) of France; Emmerich experienced the stigmata on her head, hands, and feet and chest—wounds imitating Jesus' " (*Newsweek*, 2/16/04 p. 47). In fact, Gibson added many things in the film that were derived solely from Catholic tradition and Emmerich's book, *Delorous Passions of Our Lord Jesus Christ.*

Although the movie is a mixture of Gospel accounts, Catholic tradition, mysticism and "artistic license," the majority of viewers who are unfamiliar with the Gospel accounts will accept it as an accurate portrayal of the last twelve hours of Jesus' life. The best way to separate unsubstantiated mystic tradition from biblical truth is to closely examine the records of Matthew, Mark, Luke and John. They are the true, inspired historical accounts of the passion, crucifixion, and resurrection of Jesus Christ.

Furthermore, the prophecies in the Old Testament about Jesus Christ must also be examined. Only then can one truly understand why the Son of God had to die such an ignominious, horrendous, brutal death by crucifixion.

For centuries, many of the true teachings of the Bible have been branded as "heresy" by the leaders of Orthodox Christendom. Religious doctrines and dogmas have been developed, which are founded upon a combination of the Scriptures and the traditions of men. The result has been distorted or erroneous teachings that are accepted as the true doctrines and teachings of the Bible by the faithful.

Sadly, very few religious, church-going people take the time to study their Bibles in order to prove whether the teachings of their churches are actually the true teachings of the Bible. Therefore, they do not realize that many of their church's teachings and traditions originated, not in Christianity, but in pagan religion. As such, these beliefs are contrary to what the Bible teaches, yet they are taught in the name of Jesus Christ. When these corrupt teachings are compared to the Bible, fully fifty to ninety percent are not true!

Thus, truth has been exchanged for lies, and lies have been accepted as truth, in a process Dresden James noted in this well-known quote:

> *"When a well-packaged web of lies*
> *has been sold gradually to the masses over*
> *generations, the truth will seem*
> *utterly preposterous and its*
> *speaker a raving lunatic."*

This book *The Day Jesus the Christ Died* presents the biblical facts concerning the meaning and purpose of Jesus Christ's passion, crucifixion and resurrection. The truth is more astounding and profound than all of the ideas, superstitions, traditions and misbeliefs of men!

Fred R. Coulter
May 2004

Introduction

Today, most people, even professing Christians, are ignorant of what the Bible really teaches. For example, because pagan myths and religious practices have been "Christianized" and interwoven with Scripture, most people believe that the traditional holidays, practices and traditions of Christendom came from the New Testament. They also assume that Jesus and His apostles practiced and taught them. Nothing could be further from the truth!

In a two-hour movie depicting the last twelve hours of Jesus' life, it is impossible to convey much more than an emotional impression, as moving as it may be. Mel Gibson's movie only alluded to the true biblical meaning of Jesus' passion—*The Day Jesus the Christ Died*.

In order to fully understand the meaning of Jesus Christ's passion, crucifixion and resurrection, it is necessary to unwind the historical clock. We must go back beyond 325 AD when the Emperor Constantine founded the Roman Catholic Church as a state religion—an amalgamation of apostate Christianity and pagan religions. We must go back beyond the teachings of the early church fathers of the second and third centuries. We must go back even to the first part of the first century when Jesus began His three and one-half year ministry in 26 AD and continue to the year of His crucifixion in 30 AD as recorded in the New Testament.

Furthermore, we must set aside all religious practices and traditions of men that were added after the death of the apostles. We must realize that Jesus, the original apostles and the true believers of the first century always taught and observed the seventh day Sabbath, known as Saturday today. In addition, they observed the annual feasts and holy days of God that He had commanded the children of Israel to observe. In order to keep God's feasts and holy days in their proper seasons, they used the calculated Hebrew lunar/solar calendar to reckon time, with the first month of the year being in the spring of the year (March/April), and they reckoned a day from sunset to sunset (Gen. 1:5, 8, 13, 19, cf; Lev. 23:32). Because the majority of people do not know these things, few realize the significance of the actual historical date that Jesus was crucified. This date has great significance!

Jesus Christ was not crucified on "Good Friday." He was not resurrected from the dead a day and one-half later on "Easter Sunday" morning. He was crucified and died on the Passover day, the most important feast of God. That day was the 14th day of the first month of the sacred Hebrew calendar (Lev. 23:4-5; Exodus 12), also known as Nisan 14, 30 AD. Coordinated with the Julian Roman calendar it was April 5. Moreover, Jesus was resurrected after He was in the grave a full three days and three nights as He said He would be (see Chapter Six).

A Summary of the Passover of God in the Bible

The Passover in the Old Testament: The account of the first Passover that God commanded the children of Israel to observe is found in Exodus 12. God commanded the heads of households to select a male lamb of the first year without blemish. They were to kill it just after sunset as the 14th day of the first month began. They were to place some of the blood on the doorposts and upper lintels of the entrances to their houses. The blood was a sign and a protection against the death sentence of the firstborn that God executed against the Egyptians. At midnight on the 14th, the LORD passed through the land of Egypt and killed all the firstborn of man and beast: "For I will pass through the land of Egypt this night, and will smite all the firstborn in the land of Egypt, both man and beast; and against all the gods of Egypt I will execute judgment: I am the LORD. And the blood shall be to you for a token upon the houses where ye are: and when I see the blood, I will pass over you, and the plague shall not be upon you to destroy you, when I smite the land of Egypt. And this day shall be unto you for a memorial; and ye shall keep it a feast to the LORD throughout your generations; ye shall keep it a feast by an ordinance for ever" (Ex. 12:12-14, *KJV*).

The 14th day of the first month is called "the Passover" because God passed over Israel's houses on that night and spared their firstborn: "And it shall come to pass, when your children shall say unto you, What mean ye by this service? That ye shall say, It is the sacrifice of the LORD'S passover, who passed over the houses of the children of Israel in Egypt, when he smote the Egyptians, and delivered our houses. And the people bowed the head and worshipped" (Ex. 12:26-27).

Editor's note: *The historical records show that in the time before and after the seventy-year Babylonian Captivity (605-535 BC) there was a dispute among the Jews about the date for observing the Passover. Some faithfully followed the commands of God in the Bible to observe it on the 14th day of the first month using a domestically killed lamb and eating their Passover meal in their houses on the night of the 14th. Others who observed it on the 15th day of the first month abandoned the domestic killing of the lamb in the evening of the 14th, as the day began at sunset, and substituted a temple sacrificed lamb in the afternoon of the 14th. Consequently, they ate their Passover meal a day later on the night of the 15th, which is contrary to the scriptural commands of God.*

From the New Testament records it is clear that Jesus always obeyed the commands of God concerning all things, including the scriptural observance of the Passover on the 14th day of the first month. In fact, Jesus' last Passover with His apostles was a domestic 14th Passover observed in a house in Jerusalem. The Christian Passover by Fred R. Coulter is the most comprehensive book ever written on this vital biblical teaching. Those who desire to understand more about the true Passover of God in the Old and New Testaments may order the book from Amazon.com or directly from York Publishing Company.

Introduction

The Passover in the New Testament: From the time of Israel's first Passover in Egypt to the time of Jesus Christ, the Passover was observed to commemorate God's sparing their firstborn. The male lamb without blemish that was sacrificed for the observance of the Old Testament Passover was a foretype that symbolized Jesus Christ, Who was the "Lamb of God" sacrificed for the sins of the world.

In the Gospel of John, Jesus foretold the meaning of the New Testament Passover—the true Christian Passover: "Jesus said to them, 'I am the bread of life; the one who comes to Me shall never hunger; and the one who believes in Me shall never thirst at any time ... Then the Jews were complaining against Him, because He said, 'I am the bread that came down from heaven.' And they were saying, 'Is this not Jesus, the son of Joseph, whose father and mother we know? Why then does He say, "I came down from heaven"?'

"For this reason, Jesus answered them and said, 'Do not be complaining among one another ... Truly, truly I say to you, the one who believes in Me has eternal life. **I am the bread of life**. Your fathers ate manna in the desert, but they died. This is the bread which comes down from heaven so that anyone may eat of it and not die. **I am the living bread, which came down from heaven; if anyone eats of this bread, he shall live forever; and the bread that I will give is even My flesh, which I will give for the life of the world**.' Because of this, the Jews were arguing with one another, saying, 'How is He able to give us *His* flesh to eat?'

"Therefore, Jesus said to them, 'Truly, truly I say to you, unless you eat the flesh of the Son of man, and drink His blood, you do not have life in yourselves. The one who eats My flesh and drinks My blood has eternal life, and I will raise him up in the last day; for My flesh is truly food, and My blood is truly drink. The one who eats My flesh and drinks My blood is dwelling in Me, and I in him. As the living Father has sent Me, and I live by the Father; so also the one who eats Me shall live by Me. This is the bread which came down from heaven; not as your fathers ate manna, and died. The one who eats this bread shall live forever' " (John 6:35, 41-43, 47-58).

Consequently, on the night of His last Passover with His apostles, Jesus Christ changed the symbols and meaning of the Passover to commemorate the New Covenant of eternal life that He was instituting: "And as they were eating, Jesus took the bread and blessed *it*; *then He* broke *it* and gave *it* to the disciples, and said, 'Take, eat; this is My body.' And He took the cup; and after giving thanks, He gave *it* to them, saying, 'All of you drink of it; for this is My blood, the *blood* of the New Covenant, which is poured out for many for *the* remission of sins' " (Matt. 26:26-28). See *Chapters Nine and Ten that explain the meaning of the body and blood of Jesus Christ.*

However, during supper, before Jesus instituted the symbols of the bread and wine to be taken once a year on the Passover night, He instituted the ordinance of footwashing: Jesus "rose from supper and laid aside *His* garments; and after taking a towel, He secured it around Himself. Next, He poured water into a washing basin and began to wash the disciples' feet, and to wipe *them* with the towel which He had secured … when He had washed their feet, and had taken His garments, *and* had sat down again, He said to them, 'Do you know what I have done to you? You call Me the Teacher and the Lord, and you speak rightly, because I am. **There-fore, if I, the Lord and the Teacher, have washed your feet, you also are duty-bound to wash one another's feet; for I have given you an ex-ample,** *to show* **that you also should do exactly as I have done to you**. Truly, truly I tell you, a servant is not greater than his lord, nor a messen-ger greater than he who sent him. If you know these things, blessed are you if you do them' " (John 13:4-5, 12-17). *See Chapter Eight that ex-plains the meaning of footwashing.*

On the night of the Passover, Jesus Christ instituted the New Cove-nant Christian Passover. All the events recorded in Scripture of Jesus' be-trayal and arrest, His trial, beating, scourging, crucifixion, death and burial took place within that one 24-hour day. The death of Jesus Christ for the sins of the world is the foundation of true Christianity. Without His death and the shedding of His blood, as well as His resurrection, there is no for-giveness of sins (I Cor. 15:1-23). Therefore, by virtue of this profound his-torical and spiritual fact, the Passover day is the most important commanded feast of God. Jesus Christ is the supreme sacrifice of God the Father—He is our Passover Lamb. The apostle Paul wrote to the Gentile church in Cor-inth: "**For Christ our Passover was sacrificed for us**" (I Cor. 5:7).

Part One

Crucifixion to Ascension

CHAPTER ONE

Jesus' Last Passover and Crucifixion

The greatest event since the creation of the world was about to take place. Jesus Christ, Who was God manifested in the flesh (I Tim. 3:16), was going to die! He would give His life as the supreme sacrifice for the sins of all mankind. John the Baptist understood this when he said of Jesus: "Behold the Lamb of God, Who takes away the sin of the world" (John 1:29). This momentous event had been planned before the creation of the world: "…the Lamb, slain from *the* foundation of *the* world" (Rev. 13:8).

When and how did sin enter the world? Why was it necessary for Jesus Christ to lay down His life for the sins of mankind? How can His one sacrifice purge all sin?

The sin of Adam and Eve was not the first transgression against God. The original sin was committed by Lucifer and the angels who followed him. *Lucifer* (Latin, "Light Bringer" or "Shining One") was the first created being to commit sin; therefore he is the author of sin. He boasted that he would become like the Most High and sit on God's throne (Isa. 14:14-15; Ezek. 28:12-18). One third of the angels followed him in his rebellion (Rev. 12:3-4). At that time, Lucifer became Satan the devil, the adversary of God, and the rebelling angels who followed him became known as demons.

When Satan and the demons attempted to seize the throne of God, they were cast back down to the earth (Luke 10:18). That war left the earth in ruin and parts of the heavens in shambles. Everything that Lucifer and his angels had established on earth before the rebellion was destroyed, and the earth was covered with a flood (Gen. 1:2). Then God, the one Who became Jesus Christ, recreated the surface of the earth and filled it with life.

On the sixth day of creation, God made man in His own image and likeness, male and female (Gen. 1:26-27). God gave Adam and Eve free moral agency. He set before them the way of eternal life, as symbolized by the Tree of Life. He also set before them the Tree of the Knowledge of Good and Evil, which represented the way that seemed right to them, under the sway of Satan the devil. But God commanded them not to eat of the fruit of that tree, and warned them that if they ate of it they would surely die.

Under the influence of Satan the devil, Adam and Eve chose to disobey God by eating the fruit from the Tree of the Knowledge of Good and Evil. Through their disobedience sin and death passed to all mankind (Rom. 5:12). As a result, nearly all of humanity has followed the dictates of human nature under Satan's sway, cut off from God. Although God has set limits on Satan, God has not yet removed Satan and his evil influence. In His own time, God will ultimately bring mankind out from subjection to sin and Satan. Through His plan of redemption, initiated by His Son's perfect sacrifice, God has made it possible for all mankind to be delivered from sin and the penalty of death.

God as Lawgiver and Creator has decreed that the wages of sin for all human beings is death (Rom. 6:23). Sin is the transgression of God's holy, spiritual laws and commandments (I John 3:4). All have sinned and have come short of the glory of God, so all face death unless they accept the way of salvation that God has provided (Rom. 3:23). The death that is decreed for sin is the second death in the lake of fire. From that death there is no resurrection (Rev. 20:13-15; 21:8).

After Adam and Eve sinned, God pronounced His judgment upon them. Within His sentence, we find the first prophecy of the death of the Messiah: "And I will put enmity between thee [the serpent – Satan the devil] and the woman [a type of Israel, and later, the Church of God], and between thy seed [the followers of Satan] and her Seed [Jesus Christ, the coming Messiah]; *it* [the Seed] shall bruise thy head [Satan], and thou [Satan] shalt bruise His heel [the crucifixion of Christ]" (Gen. 3:15, *KJV*).

This prophecy was spoken by God Himself, the one Who was to become Jesus Christ. As the Lord God of the Old Testament, He prophesied His own death to atone for the sins of Adam and Eve and all their descendants to come. This prophecy was spoken more than 4,000 years before His beating, scourging and crucifixion on the Passover day, Nisan 14, April 5, 30 AD.

The Promised Seed of the Covenant With Abraham

The promise of a Seed who would conquer sin and banish Satan was confirmed by the covenant that God made with Abraham. The words of the covenant were a prophecy of His own future birth as the fleshly Seed of Abraham. Let us examine the account in the book of Genesis: "And, behold, the word of the LORD *came* unto him [Abraham], saying, 'This [his steward Eliezer] shall not be thine heir; but *he* that shall come forth out of thine own bowels shall be thine heir' " (Gen. 15:4, *KJV*).

The birth of Isaac, the son of Abraham and Sarah, was only the beginning of the fulfillment of this promise to Abraham. The promise was not only for Isaac but also for his future descendant, the coming Messiah. The birth of Jesus Christ was the ultimate fulfillment of the promise, the Seed to Whom the promises were given: "Now to Abraham and to his Seed were the promises spoken. He does not say, 'and to *your* seeds,' as of many; but as of one, 'and to your Seed,' which is Christ" (Gal. 3:16). Jesus Christ is the promised Seed and true Heir of the promises God made to Abraham.

The account in Genesis 15 reveals that evening had come when God began to give the promises to Abraham. On that night, God took Abraham outside and showed him the stars of heaven. Then He gave Abraham another promise: "And He brought *him* forth abroad, and said, 'Look now toward heaven, and tell the stars, if thou be able to number *them*': and He said unto him, 'So shall thy seed be' " (Gen. 15:5, *KJV*). The New Testament shows that these words of God do not refer to Abraham's physical descendants but to those who would become the children of Abraham through faith in Jesus Christ. The apostle Paul wrote: "Because of this, *you should* understand that those who *are* of faith are the *true* sons of Abraham" (Gal. 3:7).

The true children of Abraham are not counted by their physical lineage. They are a spiritual nation, composed of individuals of every race and every bloodline who follow in the faith of Abraham (verses 8, 14). At the return of Jesus Christ, they will be resurrected to eternal life as glorified spirit beings and will shine as the stars forever (Dan. 12:3, Matt. 13:43, I Cor. 15:40-44).

Next, God promised to give to Abraham and his physical seed the land of the Canaanites: "And He said unto him, '*I am* the LORD that brought thee out of Ur of the Chaldees, to give thee this land to inherit it'" (Gen. 15:7, *KJV*). This promise was for his physical descendants, the children of Israel. Many generations would pass before the promised Seed, Jesus Christ, would come to prepare a spiritual people for a spiritual kingdom—the sons of God in the Kingdom of God. Abraham received the promises with complete faith that God would fulfill them: "And he believed in the LORD; and He counted it to him for righteousness" (verse 6, *KJV*).

The Covenant Confirmed by a Maledictory Oath

When God established His covenant with Abraham, He confirmed it with a maledictory oath, which was a pledge and prophecy of His own future death. On the morning after giving Abraham the promises, God spoke to him and instructed him to prepare a special sacrifice to seal the covenant: "And He said unto him, 'Take Me an heifer of three years old, and a she goat of three years old, and a ram of three years old, and a turtledove, and a young pigeon.' And he took unto him all these, and divided *them* in the midst [cut them down the middle], and laid each piece one against [opposite one] another: but the birds divided he not. And when the fowls came down upon the carcasses, Abram drove *them* away" (verses 9-11, *KJV*). The bloody carcasses of the sacrificial animals were laid on the ground to represent the symbolic death of the one Who would confirm the covenant. By passing between the parts, He would pledge His own life to fulfill the covenant.

By the time that Abraham had finished preparing the covenant sacrifice, it was late in the day: "And when the sun was going down, a deep sleep fell upon Abram; and, lo, an horror of great darkness fell upon him" (verse 12, *KJV*). While Abraham lay sleeping, God appeared to him in a vision and promised that his physical descendants would inherit the land. However, this would not happen until they had lived in another land for four generations: "And He said unto Abram, 'Know of a surety that thy seed shall be a stranger in a land *that is* not theirs, and shall serve them; and they shall afflict *them* four hundred years; and also that nation, whom they shall serve, will *I* judge: and afterward shall they come out with great substance. And *thou* shalt go to thy fathers in peace; thou shalt be buried in a good old age. But in the fourth generation they shall come hither again: for the iniquity of the Amorites *is* not yet full' " (verses 13-16, *KJV*).

After prophesying these events, God bound Himself to fulfill them by passing between the sacrificial animals to seal the covenant: "And it came to pass, that, **when the sun went down** [beginning the next day], and it was dark, behold a smoking furnace, and a burning lamp that passed between those pieces. In the same day the LORD made a covenant with Abram..." (verses 17-18, *KJV*).

After the sun had gone down, God passed through the middle of the sacrificial animals, revealing His presence by the smoking furnace and flaming torch. When God passed between the parts, He walked a death walk, pledging His future death. Apparently, the smoking furnace wholly consumed the sacrificial animals. That is how God ratified His unilateral covenant with Abraham.

The full account in Genesis 15 reveals that the making of the covenant took place during two consecutive days. When God first spoke to Abraham, it was night because the stars could be seen (verse 5). In the morning, God gave Abraham instructions for preparing the covenant sacrifice. Abraham prepared the sacrifice that same day. We know that he completed the preparations while the sun was still high because the birds of prey were flying about and attempting to land on the sacrifice (verse 11). The next verse records the end of the day: "And when the sun was going down, a deep sleep fell upon Abram" (verse 12). After the sun had gone down, God appeared to Abraham and ratified the covenant (verse 18).

There is great significance in the fact that the covenant was established over a two-day period, with the promises being given on the first night and the covenant being ratified on the second night. The timing of these events has an exact parallel in the chronology of the Passover and the Exodus, which were the first acts in the fulfillment of God's promises for the physical seed—the descendants of Abraham through Isaac and Jacob.

Israel's First Passover and the Exodus from Egypt

Exodus 12 records that the children of Israel kept the Passover on the 14th day of the first month, or Abib (this month was later known as Nisan). The Passover lamb, a type of the coming Messiah, was killed immediately after sunset at the beginning of the 14th. The people took some of the blood and put it on the side posts and lintel of the doors of their houses so that God would pass over their houses and spare their firstborn. Then they roasted the lamb with fire and ate it with bitter herbs.

At midnight on the 14th, God executed His final judgment on the Egyptians and their gods by killing all the firstborn of men and beasts.

When God saw the blood of the Passover lambs on the houses of the children of Israel, He passed over them, sparing their firstborn.

At sunrise, as the day portion of Nisan 14 began, the children of Israel left their houses to assemble at Rameses for the Exodus. As they journeyed to Rameses, they completely spoiled the Egyptians, fulfilling God's promise to Abraham that his descendants would depart from the land of their servitude with great substance. God commanded the children of Israel to observe this day, the 14th day of the first month, as the feast of the Passover for all generations to come, in commemoration of His final judgment against the Egyptians and their gods and His sparing of the firstborn of Israel (Ex. 12:3-14, 21- 28, Lev. 23:5).

After the children of Israel had assembled in Rameses, the Exodus from Egypt began. The people departed from Rameses as the 14th day was ending at sunset and the 15th day was beginning. The timing of this event fulfilled another promise that God had made to Abraham: "Now the sojourning of the children of Israel, who dwelt in Egypt, *was* **four hundred and thirty years**. And it came to pass at the end of the **four hundred and thirty years, EVEN THE SELFSAME DAY it came to pass, that all the hosts of the LORD went out from the land of Egypt.** *It is* **a night to be much observed unto the LORD for bringing them out from the land of Egypt...**" (Ex. 12:40-42, *KJV*).

The phrase "**the selfsame day**" refers to **a specific day exactly four hundred and thirty years before the Exodus**. What day was this? The Scriptures reveal that it was the "selfsame day" that God established His covenant with Abraham. On that day, God promised that He would bring his descendants out of bondage with great substance. On that "selfsame day," the 15th day of the first month, God fulfilled His promise. Therefore, God established the 15th day of the first month as a holy day to commemorate the beginning of the Exodus (Ex. 12:37-42; 13:3-10; Lev. 23:6-8).

The Foundation of the Christian Passover in the Covenant with Abraham

Four hundred and thirty years after establishing His covenant with Abraham, God brought the children of Israel out of Egypt. After bringing them out, He established a covenant with them now called the Old Covenant. In his epistle to the Galatians, the apostle Paul confirms that the Old Covenant was established four hundred and thirty years after God's covenant with Abraham: "Now this I say, *that the* covenant ratified beforehand by God to Christ [Abraham's true Heir] cannot be annulled by the law [the physical requirements of the Old Covenant], which was *given* four hundred and thirty years later, so as to make the promise of no effect" (Gal. 3:17).

The Old Covenant with the children of Israel did not fulfill God's promise to Abraham of a spiritual seed that would shine as the stars forever. This promise did not begin to be fulfilled until the coming of the New Covenant, the covenant of everlasting life, which was established nearly 2,000 years later. As God manifested in the flesh, Jesus Christ, the promised Seed of Abraham, instituted the New Covenant on the Passover night, the 14th day of the first month, named Nisan. The Passover that initiated the New Covenant was not a supper of lamb and bitter herbs, as was the Passover of the children of Israel under the Old Covenant. When Jesus instituted the new Christian Passover, He changed the symbols of the Passover to represent His own body and blood, which He sacrificed as the true Passover Lamb of God to ratify the New Covenant. Although He changed the symbols, He did not change the day, or the time of day, on which the Passover was to be observed.

The Christian Passover, as instituted by Jesus Christ, is to be observed on the night of Nisan 14. The new ceremony consists of three parts: 1) footwashing (John 13:2-17); 2) partaking of the broken unleavened bread, symbolizing Jesus' broken body (Matt. 26:26, Mark 14:22, Luke 22:19, I Cor. 11:23-24); and 3) partaking of the wine, symbolizing the blood of Jesus shed for the remission of sins so that all who accept His sacrifice may enter the New Covenant (Matt. 26:27-29, Mark 14:23-25, Luke 22:17-20, I Cor. 11:25-26).

Why Did God Have to Die?

As we have learned, God ratified His promises to Abraham with a maledictory oath. By passing between the parts of the covenant sacrifice, He pledged that He would give His own life to fulfill the promises. The bloody slaughter of these sacrificial animals symbolized the brutal suffering and crucifixion of Jesus Christ, which occurred in 30 AD on the Passover day—Nisan 14. The deep sleep and horror of great darkness that Abraham experienced was symbolic of Jesus Christ's burial in the tomb as Nisan 14 was ending at sunset. Thus, 2,000 years later, on the very same day that God ratified His covenant with Abraham, His lifeless body was in the tomb. He had carried out His pledge that He would die in order to fulfill the promises.

Before we can comprehend the death of God manifested in the flesh, we need to understand a fundamental truth about God. The Scriptures reveal that the Godhead is composed of more than one divine Being. In the first chapter of Genesis, the Hebrew name *Elohim* is used to describe God. In the Hebrew language, the suffix *im* added to a word makes it plural. Thus *Elohim* is a plural noun, meaning that there is more than one Being in the Godhead. When God created Adam and Eve, God said, "Let **Us** make man in **Our** image, after **Our** likeness..." (Gen. 1:26, *KJV*).

John begins his Gospel by revealing this fundamental truth: "**In *the* beginning was the Word, and the Word was with God, and the Word was God. He was in *the* beginning with God**. All things came into being through Him, and not even one *thing* that was created came into being without Him. In Him was life, and the life was the light of men....**He was in the world, and the world came into being through Him, but the world did**

not know Him....And the Word became flesh, and tabernacled [temporarily dwelt] **among us** (and we ourselves beheld His glory, *the* glory as of *the* only begotten with the Father), full of grace and truth" (John 1:1-4, 10, 14).

Jesus Himself testified that He was with the Father in glory before the world existed. In His final prayer to God the Father before He was arrested, tried and crucified, He said, "I have glorified You on the earth. I have finished the work that You gave Me to do. And now, **Father, glorify Me with Your own self, with the glory that I had with You before the world existed**" (John 17:4-5).

The Scriptures of the Old Testament and the New Testament consistently reveal that from the beginning there were two Beings Who existed together as God, or Elohim. The one of Elohim Who created all things was the one Who became Jesus Christ, the Messiah and the Savior of the world. The other one of Elohim became the Father. We find a prophecy of this in the book of Psalms: "I [the one of Elohim Who became the Son, Jesus Christ] will declare the decree: the LORD [the one of Elohim Who became the Father] hath said unto Me, ***Thou* art My Son; this day have I begotten Thee** [the day He was begotten in the womb of the virgin Mary]" (Psa. 2:7, *KJV*).

The one of Elohim Who became Jesus Christ, the Son of God and Savior of the world, had to divest himself of His power and glory as God. He had to become a pinpoint of life in order to be begotten by the Father in the womb of the virgin Mary. The apostle Paul reveals how this was accomplished: "Let this mind be in you, which *was* also in Christ Jesus; Who, although He existed [Greek υπαρχων, *huparchoon*, to exist or pre-exist] in *the* form of God, did not consider it robbery to be equal with God, but emptied Himself [of His power and glory], *and* was made in *the* likeness [Greek ομοιωμα *homoioma*, the same existence] of men, *and* took the form of a servant [Greek δουλος *doulos*, a slave]; and being found in *the* manner of man, He humbled Himself, *and* became obedient unto death, even *the* death of *the* cross" (Phil. 2:5-8).

These inspired words of Paul confirm that before Jesus Christ became human He was, in fact, Jehovah Elohim, the Lord God of the Old Testament. Existing as God, He was composed of ever-living Spirit. In this existence, it was impossible for Him to die. The only way for God to die was to become fully human—to be "manifested in the flesh." The God Who had created man in His image and likeness took on the same flesh and nature as man in order to redeem man from sin.

Jesus Christ voluntarily became a man in order to give His life as an offering for the sin of the world. The Father gave Him authority to lay down His life and to receive it back, as Jesus Himself testified: "Just as the Father knows Me, I also know the Father; and **I lay down My life for the sheep**. And I have other sheep that are not of this fold. I must bring those also, and they shall hear My voice; and there shall be one flock *and* one

Shepherd. **On account of this, the Father loves Me: because I lay down My life, that I may receive it back again. No one takes it from Me, but I lay it down of Myself. I have authority to lay it down and authority to receive it back again. This commandment I received from My Father**" (John 10:15-18).

Jesus Christ came to do the will of the Father and to give His life as the sacrifice for sin. In his epistle to the Hebrews, Paul quotes the words of the prophecy of Psalm 40:6-8: "For this reason, when He comes into the world, He says, 'Sacrifice and offering You did not desire, but You have prepared a body for Me [Christ's human body of flesh]. You did not delight in burnt offerings and *sacrifices* for sin. Then said I, "**Lo, I come** (*as* it is written of Me in *the* scroll of *the* book) **to do Your will, O God**" ' " (Heb. 10:5-7).

It was the purpose of the two Beings Who were Elohim that one of Them would be made fully human in order to die, so that through His sacrifice, all mankind might be granted grace unto salvation. Paul makes this absolutely clear: "But we see Jesus, **Who** *was* **made a little lower than** *the* **angels**, crowned with glory and honor on account of suffering the death, in order that **by** *the* **grace of God He Himself might taste [partake of] death for everyone**; because it was fitting for Him, for Whom all things *were created*, and by Whom all things *exist*, in bringing many sons unto glory, to make the Author of their salvation perfect through sufferings" (Heb. 2:9-10).

The Scriptures reveal that Jesus Christ was a mortal human being. He was not an angelic being that appeared to be a man. Paul states very clearly that He shared the same flesh and blood as all human beings: "**Therefore, since the children are partakers of flesh and blood, in like manner He also took part in the same**, in order that through death He might annul him who has the power of death—that is, the devil; and *that* He might deliver those who were subject to bondage all through their lives by *their* fear of death.

"For surely, He is not taking upon Himself to help *the* angels; but He is taking upon Himself to help *the* seed of Abraham. For this reason, it was obligatory for *Him* to be made like *His* brethren in everything [sharing the same flesh and nature], that He might be a merciful and faithful High Priest *in* things pertaining to God, in order to make propitiation for the sins of the people. For because He Himself has suffered, having been tempted *in like manner*, He is able to help those who are being tempted" (Heb. 2:14-18).

What a magnificent expression of God's love! The Creator of all mankind temporarily gave up His eternal existence as God and lowered Himself to the level of mortal man so that He could suffer and die for every human being! By the grace and love of God, through the power of the Holy Spirit, He willingly took upon Himself the death penalty that He had pronounced upon Adam and Even and their descendants.

Jesus Christ voluntarily chose to lay down His life to reconcile mankind to God so that all who accept His sacrifice may have the opportunity to receive salvation and eternal life. Jesus endured all His suffering in the flesh so that He might become the Author of eternal salvation, "Who, in the days of His flesh, offered up both prayers and supplications with strong crying and tears to Him Who was able to save Him from death, and was heard because *He* feared *God*. Although He was a Son, *yet* He learned obedience from the things that He suffered; and having been perfected, He became *the* Author of eternal salvation to all those who obey Him" (Heb. 5:7-9).

It took the death of the Creator God, manifested in the flesh, to become the perfect sacrifice for the forgiveness of human sin. No other sacrifice could bring forgiveness of sin to mankind. All the animal sacrifices and the shedding of their blood could never bring full forgiveness for human sin before God. The apostle Paul makes this truth very clear: "For the law, having *only* a shadow of the good things that are coming *and* not the image of those things, with the same sacrifices which they offer continually year by year, is never able to make perfect those who come *to worship*. Otherwise, would they not have ceased to be offered? For once those who worship had been purified, *they would* no longer be conscious of sin. On the contrary, in *offering* these *sacrifices* year by year*, there is* a remembrance of sins; **because *it is* impossible *for the* blood of bulls and goats to take away sins**" (Heb. 10:1-4).

***Man Cannot Save Himself*:** No other fleshly human being could have sacrificed his life to redeem mankind. If it were possible for a man to live perfectly in the letter of the law and never sin, his perfect human life, if sacrificed for sin, would not be sufficient to redeem even one human life. Redemption from sin and death requires greater obedience than the letter of the law. This is the whole lesson of Job's trials and suffering. Although he was perfect in the letter of the law, His own righteousness could not save him: "Moreover the LORD answered Job, and said, 'Shall he that contendeth with the Almighty instruct *Him*? he that reproveth *God*, let him answer it.'

"Then Job answered the LORD, and said, 'Behold, I am vile [all human beings have a sinful nature, regardless of perfect behavior in the letter of the law]; what shall I answer Thee? I will lay mine hand upon my mouth. Once have I spoken; but I will not answer: yea, twice; but I will proceed no further.' Then answered the LORD unto Job out of the whirlwind, and said, 'Gird up thy loins now like a man: I will demand of thee, and declare thou unto Me. Wilt thou also disannul My judgment? wilt thou condemn Me, that thou mayest be righteous?

" 'Hast thou an arm like God? or canst thou thunder with a voice like Him? Deck thyself now *with* majesty and excellency; and array thyself with glory and beauty. Cast abroad the rage of thy wrath: and behold every one *that is* proud, and abase him. Look on every one *that is* proud, *and* bring him low; and tread down the wicked in their place. Hide them in the dust together; *and* bind their faces in secret. Then will *I* also confess unto thee that thine own right hand can save thee' " (Job 40:1-14, *KJV*). As God told Job, it is impossible for any man to save himself—much less all of humanity.

Angels Cannot Save Mankind: God created angels to be ministering spirits. Angels are in a completely different category than human beings or God. While God created them out of spirit, they do not have the potential to enter into the God Family, as do human beings who will be transformed to spirit at the resurrection. Neither are they like the one of Elohim Who became the Son, as Paul wrote: "God, Who spoke to the fathers at different times in the past and in many ways by the prophets, has spoken to us in these last days by *His* Son, Whom He has appointed heir of all things, by Whom also He made the worlds; Who, being *the* brightness of *His* glory and *the* exact image of His person, and upholding all things by the word of His own power, when He had by Himself purged our sins, sat down at *the* right hand of the Majesty on high; **having been made so much greater than *any* of the angels, inasmuch as He has inherited a name exceedingly superior to them**.

"**For to which of the angels did He ever say, 'You are My Son; this day have I begotten You'**? And again, 'I will be a Father to Him, and He will be a Son to Me'? And again, when He brought the Firstborn into the world, He said, 'Let all *the* angels of God worship Him.' Now on one hand, of the angels He says, 'Who makes His angels spirits, and His ministers a flame of fire'….But unto which of the angels did He ever say, 'Sit at My right hand, until I make Your enemies a footstool for Your feet'? **Are they not all ministering spirits, sent forth to minister to those who are about to inherit salvation**?" (Heb. 1:1-7, 13-14) It was not possible for the sacrifice of angels to pay for the sins of all mankind.

Only God Can Save Man: The only Being whose life could purchase redemption from sin for all humanity is the Creator God. If the one Who had created man died, complete and total payment for human sin could be made, and reconciliation with God would be possible for all humanity. God's mercy could then be extended to all who repent and accept the death of Jesus Christ, God manifested in the flesh, as payment for their sins. This is why God had to die!

The one of Elohim Who created the heavens and the earth became Jesus Christ—God manifested in the flesh. He was divinely begotten by God the Father and born of the virgin Mary, His physical mother. He was the same as any ordinary human being, except that He had the Holy Spirit from conception. Only the death of God could reconcile man and God. Thus Jesus had to be God in the flesh—human as well as divine.

While He lived in the flesh, Jesus Christ was subject to every type of temptation that a human being can experience, but He never yielded to a single temptation of the flesh or of Satan. Jesus Christ never sinned. His obedience was perfect in the full spirit of the law. By living a sinless life, He was qualified to become not only the Savior and Redeemer of mankind but also the High Priest and Mediator between God and man: "Having therefore a great High Priest, *Who* has passed into the heavens, Jesus the Son of God, we should hold fast the confession *of our faith*. **For we do not have a high priest who cannot empathize with our weaknesses, but *one Who* was tempted in all things according to *the* likeness of *our own temptations*, yet *He was* without sin**. Therefore, we should come with boldness to the throne of grace, so that we may receive mercy and find grace to help in time of need" (Heb. 4:14-16).

Jesus' life in the flesh was able to purchase redemption from sin for all humanity because:

1) He was the Creator of all human beings.
2) He was divinely begotten by God the Father.
3) He was God manifested in the flesh.
4) He was the only human to live His entire life according to the will of God.
5) He was the only human never to sin.
6) He was the only human never to yield to a single temptation of the flesh or of Satan the devil.
7) He was the only human not to come under the death penalty for sin.

Only the precious blood of the Lamb of God could atone for all human sin. The death of God in the flesh was complete and perfect as a sacrifice and an atonement because His life in the flesh encompassed the full scope of human experience. On the human level, He suffered every type of temptation possible. He suffered the vilest of human indignities and excruciating tortures, enduring a violent beating, scourging, and crucifixion, and the shame of public death. He suffered rejection by His own people and injustice at the hands of religious and civil authorities. He was the victim of political expediency and religious hypocrisy. He overcame all, gaining total victory over Satan the devil and the pulls of the flesh through His perfect love and obedience to God the Father. The sacrifice of His perfect life opened the way for all mankind to receive salvation through faith in Jesus Christ: "For God so loved the world that He gave His only begotten Son, so that everyone who believes in Him may not perish, but may have everlasting life. For God sent not His Son into the world that He might judge the world, but that the world might be saved through Him" (John 3:16-17).

God the Father accepted the death of Jesus Christ once for all time as full payment for human sin. But before the sacrifice of Jesus Christ can be applied to an individual, he or she must first repent of sin, accept Jesus Christ as personal Savior and be baptized by full immersion in water. At baptism, he or she is conjoined into Christ's death by symbolic burial in a watery grave. Each one who is raised out of that baptismal burial is to walk in newness of life, learning to love God the Father and Jesus Christ with all the heart and to keep Their commandments in the full spirit of the law. This is the way of life that Jesus established for those who enter the New Covenant through faith in His sacrifice for sin.

All who enter the New Covenant are commanded to observe the Passover year by year as a renewal of the covenant of everlasting life. By partaking of the Passover as Jesus taught, they acknowledge that they have accepted the body and blood of Jesus Christ as full payment for their sins and have dedicated their lives to live by Him (John 6:57). When they partake of the broken unleavened bread, they acknowledge that they are healed of their diseases by the broken body of Jesus Christ: "…by Whose stripes you were healed" (I Pet. 2:24). When they partake of the wine, they acknowledge that they trust in His shed blood "for the remission of sins" (Matt. 26:28).

All true Christians have been bought with a great price. They belong to Jesus Christ, Who paid with His own blood to release them from the power of Satan and the bondage of sin, and to reconcile them to God the Father. "Christ our Passover was sacrificed for us" (I Cor. 5:7). This is the meaning of the DAY JESUS THE CHRIST DIED FOR THE SINS OF THE WHOLE WORLD!

CHAPTER TWO

The Agony of the Crucifixion

At His last Passover meal with the apostles, Jesus said, "Behold, even *now* the hand of him who is betraying Me *is* with Me at the table" (Luke 22:21). Although Jesus knew that Judas would betray Him, He washed Judas' feet along with the other apostles' (John 13:2-5, 11). Then Judas left. As Jesus administered the symbols of His body and His blood to the eleven apostles who were with Him, He knew that the time of His betrayal was near. When He departed with the apostles to the Mount of Olives, walking into the darkness of that dread night, Jesus began to feel the melancholy oppressiveness of the sins of the whole world weighing on Him, and His mind was filled with thoughts of the suffering and agony that lay ahead. Though His apostles were with Him, an overwhelming feeling of isolation penetrated every cell of His being. He could not share His sorrow with them because they did not understand what the rest of that Passover night and day would bring. He had spoken to them in the days leading up to the Passover, forewarning them of His betrayal and death, but they did not grasp the meaning of His words. They did not know that His life was about to end with a gruesome death on the cross as the TRUE PASSOVER SACRIFICE OF GOD—THE SIN OFFERING FOR THE WORLD.

The time had come! His rendezvous with destiny drew closer and closer to its ultimate climax! The Lord God of the Old Testament, Who had come to earth in the flesh, was about to die the agonizing death that He and the prophets had foretold. This was the reason He had come into the world. He had come in the flesh in order to die—to give His body to be beaten, scourged and crucified, and to offer His blood for the sins of mankind. But no human being desires to die a slow death in great pain and agony. As Jesus anticipated His suffering, His flesh cried out to be spared. Only the love of God, which had sustained Him and brought Him to this day, could give Him the strength to endure the suffering that was appointed to Him.

He had manifested the love of God during His days in the flesh, setting a perfect example for His disciples. Now the love of God would be manifested by His death. As they were walking to the Mount of Olives, He charged His apostles, "LOVE ONE ANOTHER, AS I HAVE LOVED YOU." He spoke from the depths of His innermost being, desiring to indelibly etch His words into their minds: "If you keep My commandments, you shall live in My love; just as I have kept My Father's commandments and live in His love.

"These things I have spoken to you, in order that My joy may dwell in you, and *that* your joy may be full. **This is My commandment: that you**

love one another, as I have loved you. No one has greater love than this: that one lay down his life for his friends. (John 15:10-13).

Jesus was about to manifest the greatest love of all by laying down His life for them, as well as for the whole world. But the apostles did not know this yet, nor did they know that some of them would also lose their lives for His name's sake in the days ahead. Jesus warned the disciples that the world would hate them and persecute them, just as the world had hated and persecuted Him: "If the world hates you, you know that it hated Me before *it hated* you. If you were of the world, the world would love its own. However, because you are not of the world, but I have personally chosen you out of the world, the world hates you for this. Remember the word that I spoke to you: a servant is not greater than his master. If they persecuted Me, they will persecute you also. If they kept My word, they will keep your *word* also. But they will do all these things to you for My name's sake, because they do not know Him Who sent Me.

"If I had not come and spoken to them, they would not have had sin; but now they have nothing to cover their sin. **The one who hates Me hates My Father also**. If I had not done among them the works that no other man has done, they would not have had sin; but now they have both seen and hated both Me and My Father. But this has happened so that the saying might be fulfilled which is written in their law, 'They hated Me without *a* cause.' But when the Comforter has come, which I will send to you from the Father, *even* the Spirit of the truth, which proceeds from the Father, that one shall bear witness of Me. Then you also shall bear witness, because you have been with Me from *the* beginning. I have spoken these things to you so that you will not be offended" (John 15:18-16:1).

Jesus continued to warn them, telling them that they, too, would be killed for preaching the truth of God: "They shall cast you out of the synagogues; furthermore, **the time is coming that everyone who kills you will think that he is rendering service to God.** And they shall do these things to you because they do not know the Father, nor Me. But **I have told you these things so that when the time comes, you may remember** that I said *them* to you. However, I did not say these things to you at *the* beginning because I was with you....These things I have spoken to you, so that in Me you may have peace. **In the world you shall have tribulation. But be courageous! I have overcome the world**" (John 16:2-4; 33).

When they arrived at the Mount of Olives, Jesus told His apostles, "My soul is deeply grieved, even to death. Stay here and watch with Me" (Matt. 26:38). Then, taking Peter, James and John, He went into the Garden of Gethsemane. "And when He arrived at the place, He said to them, 'Pray *that you* do not enter into temptation.' And He withdrew from them about a stone's throw; and falling to *His* knees, He prayed, saying, 'Father, if You are willing to take away this cup from Me—; NEVERTHELESS, NOT MY WILL, BUT YOUR *WILL* BE DONE' " (Luke 22:40-42).

Jesus Knew That He Could Not Escape Death

Even as He prayed to the Father, Jesus knew that the prophecies of His suffering and death must be fulfilled. As the Lord God of the Old Testament, He had given the first prophecy of His suffering to Adam and Eve in the presence of Satan, who would instigate His death (Gen. 3:15, *KJV*).

Jesus knew that He was the Lamb of God "slain from *the* foundation of *the* world" (Rev. 13:8). He knew from the beginning that He was destined to die on this Passover day—Nisan 14, April 5, 30 AD. As the Lord God of the Old Testament, He had entered into covenant with Abraham by passing between the parts of the sacrificial animals to represent His own death (Gen. 15:5-18). At the beginning of the 14th, during the dark hours of the night, He had delivered the promises of the covenant, foreshadowing the time when, as Jesus Christ, He would deliver the promises of the New Covenant. On the day portion of the 14th, the animals for the covenant sacrifice were slaughtered and their bodies were split asunder, allowing their blood to spill on the ground. During those same hours, the body of Jesus Christ would be beaten and broken open, and His blood would be poured out unto death. In the late afternoon of the 14th, the slaughtered animals lay still on the ground, and Abraham watched and waited. In like manner, Jesus' body would remain on the cross as the end of the 14th drew near, while his followers watched and waited (Luke 23:49). Although Jesus died at the "ninth hour," or approximately 3 PM, His body was not placed in the tomb until the 14th was ready to end at sunset.

At the exact time that Jesus would be buried, nearly 2000 years before, Abraham experienced a foretype of His death and burial: "And when the sun was going down, **a deep sleep fell upon Abram; and, lo, an horror of great darkness fell upon him**" (Gen. 15:12, *KJV*). Abraham remained in this symbolic burial after the sun had gone down. When the darkness of night had come, the Lord God passed between the parts of the sacrifice: "And it came to pass, that, when the sun went down, and it was dark, behold a smoking furnace, and a burning lamp that passed between those pieces" (verse 17, *KJV*).

By this maledictory oath, God Himself confirmed that He would fulfill the covenant through His own death and burial. This event, which took place during "the horror of great darkness," also had a fulfillment in Jesus Christ. The only sign that Jesus gave of His Messiahship was the length of time that He would be "in the heart of the earth" (Matt. 12:40). As He lay in the darkness of the tomb for three days and three nights, He was confirming that He was the Messiah Who would fulfill the promises of the New Covenant.

Jesus Knew That the Words of the Prophets Would All Be Fulfilled

As the covenant sacrifice had foreshadowed and the prophets had foretold, the suffering and death that were appointed to Jesus would surely come to pass. Every detail would be fulfilled, exactly as recorded in Scripture. When Judas left His presence on that Passover night, Jesus knew that Judas was on his way to the authorities to betray Him, as it was written: "Yea, mine own familiar friend, in whom I trusted, which did eat of my bread, hath lifted up *his* heel against me" (Psa. 41:9, *KJV*). Jesus also knew that the elders and the chief priests would pay Judas thirty pieces of silver to betray Him: "And I said unto them, 'If ye think good, give me my price; and if not, forbear.' So **they weighed for my price thirty** *pieces* **of silver**" (Zech. 11:12, *KJV*). Thirty pieces of silver was the price of a dead slave (Ex. 21:32).

Jesus also remembered the prophecy of Isaiah that He would be led as a lamb to the slaughter: "**He is despised and rejected of men**; a man of sorrows, and acquainted with grief: and we hid as it were *our* faces from him; he was despised, and we esteemed him not. Surely he hath borne our griefs, and carried our sorrows: yet we did esteem him stricken, smitten of God, and afflicted.

"**But he** *was* **wounded for our transgressions,** *he was* **bruised for our iniquities: the chastisement of our peace** *was* **upon him; and with his stripes we are healed**. All we like sheep have gone astray; we have turned every one to his own way; and **the LORD hath laid on him the iniquity of us all. He was oppressed, and he was afflicted, yet he opened not his mouth: he is brought as a lamb to the slaughter, and as a sheep before her shearers is dumb, so he openeth not his mouth**....for he was cut off out of the land of the living: for the transgression of my people was he stricken....Yet it pleased the LORD to bruise him; he hath put *him* to grief: when thou shalt make his soul an offering for sin,....he shall see of the travail of his soul, *and* shall be satisfied: by his knowledge shall my righteous servant justify many; for he shall bear their iniquities....because he hath poured out his soul unto death: and he was numbered with the transgressors; and he bare the sin of many, and made intercession for the transgressors" (Isa. 53:3-12, *KJV*).

Jesus was fully aware that He would be mocked, beaten and spit upon, and would suffer a terrible scourging. The whip that would inflict His scourging would have tips of nails and glass and would literally rip the flesh off His body. After forty lashes, He would be near death. He knew that this torturous ordeal would leave Him so horribly disfigured that He would be almost unrecognizable. Isaiah prophesied all of these things: "**I gave my back to the smiters, and my cheeks to them that plucked off the hair**: I hid not my face from shame and spitting....As many were astonied at thee; **his visage was so marred more than any man, and his form more than the sons of men**" (Isa. 50:6; 52:14, *KJV*).

Jesus knew that the prophecy of David in Psalm 22 was about to be fulfilled. He would cry out these very words while He was hanging on the cross: "**My God, my God, why hast thou forsaken me?** *why art thou so* far from helping me, *and from* the words of my roaring? O my God, I cry in the daytime, but thou hearest not; and in the night season, and am not silent….But *I am* a worm, and no man; **a reproach of men, and despised of the people**. All they that see me laugh me to scorn: they shoot out the lip, they shake the head, *saying*, 'He trusted on the LORD *that* he would deliver him: let him deliver him, seeing he delighted in him" (Psa. 22:1-2, 6-8, *KJV*).

Even during the mocking and jeering of the people, priests and Pharisees, He would trust God the Father, as He had from His earliest days in the flesh: "But thou *art* he that took me out of the womb: thou didst make me hope *when I was* upon my mother's breasts. I was cast upon thee from the womb: thou *art* my God from my mother's belly. Be not far from me; for trouble *is* near; for *there is* none to help. Many bulls [the demons] have compassed me: strong *bulls* of Bashan [Satan and his chief demons] have beset me round. They gaped upon me *with* their mouths, *as* a ravening and a roaring lion" (verses 9-13, *KJV*).

The next prophecies of David reveal the excruciating agony that He would suffer during His crucifixion as His physical life drained away: "I am poured out like water, and all my bones are out of joint [from the jolt of the cross falling into its hole]: my heart is like wax; it is melted in the midst of my bowels [from loss of blood]. My strength is dried up like a potsherd; and my tongue cleaveth to my jaws; and thou hast brought me into the dust of death.

"For dogs [the soldiers] have compassed me: the assembly of the wicked [the priests and Pharisees] have inclosed me: **they pierced my hands and my feet** [nailing Him to the cross]. **I may tell** [count] **all my bones** [because the flesh had been ripped open]: they look *and* stare upon me [in astonishment because He was so disfigured]. **They part my garments among them, and cast lots upon my vesture**" (verses 14-18, *KJV*).

In the midst of this agonizing ordeal, Jesus would pray to God the Father for strength to endure: "But be not thou far from me, O LORD: **O my strength, haste thee to help me**. Deliver my soul from the sword; my darling from the power of the dog. Save me from the lion's mouth: **for thou hast heard me**….For he hath not despised nor abhorred the affliction of the afflicted [Jesus Christ]; **neither hath he hid his face from him; but when he cried unto him, he heard**" (verses 19-24, *KJV*). These prophetic words of David show that God the Father would not truly forsake His Son at any time during His suffering and crucifixion but would be with Him as He bore the sins of all mankind.

In Psalm 69, God inspired David to write more of the thoughts that Jesus would have while on the cross. Although He had done no wrong, He would be hated and condemned to die by crucifixion, which was the lot of criminals. His death would bring great disrepute upon His disciples, and He would be rejected by His own physical brothers and sisters: "**They that hate me without a cause are more than the hairs of mine head**: they that would destroy me, *being* mine enemies wrongfully, are mighty….Let not them that wait on thee, O Lord GOD of hosts, be ashamed for my sake: **let not those that seek thee be confounded for my sake**, O God of Israel. Because **for thy sake I have borne reproach; shame hath covered my face**. I am become a stranger unto my brethren, and an alien unto my mother's children" (Psa. 69:4-8, *KJV*).

Jesus would suffer all the shame and agony of the crucifixion because of His profound love and zeal for God the Father: "**For the zeal of thine house hath eaten me up; and the reproaches of them that reproached thee are fallen upon me**....Hear me, O LORD; for thy lovingkindness *is* good: turn unto me according to the multitude of thy tender mercies. And hide not thy face from thy servant; for I am in trouble: hear me speedily. Draw nigh unto my soul, *and* redeem it: deliver me because of mine enemies. **Thou hast known my reproach, and my shame, and my dishonour** [being executed like a criminal]: mine adversaries *are* all before thee. **Reproach hath broken my heart; and I am full of heaviness: and I looked *for some* to take pity, but *there was* none; and for comforters, but I found none**. They gave me also gall for my meat; and **in my thirst they gave me vinegar to drink**" (verses 9, 16-21, *KJV*).

Jesus knew that He would have to bear this shameful and agonizing ordeal to the end. He knew that His suffering would become so unbearable that He would feel as if the Father had abandoned Him. He knew that a spear would be thrust into the side of His body, as the prophet Zechariah was inspired to write: "...and **they shall look upon me whom they have pierced**, and they shall mourn for him, as one mourneth for *his* only *son*, and shall be in bitterness for him, as one that is in bitterness for *his* firstborn" (Zech. 12:10, *KJV*).

Knowing that every one of these prophecies must be fulfilled, Jesus was in great anguish as He prayed to the Father. The thought of suffering such a hideous and merciless death was nearly overwhelming. Luke records, "Then an angel from heaven appeared to Him, strengthening Him. **And being in AGONY** [in His mind and spirit, knowing that all eternity hinged on this day], **He prayed more earnestly. And His sweat became as great drops of blood falling down to the ground**" (Luke 22:43-44).

Jesus Looked Forward to the Kingdom of God

Throughout His suffering, Jesus would keep His mind on His coming resurrection and the Kingdom of God. He knew that He would be raised from the dead by the power of God the Father and would give praise and glory to Him at the future resurrection of the saints, when His kingdom would be established over all the earth: "My praise *shall be* of thee in the great congregation: I will pay my vows before them that fear him [the resurrected saints]. The meek shall eat and be satisfied: they shall praise the LORD that seek him: your heart shall live for ever. All the ends of the world shall remember and turn unto the LORD [because of Jesus Christ's sacrifice for sin]: and all the kindreds of the nations shall worship before thee [at His return]. For the kingdom *is* the LORD'S: and he *is* the governor [Ruler] among the nations.

"All *they that be* fat upon earth shall eat and worship: all they that go down to the dust shall bow before him: and none can keep alive his own soul. A seed shall serve him; it shall be accounted to the LORD for a generation. They shall come, and shall declare his righteousness unto a people that shall be born, that he hath done *this* [through the crucifixion and resurrection of Jesus Christ]" (Psa. 22:25-31, *KJV*).

In the final words of His prayer, Jesus asked God the Father to restore Him to the glory that He had with the Father before the world existed. He also prayed for His disciples and for those who would become His disciples through the preaching of the gospel, that they all might be one with Him and the Father: "Jesus spoke these words, and lifted up His eyes to heaven and said, 'Father, **the hour has come**; glorify Your own Son, so that Your Son may also glorify You; since You have given Him authority over all flesh, in order that He may give eternal life to all whom You have given Him. For this is eternal life, that they may know You, the only true God, and Jesus Christ, Whom You did send. **I have glorified You on the earth. I have finished the work that You gave Me to do.**

"And now, **Father, glorify Me with Your own self, with the glory that I had with You before the world existed**. I have manifested Your name to the men whom You have given Me out of the world. They were Yours, and You have given them to Me, and they have kept Your Word. Now they have known that all things that You have given Me are from You. For I have given them the words that You gave to Me; and they have received *them* and truly have known that I came from You; and they have believed that You did send Me.

"I am praying for them; I am not praying for the world, but for those whom You have given Me, for they are Yours. All Mine are Yours, and all Yours *are* Mine; and I have been glorified in them. **And I am no longer in the world, but these are in the world, and I am coming to You. Holy Father, keep them in Your name, those whom You have given Me, so that they may be one, even as We *are one*.** When I was with them in the world, I kept them in Your name. I protected those whom You have given Me, and not one of them has perished except the son of perdition, in order that the Scriptures might be fulfilled.

"But now I am coming to You; and these things I am speaking *while yet* in the world, that they may have My joy fulfilled in them. **I have given them Your words, and the world has hated them** because they are not of the world, just as I am not of the world. I do not pray that You would take them out of the world, but that You would **keep them from the evil one**. They are not of the world, just as I am not of the world. **Sanctify them in Your truth; Your Word is the truth.**

"Even as You did send Me into the world, I also have sent them into the world. **And for their sakes I sanctify Myself, so that they also may**

be sanctified in *Your* truth. I do not pray for these only, but also for those who shall believe in Me through their word; that **they all may be one, even as You, Father, *are* in Me, and I in You; that they also may be one in Us**, in order that the world may believe that You did send Me.

"And I have given them the glory that You gave *to* Me, in order that they may be one, in the same way *that* We are one: I in them, and You in Me, that they may be perfected into one; and that the world may know that You did send Me, and have loved them as You have loved Me. Father, I desire that those whom You have given Me may also be with Me where I am, so that they may behold My glory, which You have given Me; because **You did love Me before *the* foundation of *the* world**. Righteous Father, the world has not known You; but I have known You, and these have known that You did send Me. **And I have made known Your name to them, and will make *it* known** [through His death and resurrection]; **so that the love with which You have loved Me may be in them, and I in them**" (John 17:1-26).

When Jesus finished this prayer, He arose and returned to His disciples. "After saying these things, Jesus went out with His disciples *to a place* beyond the winter stream of Kidron, where *there* was a garden into which He and His disciples entered. And Judas, who was betraying Him, also knew of the place because Jesus had often gathered there with His disciples" (John 18:1-2).

The time had come for Jesus to be betrayed into the hands of sinners, and to give His life for their sins and for the sins of the world. It was the death of God manifested in the flesh—THE CREATOR GOD! **His death and only His death could pay for the sins of all mankind.** Because of God's profound love for mankind, He personally and willingly took upon Himself the penalty for sin, which is death. Though He was made in the likeness of sinful flesh (Rom. 8:2-3), He never sinned. Thus He could offer Himself as the perfect sacrifice for sin.

He would experience a cruel death not only at the hands of wicked and treacherous men, **but at the hands of Satan the devil, the author of sin and the enemy of God and man!** Could God manifested in the flesh conquer sin and overcome Satan by enduring the suffering and shame of the cross?

In fact, there was no question about whether He would be able to endure the pain and agony of the beating, scourging and crucifixion. Why? What was Jesus' mindset? In the book of Hebrews, the apostle Paul wrote of Jesus' attitude: "... **Who for the joy that lay ahead of Him endured *the* cross, *although* He despised *the* shame**, and has sat down at *the* right hand of the throne of God" (Heb. 12:2).

The very fact that Jesus was to die in this manner was the ultimate purpose of His coming in the flesh. He was to taste death for every person because He alone was the Savior of mankind: "But we see Jesus, Who *was* made a little lower than *the* angels, crowned with glory and honor **on ac-**

count of suffering the death, in order that by *the* grace of God He Himself might taste death for everyone; because it was fitting for Him, for Whom all things *were created*, and by Whom all things *exist*, in bringing many sons unto glory, to make the Author of their salvation perfect through sufferings. For both He Who is sanctifying and those who are sanctified *are* all of one; for which cause He is not ashamed to call them brethren, saying, 'I will declare Your name to My brethren; in *the* midst of *the* church I will sing praise to You.' And again, 'I will be trusting in Him.' And again, 'Behold, I and the children whom God has given Me' " (Heb. 2:9-13).

This is what Jesus must have been thinking as He finished His prayer. Now the moment had arrived! The time of His betrayal was at hand. Judas was coming. Jesus was ready.

The Ordeal Begins

His fervent prayers in the Garden of Gethsemane had brought Jesus strength from the Father (Luke 22:43). Determined to do His Father's will, Jesus said to His apostles, "Behold, the hour has drawn near, and the Son of man is betrayed into *the* hands of sinners. Arise! Let us be going. Look, the one who is betraying Me is approaching" (Matt. 26:45-46).

Then Jesus stepped forward to meet Judas, who was now possessed of Satan. The prophecy of His arrest was being fulfilled: "And immediately, while He was speaking, Judas, being one of the twelve, came up with a great multitude with swords and clubs, from the chief priests and the scribes and the elders. Now the one who was betraying Him had given them a sign, saying, '**Whomever I shall kiss, He is *the one*. Arrest Him** and take Him securely away.' And as soon as he came up to Him, he said, 'Master, Master,' and kissed Him earnestly . Then they laid their hands on Him and arrested Him" (Mark 14:43-46).

Jesus was arrested like a common criminal, exactly as the Scriptures had prophesied: "At that point Jesus said to the crowd, 'Have you come out to take Me with swords and clubs, as against a robber? I sat day after day with you, teaching in the temple, and you did not arrest Me. **But all this has happened so that the Scriptures of the prophets might be fulfilled**.' Then all the disciples forsook Him and fled [fulfilling the prophecy in Zechariah 13:7]" (Matt. 26:55-56).

As the chain of agonizing events unfolded—the false accusations and unjust trials, the cruel beatings, the humiliating mocking and spitting, the brutal scourging and a slow death by crucifixion—Jesus Christ remained steadfast in His love and loyalty to God the Father. But the disciples and women who looked upon Jesus' mutilated and bloodied body did not understand what they were witnessing. They stood afar off, watching His crucifixion in stunned bewilderment and disbelief that this could be happening to Jesus Christ, Whom they believed to be the Son of God. How could the promised Savior be nailed to the cross in naked shame, dying before their very eyes? They had hoped that He would save them from the Roman oppression and establish the Kingdom of God. Now there would be no salvation, not at that time or ever, so they thought, as they witnessed Jesus drawing His last breath on the cross. They did not realize until after the resurrection that **the outpouring of Jesus' blood was the beginning of the salvation of the world.**

The Son of God had died to atone for the sins of the world! As the God Who had created man, His death paid the penalty for the sins of every human being, opening the way for all mankind to receive the gift of eternal life. This was the beginning of the New Covenant, sealed with the body and the blood of Jesus Christ, which would bring salvation to all the world.

CHAPTER THREE

Who Killed Jesus the Christ?

Since the crucifixion of Jesus Christ in 30 AD until our day, people have questioned who killed Jesus Christ. Was it the Jews? Was it the Jewish priesthood? Was it the Romans? The answers to these questions are found in the Scriptures themselves, conveying the awesome love, power and plan of God in His intimate dealings with mankind.

Jesus Christ's Sacrificial Death
Planned From the Beginning

Before the creation of the world, God the Father had His predetermined plan of redemption and salvation through His only begotten Son, Jesus Christ, Who was the "the Lamb slain from *the* foundation of *the* world" (Rev. 13:8) for the sins of the whole world—all mankind (I John 2:2). In fulfilling this as well as hundreds of other prophecies, God the Father demonstrated His love by sending His Son: "For God so loved the world that He gave His only begotten Son, so that everyone who believes in Him may not perish, but may have everlasting life. For God sent not His Son into the world that He might judge the world, but that the world might be saved through Him" (John 3:16-17).

The apostle Paul wrote of God's divine plan of salvation in the death and resurrection of Jesus Christ: "In Whom we have redemption through His blood, *even* the remission of sins, according to the riches of His grace, which He has made to abound toward us in all wisdom and intelligence; **having made known to us the mystery of His own will**, according to His good pleasure, **which He purposed in Himself; that in *the divine* plan for the fulfilling of *the* times … Who is working out all things according to the counsel of His own will**" (Eph. 1:7-11).

Jesus Voluntarily Laid Down His Life: Because no man has power over God, nor can anyone command God or exercise authority over Him—whether in heaven or on earth—Jesus made it clear that in the fulfilling of God's plan He would voluntarily lay down His own life, saying, "I am the good Shepherd, and I know those who *are* Mine, and am known of those who *are* Mine. Just as the Father knows Me, I also know the Father; and I lay down My life for the sheep … No one takes it from Me, but I lay it down of Myself. I have authority to lay it down and authority to receive it back again. This commandment I received from My Father' " (John 10:14, 18).

On the night of Jesus' last Passover, as He and the apostles were walking to the Garden of Gethsemane, He began to explain many things to

24

them. Most importantly, He expressed His profound love for them as friends, for whom He was going to lay down His life: "This is My commandment: that you love one another, as I have loved you. **No one has greater love than this: that one lay down his life for his friends**. You are My friends, if you do whatever I command you. No longer do I call you servants, because the servant does not know what his master is doing. But I have called you friends because I have made known to you all *the* things that I have heard from My Father" (John 15:12-15).

In spite of the fact that Jesus willingly laid down His life to suffer death by beating, scourging and crucifixion, the men who were involved had their part in killing Him. As we will see, they were instruments of God to fulfill His will. Those directly involved were: Judas Iscariot; the high priest Caiaphas and the Jewish religious authorities; the Roman governor Pontius Pilate; the Jewish people who demanded that He be crucified; and the Roman soldiers who beat, scourged and crucified Him.

Judas Iscariot: When Jesus personally chose Judas Iscariot, He knew that he would betray Him and deliver Him up to the Jewish and Roman authorities (Mark 3:19). On another occasion, Jesus told the twelve, " 'Did I not choose you twelve, and one of you is *the* devil?' Now He spoke of Judas Iscariot, Simon's *son*; for he was about to betray Him, being one of the twelve" (John 6:70-71).

Before Judas Iscariot betrayed Jesus, he covenanted with the chief priests to do so for thirty pieces of silver—the price of a dead slave: "Then one of the twelve, who was called Judas Iscariot, went to the chief priests, *and* said, 'What are you willing to give me, and I will deliver Him up to you?' And they offered him thirty pieces of silver. And from that time he sought an opportunity to betray Him" (Matt. 26:14-16).

During Jesus' last Passover, when the time came for Judas to betray Him, Jesus said, "Truly I say to you, one of you shall betray Me, *even* he who is eating with Me … The Son of man indeed goes, just as it has been written of Him; but woe to that man by whom the Son of man is betrayed! It would be better for that man if he had not been born" (Mark 14:18, 21). Then Jesus dipped the sop and gave it to Judas, and Satan entered into him. He immediately departed to betray Jesus to the priests (John 13:26). At midnight, as Judas was receiving the band of soldiers who came to arrest Jesus, Caiaphas and the religious authorities were undoubtedly assembling for their final judgment against Jesus. For his part in killing Jesus, Judas hanged himself (Matt. 26:5).

Caiaphas the High Priest and the Jewish Religious Authorities: After the spectacular miracle of raising Lazarus from the dead, the Jewish religious authorities—the priests, the Levites, the scribes, the Pharisees and the Sadducees—were fearful that the Romans would remove them from power. Consequently, they held a special council and decided to kill Jesus: "Then the chief priests and the Pharisees gathered a council and said, 'What shall we do? For this man does many miracles. If we allow Him to continue in this manner, all will believe in Him, and the Romans will come and take away from us both this place and the nation.' But a certain one of them, Caiaphas, being high priest that year, said to them, 'You have no understanding, nor consider that it is better for us that one man die for the people, than that the whole nation should perish.' Now he did not say this of himself, but being high priest that year, he prophesied that Jesus would die for the nation; and not for the nation only, but also that He might gather together into one the children of God who were scattered abroad. Therefore, from that day they took counsel together, so that they might kill Him" (John 11:47-53).

As both the leaders and the supreme court of the Jewish nation, Caiaphas and the religious authorities of the Sanhedrin were the only ones who had the authority to condemn Jesus to death. They did not believe that Jesus was the Son of God, the anointed Messiah of God, and falsely accused Him of blasphemy when He declared that He was (Matt. 26:63-66; Mark 14:60-64). Although God the Father was fulfilling His will, Caiaphas and the Jewish religious authorities had their part in conspiring to kill Jesus. Because they were forbidden by the Romans to execute anyone, they turned Him over to Pontius Pilate for Roman judgment and crucifixion.

From the time of John the Baptist until His crucifixion, the priests and religious authorities had had nearly four years to repent and believe that Jesus was the Christ—the anointed Messiah of God. Because they did not, in the days before His crucifixion, Jesus gave them a final warning: " 'Have you never read in the Scriptures, "*The* Stone that the builders rejected, this has become *the* head of *the* corner. This was from *the* Lord, and it is wonderful in our eyes"? Because of this, I say to you, the kingdom of God shall be taken from you, and it shall be given to a nation *that* produces the fruits of it. And the one who falls on this Stone [in repentance] shall be broken; but on whomever it shall fall [because of failure to repent], it will grind him to powder.' Now after hearing His parables, **the chief priests and the Pharisees knew that He was speaking about them**. And they sought to arrest Him, but they were afraid of the multitudes, because they held Him as a prophet" (Matt. 21:42-46).

Just as they did not heed John the Baptist's warning or Jesus' warnings during His three and one-half year ministry, they did not heed His final warning. They viewed Jesus as a competitor (John 12:19) and were mostly concerned with maintaining their power and religious authority. Although some secretly believed that He was the Messiah, they refused to repent and confess Him: "But even so, many among the rulers believed in Him; but because of the Pharisees they did not confess *Him,* so that they would not be put out of the synagogue; for they loved the glory of men more than the glory of God" (John 12:42-43).

In the greatest act of mercy, Jesus personally offered them forgiveness while He was dying on the cross as they taunted and ridiculed Him (Luke 23:43), but they did not accept it. However, if they had chosen to repent, they would have fulfilled the will of God for those who repent and believe, rather then receiving the judgment of God unto condemnation.

After Jesus' resurrection, through the witness of the apostles, the chief priests and Jewish religious authorities had many opportunities to repent and to accept the forgiveness that Jesus had extended to them while He was dying on the cross. In Acts 4 and 5, the apostles were arrested and brought before Caiaphas, the priests and the full Sanhedrin. The apostles witnessed to them that Jesus Christ was the Savior, the Son of God. Although the chief priests refused to repent and believe, a multitude of priests did (Acts 6:7).

Later, Stephen was brought before them in what might have been their final witness. They resisted his words, also, and killed him as described in the account in Acts: " 'O stiff-necked and uncircumcised in heart and ears! You do always resist the Holy Spirit; as your fathers *did*, so also *do* you. Which of the prophets did your fathers not persecute? And they killed those who foretold the coming of the Righteous One, of Whom you have become the betrayers and murderers; Who received the law by *the* disposition of angels, but have not kept *it.*'

"And when they heard these things, they were cut to their hearts, and they gnashed their teeth at him. But he, being filled with *the* Holy Spirit, looked intently into heaven *and* saw *the* glory of God, and Jesus standing at the right hand of God. And he said, 'Behold, I see the heavens opened, and the Son of man standing at the right *hand* of God.' Then they cried out with a loud voice, *and* stopped their ears, and rushed upon him with one accord, and cast *him* out of the city *and* stoned *him.* And the witnesses laid down their garments at the feet of a young man called Saul. And they stoned Stephen, who called upon *God,* saying, 'Lord Jesus, receive my spirit.' And he fell to his knees *and* cried with a loud voice, 'Lord, do not lay this sin to their charge.' And after he had said this, he died" (Acts 7:51-60).

So heated was the exchange between Stephen and the members of the Sanhedrin, it is recorded that Jesus Christ was standing at the right hand of God in heaven intently watching the whole incident transpire. Yet, they still did not repent and believe. Therefore, they suffered the harsh judgment of God for rejecting Jesus Christ as the anointed Messiah, the Son of God, and for instigating His death by crucifixion. In 70 AD, God's final judgment came. The city of Jerusalem and its Temple were destroyed by the Roman armies.

Pontius Pilate, the Roman Governor: After Caiaphas and the religious authorities had condemned Jesus to death, they brought Him to Pontius Pilate. The Roman governor was the only one who could condemn Jesus to be crucified, as He had prophesied (John 8:28; 12:32, 34). Although secular histories record that Pontius Pilate was a harsh, vicious ruler, many critics have complained that in the film, *The Passion* by Mel Gibson, he was depicted as a wimp. While it is undoubtedly true that Pilate was an oppressive, cruel ruler, such criticisms about his wimpiness reveal a lack of knowledge about the biblical account and the power of God to carry out His will.

While the Jewish authorities condemned Jesus to death because He claimed to be the Son of God, when they brought Jesus before Pilate they falsely accused Him of subverting the nation and making Himself a king. When Pilate questioned Jesus, he did not find any fault against Him. Several times Pilate was willing to let Him go, knowing that the Jewish leaders had had Him arrested because of envy. Moreover, Pilate's wife had a dream about Jesus and warned her husband not to have anything to do with condemning "this righteous man" (Matt. 27:19). Jesus also told Pilate that those who had delivered Him up had the greater sin (John 19:11).

By the time Pilate offered to release Jesus, a huge crowd had gathered that was demanding Jesus' crucifixion and Barabbas' release. Pilate, wanting to appease the priests and the crowd in order to avoid a riot, had Jesus beaten and scourged. Then he released Barabbas to them, and the soldiers led Jesus away to be crucified.

For his part in the crucifixion of Jesus Christ, Pontius Pilate received the judgment of God. In 36 AD, he was recalled to Rome by Tiberius for the ruthless slaughter of thousands of pilgrims. However, Tiberius died before Pilate arrived, and Caligula was Emperor. He exiled Pilate to Gaul, where, in public disgrace, Pilate committed suicide in 38 AD.

The Jewish People: At the instigation of the priests and the religious authorities, a crowd of Jewish people gathered to demand that Jesus be crucified. In a public show before the people, Pilate washed his hands to demonstrate that he was guiltless of Jesus' blood—but he was not. All the people shouted, "His blood be upon us and our children" (Matt. 27:23).

To this day, the Jews detest and reject this record. All denials and claims to the contrary, the historical record is true, and the people did make this statement. But, as we will see, this statement does not apply only to the Jews in the crowd, who uttered those words when Jesus was condemned; it also applies to every human being because all have sinned (Rom. 3:9-10, 19) and are guilty of the blood of Jesus Christ. We must never forget that, while Jesus was dying on the cross, He personally offered forgiveness to those who condemned Him and participated in His death, saying, "Father, forgive them for they do not know what they are doing."

After Jesus' Resurrection Forgiveness Was Offered to All: The day after Jesus' resurrection, He revealed Himself to His apostles and disciples and commanded them to preach the gospel of repentance and remission of sins. "And [He] said to them, 'According as it is written, it was necessary for the Christ to suffer, and to rise from *the* dead the third day. And in His name, **repentance and remission of sins should be preached to all nations, beginning at Jerusalem**. For you are witnesses of these things" (Luke 24:46-48).

At the Temple in Jerusalem on the Day of Pentecost fifty days later, God inspired the apostles to preach repentance and forgiveness to the very ones who had killed Christ: " 'Men, Israelites, listen to these words: Jesus the Nazarean, a man sent forth to you by God, as demonstrated by works of power and wonders and signs, which God performed by Him in your midst, as you yourselves also know; Him, having been delivered up by the predetermined plan and foreknowledge of God, **you have seized by lawless hands *and* have crucified and killed**. *But* God has raised Him up, having loosed the throes of death, because it was not possible *for* Him to be held by it ... **Therefore, let all *the* house of Israel know with full assurance that God has made this *same* Jesus, Whom you crucified, both Lord and Christ**.'

"Now after hearing *this*, they were cut to the heart; and they said to Peter and the other apostles, 'Men *and* brethren, what shall we do?' Then Peter said to them, '**Repent and be baptized each one of you in the name of Jesus Christ for *the* remission of sins, and you yourselves shall receive the gift of the Holy Spirit**. For the promise is to you and to your children, and to all those who are afar off, as many as *the* Lord our God may call.' And with many other words he earnestly testified and exhorted, saying, 'Be saved from this perverse generation.' Then those who joyfully received his message were baptized; and about three thousand souls were added that day" (Acts 2:22-24, 36-41). Undoubtedly, many of those who repented and were baptized were the very ones who, less than two months earlier, were shouting with the rest of the crowd: "Crucify Him! Crucify Him!"

Twice in the weeks and months that followed, the apostles were arrested by the authorities for performing miracles and preaching the resurrection of Jesus Christ. When they were brought before the high priests and the full Sanhedrin of religious leaders, the apostles witnessed to them that they were responsible for killing Jesus (Acts 4:6-23; 5:17-23). They did not repent in spite of the apostles' witness.

Yet, in Jerusalem alone, as the apostles continued to preach, heal the sick and perform miracles "...the Word of God spread, and the number of the disciples in Jerusalem was multiplied exceedingly, and a great multitude of the priests were obedient to the faith" (Acts 6:7). Multiple thousands of Jews believed, repented and received forgiveness, becoming heirs of salvation through Jesus Christ—the one Whom they had killed.

Unfortunately, the majority of the Jewish religious leaders did not repent. Yet, God gave them a third powerful witness through Stephen, whose stinging testimony moved them to kill him (Acts 7). After Stephen was martyred the Jews launched major persecution against the Jewish Christians (Acts 8 and 9).

In His mercy, God gave the rest of the Jewish nation 40 years to repent and believe. Multiple thousands did, but the majority did not. Consequently, true to the prophecies of Jesus, the Roman armies destroyed the Temple and Jerusalem. Hundreds of thousands of Jews died, and the survivors were carried into captivity and dispersed throughout the Roman Empire.

True to Jesus' final warning, those who were directly involved in His crucifixion and who did not repent suffered the judgment of God. Those who accepted His forgiveness when the apostles preached to them received mercy and remission of sins through His sacrifice, as Jesus said in His final warning, "And the one who falls on this Stone shall be broken [in repentance]; but on whomever it shall fall, it will grind him to powder" (Matt. 21:44).

A Biblical Perspective of
Who Killed Jesus Christ

From a human point of view, it is natural to think that greater blame and condemnation should be placed on those who were directly involved in Jesus' death. This may be true; however, we need to remember that they were carrying out God's will in fulfilling the many prophecies about the Messiah, even though they did not realize it.

Before Jesus was crucified, He was beaten and scourged, as Isaiah prophesied (Isa. 50:7-8). So vicious was His scourging that Jesus was hardly recognizable. His body was literally ripped to shreds, with His flesh hanging from the lashings of the scourging whip, exposing His ribs (Isa. 52:14; Psa. 22:17). Jesus was beaten because God the Father laid upon Him the sins of the whole world (Isa. 53:5-6, 11). He was led as a lamb to the slaughter (Isa. 53:7).

The apostle John wrote that those who condemned Jesus to death were fulfilling the will of God. After Caiaphas and the Sanhedrin condemned Him: "… they led Jesus from Caiaphas to the judgment hall, and it was early … Therefore, Pilate came out to them and said, 'What accusation do you bring against this man?' They answered and said to him, 'If He were not an evildoer, we would not have delivered Him up to you.' Then Pilate said to them, 'You take Him and judge Him according to your *own* law.' But the Jews said to him, 'It is not lawful for us to put anyone to death'; so that **the saying of Jesus might be fulfilled, which He had spoken to signify by what death He was about to die**" (John 18:28-32).

Upon questioning, Jesus told Pilate that He was indeed born to be a king, but His kingdom was not of this world. After Pilate heard this he again went out and told the Jews that he found no fault in Him. But the crowd would not listen to him and demanded that Jesus be crucified and Barabbas released (verses 33-40).

"Then Pilate therefore took Jesus and scourged *Him*. And after platting a crown of thorns, the soldiers put *it* on His head; and they threw a purple cloak over Him, and *kept on* saying, 'Hail, King of the Jews!' And they struck Him with the palms of their hands. Then Pilate went out again and said to them, 'Behold, I bring Him out to you, so that you may know that I do not find any fault in Him.' Then Jesus went out, wearing the crown of thorns and the purple cloak; and he said to them, 'Behold the man!'

"But when the chief priests and the officers saw Him, they cried aloud, saying, 'Crucify *Him*, crucify *Him*!' Pilate said to them, 'You take Him and crucify *Him* because I do not find any fault in Him.' The Jews answered him, 'We have a law, and according to our law it is mandatory that He die, because He made Himself *the* Son of God.' Therefore, when Pilate heard this saying, he was even more afraid. And he went into the judgment hall again, and said to Jesus, 'Where have You come from?' But Jesus did not give him an answer.

"Then Pilate said to Him, 'Why don't You speak to me? Don't You know that **I have authority to crucify You, and authority to release You?**' Jesus answered, '**You would not have any authority against Me if it were not given to you from above. For this reason, the one who delivered Me to you has *the* greater sin.**'

"Because of this *saying*, Pilate sought to release Him; but the Jews cried out, saying, 'If you release this *man*, you are not a friend of Caesar. Everyone who makes himself a king speaks against Caesar.' Therefore, after hearing this saying, Pilate *had* Jesus led out, and sat down on the judgment seat at a place called *the* Pavement; but in Hebrew, Gabbatha ... And he said to the Jews, 'Behold your King!' But they cried aloud, 'Away, away *with Him*! Crucify Him!' Pilate said to them, 'Shall I crucify your King?' The chief priests answered, 'We have no king but Caesar.' Therefore, he then delivered Him up to them so that He might be crucified. And they took Jesus and led *Him* away [to be crucified]" (John 19:1-16).

Thus all those involved in killing Jesus Christ were unwittingly fulfilling the Scriptures. John wrote in seven additional places that everything was done to fulfill the will and the Word of God (John 12:38; 15:25; 17:12; 18:9; 19:24, 28, 36). Although they were carrying out the will of God, they were still guilty of and would be held accountable for directly participating in the murder of Christ. Yet, as we have seen, Jesus offered them forgiveness while He was dying on the cross because what they had done was not an unpardonable sin.

A Prophetic View of Those Directly Involved in Crucifying Jesus

The apostle Paul wrote in the book of Hebrews, "But now, once and for all, in *the* consummation of the ages, He has been manifested for *the* purpose of removing sin through His sacrifice *of Himself*.... By Whose will we are sanctified through the offering of the body of Jesus Christ once for all" (Heb. 9:26; 10:10). The unique sacrifice of Jesus Christ was the one offering for sin for all time—all human sin—past, present and future.

From the beginning the apostles had a prophetic view of the sacrifice of Jesus Christ because after His resurrection He opened their minds to understand the Scriptures (Luke 24:44-45). When the apostles were arrested and appeared before the Sanhedrin, they gave a profound witness about Jesus Christ (Acts 4:5-23). After they returned, they reported to the brethren all that had transpired, and they all praised God by referring to Psalm Two: "And when they heard *this*, they lifted up *their* voices to God with one accord and said, 'O Master, You *are* the God Who made the heaven and the earth and the sea, and all that *are* in them, Who by *the* mouth of Your servant David did say, "Why did **the nations** insolently rage, and **the people** imagine vain things? The **kings of the earth** stood up, and **the rulers were gathered together against the Lord and against His Christ**." For of a truth they did gather together against Your holy Son, Jesus, Whom You did anoint, both **Herod and Pontius Pilate**, with *the* **Gentiles and** *the* **people of Israel**, to do whatever Your hand and Your counsel had predetermined to take place' " (Acts 4:24-28).

It is clear from these scriptures that from a prophetic view, those directly involved in killing Jesus Christ represented more than themselves.

Caiaphas and the Religious Rulers: While the priesthood and the religious leaders had the law of Moses and the order of God's Temple service in Jerusalem, they actually rejected the commandments of God by observing their own traditions as Jesus said: "Well did Isaiah prophesy concerning you hypocrites, as it is written, 'This people honors Me with their lips, but their hearts are far away from Me.' But in vain do they worship Me, teaching *for* doctrine the commandments of men. For leaving the commandment of God, you hold fast the tradition of men ... Full well do you reject the commandment of God, so that you may observe your *own* tradition" (Mark 7:6-9).

Because of this they were no different than the pagan religions of the world. As such then, apostate Judaism, **in prophetic type represented all the religions of the world** in the persons of Caiaphas and the religious rulers.

Pontius Pilate and Herod: God gave to the prophet Daniel the prophecies of all the governments of the world from the reign of Nebuchadnezzar king of Babylon to the return of Jesus Christ. At the time of Jesus, the Roman Empire, represented by the fourth beast of Daniel 7, was the ruling power in the world. Therefore, as rulers of Rome, Pontius Pilate and Herod **in prophetic type represented all the governments and nations of the world**.

The Jewish People: The Jewish people living in Judea and Jerusalem, the city where God had placed His name, were the remnant of the twelve tribes of Israel. However, the crowd of Jews, who had gathered before Pilate to demand that Jesus be crucified, **in prophetic type represented all the people of the world**.

Thus, Psalm Two was fulfilled when Jesus Christ was condemned to death and crucified on that fateful day—the Passover day 30 AD.

Every Human Being Had a Part in Killing Jesus Christ

How can those who were not even there or had not yet been born be held accountable? God has decreed, "The wages of sin is death" (Rom. 6:23). "Sin is the transgression of the law" (I John 3:4, KJV), or literally, "Everyone who practices sin is also practicing lawlessness, for sin is lawlessness."

In his epistle to the Romans, Paul wrote, "All have sinned, and come short of the glory of God" (3:23). Since Christ died for the sins of the whole world (I John 2:2), this means that all are guilty of killing Jesus Christ—guilty of the blood of Jesus Christ—and not just the Jews who uttered the words, "Let His blood be upon us and our children." Spiritually speaking, because of sin, all human beings have the blood of Jesus Christ upon them.

Paul charges that all are under sin—Jews and Gentiles—and no one is exempt: "… we have already charged both **Jews and Gentiles—ALL—** *with* **being under sin**, exactly as it is written: 'For there is not a righteous one—not even one! There is not one who understands; there is not one who seeks after God' … Now then, we know that whatever the law says, it speaks to those who are under the law [because all have sinned], so that every mouth may be stopped, **and all the world may become guilty before God**" (Rom. 3:9-11, 19).

The apostle Peter wrote: "Christ also suffered for us, leaving us an example, that you should follow in His footsteps Who committed no sin; neither was guile found in His mouth; Who, when He was reviled, did not revile in return; *when* suffering, He threatened not, but committed *Himself* to Him Who judges righteously; **Who Himself bore our sins within His own body on the tree** [the cross].… Christ indeed once suffered for sins, *the* Just for *the* unjust, so that He might bring us to God; on the one hand, He was put to death in *the* flesh; but on the other hand, He was made alive by the Spirit" (I Pet. 2:21-24; 3:18).

Who is guilty of killing Jesus Christ? The whole world! It was not only those who were directly involved when Jesus was crucified, but beginning with Adam and Eve, every human being—past, present and future—is guilty of killing Jesus Christ. All people, all nations, all religions are guilty of killing Jesus Christ because they are walking contrary to the laws and commandments of God. They have been deceived by Satan the devil, who is the god of this world (Rev. 12:9; II Cor 4:4).

Because of this human condition, the love of God the Father and Jesus Christ was demonstrated not only because Jesus laid down His life to die but also because He did so while we were still enemies of God: "For even when we were without strength, **at the appointed time Christ died for *the* ungodly**. For rarely will anyone die for a righteous man, although perhaps someone might have the courage even to die for a good man. **But God commends His own love to us because, when we were still sinners,**

Christ died for us" (Rom. 5:6-8)

The full meaning of the day that Jesus the Christ died—as our Passover lamb on the Passover day—is summed up by the apostle Paul when he wrote to the Gentiles in Corinth: "For He made Him Who knew no sin *to be* sin for us, so that we might become *the* righteousness of God in Him" (II Cor. 5:21).

CHAPTER FOUR

Twenty-eight Prophecies Fulfilled On the Crucifixion Day

On that Passover day, the day of the crucifixion, all the words of the prophets concerning the suffering of the Christ, or the Anointed One, were fulfilled. Their fulfillment in every detail stands today as a lasting testimony to the Messiahship of Jesus Christ.

The first prophecy, the oldest of all, had been given by the Lord Himself at the time of Adam and Eve's first sin:

1) The serpent would bruise the seed of the woman.

Prophesied: "And I will put enmity between thee and the woman, and between thy seed and her seed; *it* shall bruise thy head, and *thou* shalt bruise his heel" (Gen. 3:15, *KJV*).

Fulfilled: " 'Now is *the* judgment of this world. Now shall the prince of this world be cast out. And if I be lifted up from the earth, I will draw all to Myself.' But He said this to signify by what death He was about to die" (John 12:31-33).

2) The Messiah would be cut off, but not for Himself, as prophesied by Daniel.

Prophesied: "And after threescore and two weeks shall Messiah be cut off, but not for himself..." (Dan. 9:26, *KJV*).

Fulfilled: " 'Nor consider that it is better for us that one man die for the people, than that the whole nation should perish.' Now he did not say this of himself, but being high priest that year, prophesied that Jesus would die for the nation; and not for the nation only, but also that He might gather together into one the children of God who were scattered abroad" (John 11:50-52).

3) The betrayal of Jesus by Judas was foretold by David.

Prophesied: "Yea, mine own familiar friend, in whom I trusted, which did eat of my bread, hath lifted up *his* heel against me" (Psa. 41:9, *KJV*).

Fulfilled: "Then Judas Iscariot, one of the twelve, went to the chief priests in order that he might deliver Him up to them. And after hearing *this*, they were delighted and promised to give him money. And he sought how he might conveniently betray Him" (Mark 14:10-11).

4) Jesus Christ would be forsaken

by His disciples, as prophesied by Zechariah.

Prophesied: "Awake, O sword, against my shepherd, and against the man *that is* my fellow, saith the LORD of hosts: smite the shepherd [Jesus], and the sheep shall be scattered..." (Zech. 13:7, *KJV*).

Fulfilled: "Then they all forsook Him and fled" (Mark 14:50).

5) The price of His betrayal was also foretold by Zechariah.

Prophesied: "And I said unto them, If ye think good, give *me* my price; and if not, forbear. So they weighed for my price thirty *pieces* of silver" (Zech. 11:12, *KJV*).

Fulfilled: "*And* said, 'What are you willing to give me, and I will deliver Him up to you?' And they offered him thirty pieces of silver" (Matt. 26:15).

6) Zechariah also foretold what would be done with the betrayal money.

Prophesied: "And the LORD said unto me, Cast it unto the potter: a goodly price that I was prised at of them. And I took the *thirty* pieces of silver, and cast them to the potter in the house of the LORD" (Zech. 11:13, *KJV*).

Fulfilled: "Now when Judas, who had betrayed Him, saw that He was condemned, he changed his mind *and* returned the thirty pieces of silver to the chief priests and the elders, saying, 'I have sinned and have betrayed innocent blood.' But they said, 'What *is that* to us? You see *to it* yourself.' And after throwing down the pieces of silver in the temple, he went out and hanged himself. But the chief priests took the pieces of silver *and* said, 'It is not lawful to put them into the treasury, since it is *the* price of blood.' And after taking counsel, they bought a potter's field with the *pieces of silver*, for a burial ground for strangers" (Matt. 27:3-7).

7) Isaiah prophesied that Jesus Christ would be sacrificed as the Passover Lamb of God.

Prophesied: "...He is brought as a lamb to the slaughter..." (Isa. 53:7, *KJV*).

Fulfilled: "For Christ our Passover was sacrificed for us" (I Cor. 5:7). "Knowing that you were not redeemed by corruptible things...but by *the* precious blood of Christ, as of a lamb without blemish and without spot; Who truly was foreknown before *the* foundation of *the* world, but was manifested in *these* last times for your sakes" (I Pet. 1:18-20).

8) Isaiah also prophesied the scourging and mocking that He would suffer.

Prophesied: "I gave my back to the smiters [scourgers], and my cheeks to them that plucked off the hair: I hid not my face from shame and spitting" (Isa. 50:6, *KJV*).

Fulfilled: "Then he released Barabbas to them; but after scourging Jesus, he delivered *Him* up so that He might be crucified. Then the governor's soldiers, after taking Jesus with *them* into the Praetorium, gathered the entire band against Him; and they stripped Him *and* put a scarlet cloak around Him. And after platting a crown of thorns, they put *it* on His head; and a rod in His right hand; and bowing *on* their knees before Him, they mocked Him, and *kept on* saying, 'Hail, king of the Jews!' Then, after spitting on Him, they took the rod and struck *Him* on the head" (Matt. 27:26-30).

9) Both Isaiah and David prophesied that Jesus' body would be mutilated.

Prophesied: "As many were astonied at thee; his visage was so marred more than any man, and his form more than the sons of men" (Isa. 52:14, *KJV*). "I may tell [count] all my bones: *they* look *and* stare upon me" (Psa. 22:17, *KJV*).

Fulfilled: "...But after scourging Jesus, he delivered *Him* up so that He might be crucified" (Matt. 27:26*). "Then Pilate therefore took Jesus and scourged *Him*" (John 19:1).

10) David prophesied the shame and dishonor that Jesus would suffer, being condemned as a criminal.

Prophesied: "...The reproaches of them that reproached thee are fallen upon me....*Thou* hast known my reproach, and my shame, and my dishonour: mine adversaries *are* all

before thee. Reproach hath broken my heart; and I am full of heaviness: and I looked *for some* to take pity, but *there was* none; and for comforters, but I found none" (Psa. 69:9, 19-20, *KJV*).

Fulfilled: "At that point Jesus said to the crowd, 'Have you come out to take Me with swords and clubs, as against a robber?' " (Matt. 26:55) "...They answered *and* said, 'He is deserving of death!' " (Matt. 26:66)

11) David also foretold that false witnesses would testify against Christ.

Prophesied: "False witnesses did rise up; they laid to my charge *things* that I knew not" (Psa. 35:11, *KJV*).

Fulfilled: "And the chief priests and the whole Sandhedrin were trying to find testimony against Jesus, to put Him to death; but they did not find *any*. For many bore false witness against Him, but their testimonies did not agree. And some rose up and bore false witness against Him, saying..." (Mark 14:55-57).

12) Isaiah prophesied that Jesus would not make an effort to defend Himself at the trial.

Prophesied: "He was oppressed, and *he* was afflicted, yet he opened not his mouth: he is brought as a lamb to the slaughter, and as a sheep before her shearers is dumb, so he openeth not his mouth" (Isa. 53:7, *KJV*).

Fulfilled: "Then Pilate said to Him, 'Don't You hear how many things they testify against You?' And He did not answer even one word to him, so that the governor was greatly amazed" (Matt. 27:13-14).

13) Isaiah also foretold Jesus Christ's crucifixion as the sin offering for the world.

Prophesied: "Surely *he* hath borne our griefs, and carried our sorrows: yet *we* did esteem him stricken, smitten of God, and afflicted. But *he was* wounded for our transgressions, *he was* bruised for our iniquities: the chastisement of our peace *was* upon him; and with his stripes we are healed. All we like sheep have gone astray; we have turned every one to his own way; and the LORD hath laid on him the iniquity of us all....Yet it pleased the LORD to bruise him; he hath put *him* to grief: when thou shalt make his soul an offering for sin, he shall see *his* seed, he shall prolong *his* days, and the pleasure of the LORD shall prosper in his hand. He shall see of the travail of his soul, and shall be satisfied: by his knowledge shall my righteous servant justify many; for *he* shall bear their iniquities" (Isa. 53:4-6, 10-11, *KJV*).

Fulfilled: "Therefore, he then delivered Him up to them so that He might be crucified. Now they took Jesus and led *Him* away; and He went out bearing His own cross to the place called 'A Skull,' which is called in Hebrew, 'Golgotha'; where they crucified Him, and with Him two others, one on this side and *one* on the other side, and Jesus

in the middle. Now Pilate also wrote a title and put it on the cross. And it was written, 'Jesus the Nazarean, the King of the Jews' " (John 19:16-19).

14) As Isaiah had prophesied, He was numbered among lawbreakers.

Prophesied: "...He was numbered with the transgressors...(Isa. 53:12, *KJV*).

Fulfilled: "And also two other malefactors were led away with Him to be put to death. And when they came to the place called 'Skull,' there they crucified Him and the malefactors, one on *the* right and one on *the* left" (Luke 23:32-33).

15) David prophesied that His hands and His feet would be pierced.

Prophesied: "For dogs have compassed me: the assembly of the wicked have inclosed me: they pierced my hands and my feet" (Psa. 22:16, *KJV*).

Fulfilled: "And they crucified Him" (Mark 15:25). "Then the other disciples said to him, 'We have seen the Lord!' But he said to them, 'If I do not see the nail marks in His hands, and put my finger into the nail marks, and put my hand into His side, I will not believe at all!' Now after eight days, His disciples were within, and Thomas with them. After the doors were shut, Jesus came and stood in the midst, and said, 'Peace to you.' Then He said to Thomas, 'Bring forth your finger, and see My hands; and bring *forth* your hand, and put *it* into My side; and be not unbelieving, but believing' " (John 20:25-27).

16) The parting of His garments was also prophesied by David.

Prophesied: "They part my garments among them, and cast lots upon my vesture" (Psa. 22:18, *KJV*).

Fulfilled: "Then they said to one another, 'Let us not tear it, but let us cast lots for it *to determine* whose it shall be'; that the Scripture might be fulfilled, which says, 'They divided My garments among them, and they cast lots for My vesture.' Therefore the soldiers did these things" (John 19:24).

17) In another psalm, David prophesied that they would give Him vinegar to drink.

Prophesied: "They gave me also gall for my meat; and in my thirst they gave me vinegar to drink" (Psa. 69:21, *KJV*).

Fulfilled: "They gave Him vinegar mingled with gall to drink; but after tasting *it*, He would not drink" (Matt. 27:34).

18) David also prophesied that many would be watching Jesus during the crucifixion.

Prophesied: "...*They* look *and* stare upon me" (Psa. 22:17, *KJV*).

Fulfilled: "And the guards sat down there to guard Him" (Matt. 27:36). "And all the people who were gathered together to this sight, after seeing the things that took place, beat their breasts *and* returned" (Luke 23:48).

19) Among those watching would be Jesus' family and friends, who would stand at a distance.

Prophesied: "...My friends stand aloof from my sore [wounds]; and my kinsmen stand afar off" (Psa. 38:11, *KJV*).

Fulfilled: "Now all those who knew Him stood afar off observing these things, *the* women also who followed Him from Galilee" (Luke 23:49).

20) Some of His observers would shake their heads at Him.

Prophesied: "*I* became also a reproach unto them: *when* they looked upon me they shaked their heads" (Psa. 109:25, *KJV*).

Fulfilled: "But those who were passing by railed at Him, shaking their heads and saying, "You who *would* destroy the temple and build *it* in three days, save Yourself! If You are the Son of God, come down from the cross!" (Matt. 27:39-40)

21) Even the words of His reproachers were prophesied by David.

Prophesied: "He trusted on the LORD *that* he would deliver him: let him deliver him, seeing he delighted in him" (Psa. 22:8, *KJV*).

Fulfilled: " 'He trusted in God; let Him deliver Him now, if He will *have* Him; for He said, "I am the Son of God." ' And the two robbers who were also crucified with Him reproached Him with the same *words*" (Matt. 27:43-44).

22) Isaiah prophesied that Jesus would make intercession for sinners. This intercession began even during His crucifixion.

Prophesied: "...*He* bare the sin of many, and made intercession for the transgressors" (Isa. 53:12, *KJV*).

Fulfilled: "Then Jesus said, 'Father, forgive them, for they do not understand what they are doing.' And they divided His garments, and cast lots" (Luke 23:34).

23) David prophesied the thoughts of Jesus at the height of His suffering.

Prophesied: "My God, my God, why hast thou forsaken me? *why art thou so* far from helping me, *and from* the words of my roaring?" (Psa. 22:1, *KJV*.)

Fulfilled: "And about the ninth hour, Jesus cried out with a loud voice, saying, 'Eli, Eli, lama sabachthani?' That is, 'My God, My God, why have You forsaken Me?' " (Matt. 27:46)

24) Zechariah prophesied that His body would be pierced with a spear.

Prophesied: "...And they shall look upon me whom they have pierced..." (Zech. 12:10, *KJV*).

Fulfilled: "But one of the soldiers had pierced His side with a spear, and immediately water and blood had come out....And again another scripture says, 'They shall look upon Him Whom they pierced' " (John 19:34, 37).

25) David prophesied that Jesus would commit His spirit to God.

Prophesied: "Into thine hand I commit my spirit..." (Psa. 31:5, *KJV*).

Fulfilled: "And after crying out with a loud voice, Jesus said, 'Father, into Your hands I commit My spirit.' And when He had said these things, He expired" (Luke 23:46).

26) David also prophesied Jesus' last words.

Prophesied: "...that he hath done *this*" (Psa. 22:31, *KJV*). The Hebrew literally reads, "For it is finished."

Fulfilled: "Therefore, when Jesus had received the vinegar, He said, 'It is finished.' And after bowing His head, He yielded up *His* spirit" (John 19:30).

27) As no bone of the Passover lamb was to be broken (Ex. 12:46), not a bone of His would be broken.

Prophesied: "He keepeth all his bones: not one of them is broken" (Psa. 34:20, *KJV*).

Fulfilled: "Then the soldiers came and broke the legs of the first *one*, and *the legs* of the other who was crucified with Him. But when they came to Jesus *and* saw that He was already dead, they did not break His legs....For these things took place so that the Scripture might be fulfilled, 'Not a bone of Him shall be broken' " (John 19:32-33, 36).

28) His burial in the tomb of a rich man was foretold by Isaiah.

Prophesied: "He was taken from prison and from judgment: and who shall declare his generation? for he was cut off out of the land of the living: for the transgression of my people was he stricken. And he made his grave with the wicked [criminals], and with the rich in his death; because he had done no vio-lence, neither *was any* deceit in his mouth" (Isa. 53:8-9, *KJV*).

Fulfilled: "And when evening was coming on, a rich man of Arimathea came, named Joseph, who was himself a disciple of Jesus. After going to Pilate, he begged *to have* the body of Jesus. [Jesus would otherwise have been buried among the criminals] Then Pilate commanded the body to be given over *to him.* And after taking the body, Joseph wrapped it in clean linen cloth, and placed it in his new tomb which he had hewn in the rock; and after rolling a great stone to the door of the tomb, he went away" (Matt. 27:57-60). All these prophecies were fulfilled by the suffering, death and burial of Jesus Christ on the Passover day. In the next chapter, we will learn the significance of the timing of Jesus'

Jesus' Last Passover - Nisan 14
From Sunset - Tuesday, April 4 to Sunset - Wednesday, April 5, AD 30

HEBREW TIME		ROMAN TIME
	The Place For The Passover Already Prepared Earlier	
12th Hour	**SUNSET - NISAN 13 ENDS**	6 P.M.
	NISAN 14 BEGINS	
1st Hour		7 P.M.
2nd Hour	1. Passover Begins 2. During Supper Jesus Institutes New Testament Passover With Footwashing 3. Judas Dips The Sop And Leaves To Betray Jesus 4. Breaking And Eating Unleavened Bread As Broken Body of Jesus 5. Drinking Of Wine As Blood Of Jesus For Forgiveness of Sin 6. Contention - Which Disciple Would Be Greatest 7. Jesus Prophesies That Peter Will Deny Him Three Times 8. Final Message To Disciple 9. Final Instruction Take a Sword 10. Sing a Hymn And Leave Toward Mount Of Olives	8 P.M.
3rd Hour		9 P.M.
4th Hour	1. On The Way To Gethsemane Jesus Tells Disciples He Is The True Vine. 2. Final Words of Encouragement 3. Tells Disciples All Would Be Scattered	10 P.M.
5th Hour	1. Prays The Lord's Prayer The Third Hour - John 17 2. Jesus Takes Peter, James And John with Him And Prays For Three Hours But The Disciples Sleep 3. Jesus Prays So Hard That His Sweat Appears Like Great Drops Of Blood	11 P.M.
6th Hour	**MIDNIGHT** **April 4 Ends** / **April 5 Begins**	12 Midnight
7th Hour	1. Judas Comes With Crowd Of Soldiers And Betrays Jesus With a Kiss 2. Peter Cuts Off An Ear Of The High Priest's Servant - Jesus Heals Him 3. All Is Done To Fulfill Prophesy - Disciples Escape - Mark Escapes Naked	1 A.M.
8th Hour	1. Jesus Led Away To Annas The Priest First 2. Peter Follows At A Distance And Goes Into The Courtyard 3. Annas Questions Jesus And Beats Him And Sends Him To Caiaphas	2 A.M.
9th Hour		3 A.M.
10th Hour	1. The Chief Priests And Sanhedrin Question Jesus - Hear False Witnesses - Condemn Jesus 2. Peter Denies Jesus Twice - Cock Crows Once 3. About An Hour Later Peter Denies Jesus The Third Time The Cock Crows Again - Jesus Looks Right At Peter	4 A.M.
11th Hour	1. At Daybreak - The Whole Sanhedrin Condemns Jesus To Death and Sends Him To Pilate 2. Jesus Accused Before Pilate - He Questions Jesus and Finds He is From Galilee, Then Sends Him To Herod. Herod Sends Him Back to Pilate	5 A.M.
12th Hour	**SUNRISE**	6 A.M.

Twenty-eight Prophecies Fulfilled on the Crucifixion Day

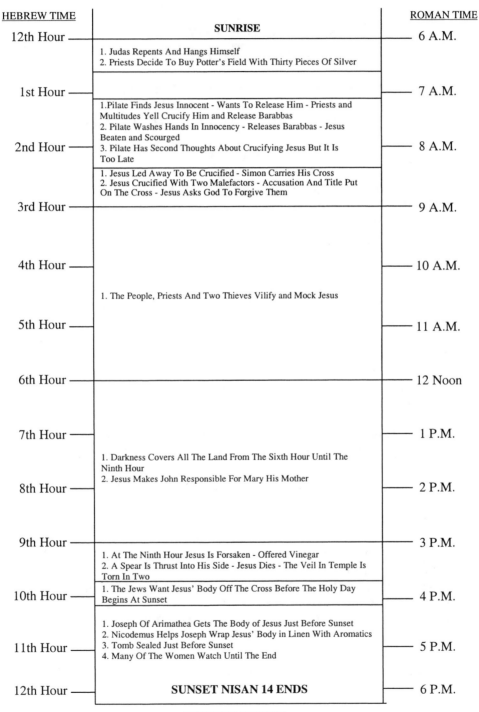

HEBREW TIME		ROMAN TIME
	SUNRISE	
12th Hour		6 A.M.
	1. Judas Repents And Hangs Himself 2. Priests Decide To Buy Potter's Field With Thirty Pieces Of Silver	
1st Hour		7 A.M.
	1. Pilate Finds Jesus Innocent - Wants To Release Him - Priests and Multitudes Yell Crucify Him and Release Barabbas 2. Pilate Washes Hands In Innocency - Releases Barabbas - Jesus Beaten and Scourged 3. Pilate Has Second Thoughts About Crucifying Jesus But It Is Too Late	
2nd Hour		8 A.M.
	1. Jesus Led Away To Be Crucified - Simon Carries His Cross 2. Jesus Crucified With Two Malefactors - Accusation And Title Put On The Cross - Jesus Asks God To Forgive Them	
3rd Hour		9 A.M.
4th Hour		10 A.M.
	1. The People, Priests And Two Thieves Vilify and Mock Jesus	
5th Hour		11 A.M.
6th Hour		12 Noon
7th Hour		1 P.M.
	1. Darkness Covers All The Land From The Sixth Hour Until The Ninth Hour 2. Jesus Makes John Responsible For Mary His Mother	
8th Hour		2 P.M.
9th Hour		3 P.M.
	1. At The Ninth Hour Jesus Is Forsaken - Offered Vinegar 2. A Spear Is Thrust Into His Side - Jesus Dies - The Veil In Temple Is Torn In Two	
10th Hour	1. The Jews Want Jesus' Body Off The Cross Before The Holy Day Begins At Sunset	4 P.M.
	1. Joseph Of Arimathea Gets The Body of Jesus Just Before Sunset 2. Nicodemus Helps Joseph Wrap Jesus' Body in Linen With Aromatics 3. Tomb Sealed Just Before Sunset 4. Many Of The Women Watch Until The End	
11th Hour		5 P.M.
12th Hour	**SUNSET NISAN 14 ENDS**	6 P.M.

NISAN 15 BEGINS

CHAPTER FIVE

Scriptures: The Day
Jesus the Christ Died

NISAN 13 - TUESDAY, APRIL 4, 30 AD

1. THE DISCIPLES PREPARE FOR THE PASSOVER

MARK 14

12. And on the first day of the unleaveneds,* when they were killing the Passover *lambs*, His disciples said to Him, "Where do You desire that we go and prepare, so that You may eat the Passover?"
13. And He sent two of His disciples, and said to them, "Go into the city, and you shall meet a man carrying a pitcher of water; follow him.
14. And whatever house he shall enter, say to the master of the house *that* the Teacher says, 'Where is the guest chamber, where I may eat the Passover with My disciples?'
15. And he shall show you a large upper room, furnished *and* ready. There prepare for us."
16. And His disciples went away: and *when* they came into the city, they found *it* exactly as He had said to them; and they prepared the Passover.

PASSOVER DAY NISAN 14 - TUESDAY EVENING, APRIL 4, 30 AD, APPROXIMATELY 7 - 7:30 PM

2. JESUS' LAST PASSOVER BEGINS AT EVENING

LUKE 22

14. Now when the hour had come, He sat *down,* and the twelve apostles with Him.
15. And He said to them, "With *earnest* desire I have desired to eat this Passover with you before I suffer.
16. For I tell you that I will not eat of it again until it be fulfilled in the kingdom of God."

---

*See Appendix A, page 144.

44

3. JESUS INSTITUTES THE NEW COVENANT PASSOVER: 1) FOOTWASHING 2) EATING THE UNLEAVENED BREAD 3) DRINKING THE WINE

FIRST PART OF THE NEW COVENANT PASSOVER: THE FOOTWASHING

JOHN 13

2. And during supper (the devil having already put into the heart of Judas Iscariot, Simon's *son,* that he should betray Him),

3. Jesus, knowing that the Father had given all things into *His* hands, and that He had come from God and was going to God,

4. Rose from supper and laid aside *His* garments; and after taking a towel, He secured it around Himself.

5. Next, He poured water into a washing basin and began to wash the disciples' feet, and to wipe *them* with the towel which He had secured.

6. Then He came to Simon Peter; and he said to Him, "Lord, are You going to wash my feet?"

7. Jesus answered and said to him, "What I am doing you do not understand now, but you shall know after these things."

8. Peter said to Him, "You shall not wash my feet, not ever." Jesus answered him, "If I do not wash you, you have no part with Me."

9. Simon Peter said to Him, "Lord, not my feet only, but also *my* hands and *my* head."

10. Jesus said to him, "The one who has been washed does not need to wash *anything other* than the feet, but is completely clean; and you are clean, but not all."

11. For He knew the one who was betraying Him; this was the reason He said, "Not all of you are clean."

12. Therefore, when He had washed their feet, and had taken His garments, *and* had sat down again, He said to them, "Do you know what I have done to you?

13. You call Me the Teacher and the Lord, and you speak rightly, because I am.

14. Therefore, if I, the Lord and the Teacher, have washed your feet, you also are duty-bound to wash one another's feet;

15. For I have given you an example, *to show* that you also should do exactly as I have done to you.

16. Truly, truly I tell you, a servant is not greater than his lord, nor a messenger greater than he who sent him.

17. If you know these things, blessed are you if you do them."

4. JUDAS DIPS THE SOP AND LEAVES
TO BETRAY JESUS

JOHN 13

18. "I am not speaking of you all; *for* I know whom I have chosen, in order that the scripture might be fulfilled: 'He who eats bread with Me has lifted up his heel against Me.'

19. I am telling you at this time, before it happens, so that when it does happen, you may believe that I AM.

20. Truly, truly I tell you, the one who receives whomever I send is receiving Me; and the one who receives Me is receiving Him Who sent Me."

21. *As He* was saying these things, Jesus was troubled in spirit, and testified, saying, "Truly, truly I tell you, one of you shall betray Me."

22. Then the disciples looked at one another, wondering of whom He was speaking.

23. Now one of His disciples, the one whom Jesus loved, was leaning on Jesus' chest.

24. And so, Simon Peter motioned to him to ask who was the one of whom He was speaking.

25. Then he leaned back on Jesus' chest *and* asked Him, "Lord, who is it?"

26. Jesus answered, "It is the one to whom I shall give a sop after I have dipped *it*." And when He had dipped the sop, He gave *it* to Judas Iscariot, Simon's *son*.

27. And after the sop, Satan entered into him. Then Jesus said to him, "What you do, do quickly."

28. But not one of those sitting at the table knew why He said *this* to him;

29. For some thought, since Judas had the bag, that Jesus was telling him, "Buy the things that we need for the feast"; or that he should give something to the poor.

30. So then, after receiving the sop, he immediately went out; and it was night.

31. When he was gone, Jesus said, "Now has the Son of man been glorified, and God has been glorified in Him.

32. If God has been glorified in Him, God shall also glorify Him in Himself, and shall immediately glorify Him."

5. SECOND PART: EATING THE UNLEAVENED BREAD

LUKE 22

19. And He took bread; *and* after giving thanks, He broke *it* and gave *it* to them, saying, "This is My body, which is given for you.

This do in the remembrance of Me."

6. THIRD PART: DRINKING THE WINE

MARK 14

23. And He took the cup; *and* after giving thanks, He gave *it* to them; and they all drank of it.
24. And He said to them, "This is My blood, the blood of the New Covenant, which is poured out for many.
25. Truly I say to you, I will not drink again at all of the fruit of the vine until that day when I drink it new in the kingdom of God."

LUKE 22

17. And He took a cup; *and* after giving thanks, He said, "Take this, and divide *it* among yourselves.
18. For I say to you, I will not drink at all of the fruit of the vine until the kingdom of God has come."
20. In like manner also, *He took* the cup after supper, saying, "This cup *is* the new covenant in My blood, which is poured out for you."

7. CONTENTIONS AMONG THE DISCIPLES AS TO WHO WOULD BE THE GREATEST

LUKE 22

24. And there was also an argument among them, *even* this: which of them should be considered *the* greatest.
25. And He said to them, "The kings of the nations lord over them, and those who exercise authority over them are called benefactors.
26. But *it shall* not be this way *among* you; rather, let the one who is greatest among you be as the younger, and the one who is leading as the one who is serving.
27. For who *is* greater, the one who is sitting *at the table*, or the one who is serving? *Is* not the one who sits *at the table*? But I am among you as one who is serving.
28. Now you are the ones who have continued with Me in My temptations.
29. And I appoint to you, as My Father has appointed to Me, a kingdom;
30. So that you may eat and drink at My table in My kingdom, and may sit on thrones judging the twelve tribes of Israel."

8. A NEW COMMANDMENT -
LOVE EACH OTHER AS JESUS LOVED HIS DISCIPLES

JOHN 13

33. "Little children, I am with you yet a little while. You shall seek Me; but as I told the Jews, 'Where I am going, you cannot come,' I am now telling you also.
34. A new commandment I give to you: that you love one another in the same way that I have loved you, that *is how* you are to love one another.
35. By this shall everyone know that you are My disciples—if you love one another."

9. JESUS PROPHESIES THAT PETER
WILL DENY HIM THREE TIMES

MARK 14

27. Then Jesus said to them, "All of you shall be offended in Me in this night; for it is written, 'I will smite the Shepherd, and the sheep shall be scattered.'
28. But after I have risen, I will go before you into Galilee."
29. Then Peter said to Him, "Even if all shall be offended, yet I *shall* not."
30. And Jesus said to him, "Truly I say to you, today, in this *very* night, before *the* cock crows twice, you shall deny Me three times."
31. But he spoke more adamantly, "If it were necessary for me to die with You, I would not deny You in any way." And they all spoke in the same manner also.

10. THE BEGINNING OF THE FINAL
MESSAGE TO HIS DISCIPLES

JOHN 14

1. "Let not your heart be troubled. You believe in God; believe also in Me.
2. In My Father's house are many dwelling places; if it were otherwise, I would have told you. I am going to prepare a place for you.
3. And if I go and prepare a place for you, I will come again and receive you to Myself; so that where I am, you may be also.
4. And where I am going you know, and the way you know."
5. Thomas said to Him, "Lord, we do not know where You are going; how then can we know the way?"
6. Jesus said to him, "I am the way, and the truth, and the life; no

one comes to the Father except through Me.

7. If you had known Me, you would have known My Father also. But from this time forward, you know Him and have seen Him."

8. Philip said to Him, "Lord, show us the Father, and that will be sufficient for us."

9. Jesus said to him, "Have I been with you so long a time, and you have not known Me, Philip? The one who has seen Me has seen the Father; why then do you say, 'Show us the Father'?

10. Don't you believe that I am in the Father, and the Father is in Me? The words that I speak to you, I do not speak from My own self; but the Father Himself, Who dwells in Me, does the works.

11. Believe Me that I am in the Father and the Father is in Me; but if not, believe Me because of the works themselves.

12. Truly, truly I say to you, the one who believes in Me shall also do the works that I do; and greater works than these shall he do because I am going to the Father.

13. And whatever you shall ask in My name, this will I do that the Father may be glorified in the Son.

14. If you ask anything in My name, I will do *it*.

15. If you love Me, keep the commandments—namely, My commandments.

16. And I will ask the Father, and He shall give you another Comforter, that it may be with you throughout the age:

17. *Even* the Spirit of the truth, which the world cannot receive because it perceives it not, nor knows it; but you know it because it dwells with you, and shall be within you.

18. I will not leave you orphans; I will come to you.

19. Yet a little while and the world shall see Me no longer; but you shall see Me. Because I live, you shall live also.

20. In that day, you shall know that I am in My Father, and you *are* in Me, and I am in you.

21. The one who has My commandments and is keeping them, that is the one who loves Me; and the one who loves Me shall be loved by My Father, and I will love him and will manifest Myself to him."

22. Judas (not Iscariot) said to him, "Lord, what has happened that You are about to manifest Yourself to us, and not to the world?"

23. Jesus answered and said to him, "If anyone loves Me, he will keep My word; and My Father will love him, and We will come to him and make Our abode with him.

24. The one who does not love Me does not keep My words; and the word that you hear is not Mine, but the Father's, Who sent Me.

25. I have spoken these things to you while I am yet present with you.

26. But *when* the Comforter *comes, even* the Holy Spirit, which the

Father will send in My name, that one shall teach you all things, and shall bring to your remembrance everything that I have told you.

27. Peace I leave with you; My peace I give to you; not as the world gives do I give *it* to you. Let not your heart be troubled, nor let it fear.

28. You have heard Me say to you that I am going away, and *that* I will come to you *again*. If you loved Me, you would have rejoiced that I said, 'I am going to the Father' because My Father is greater than I.

29. And now I have told you before it happens, so that when it comes to pass, you may believe.

30. I will not speak with you much longer because the ruler of this world is coming; but he does not have a single thing in Me.

31. Yet *he comes* so that the world may know that I love the Father, and that I do exactly as the Father has commanded Me. Arise, let us go out."

11. SOME FINAL INSTRUCTIONS TO THE DISCIPLES

LUKE 22

35. And He said to them, "When I sent you without purse and provision bag and sandals, did you lack anything?" And they said, "Nothing."

36. Then He said to them, "Now, however, let the one who has a purse take *it, and* likewise *his* provision bag; and let the one who does not have a sword sell his garment and buy *one*.

37. For I say to you, that which has been written must yet be accomplished in Me: 'And He was reckoned with *the* lawless'; for the things concerning Me have a fulfillment."

12. TAKE TWO SWORDS

LUKE 22

38. And they said, "Lord, see, here *are* two swords." And He said to them, "It is enough."

13. THEY SING A HYMN AND LEAVE

MATTHEW 26

30. And after singing a hymn, they went out to the Mount of Olives.

14. JESUS THE CHRIST IS THE TRUE VINE - LAST COMMAND TO HIS DISCIPLES

JOHN 15

1. "I am the true vine, and My Father is the husbandman.

2. He takes away every branch in Me *that* does not bear fruit; but He cleanses each one that bears fruit, in order that it may bear more fruit.

3. You are already clean through the word that I have spoken to you.

4. Dwell in Me, and I in you. As a branch cannot bear fruit of itself, but only if it remains in the vine, neither *can* you *bear fruit* unless you are dwelling in Me.

5. I am the vine, *and* you *are* the branches. The one who is dwelling in Me, and I in him, bears much fruit; because apart from Me you can do nothing.

6. If anyone does not dwell in Me, he is cast out as a branch, and is dried up; and men gather them and cast *them* into a fire, and they are burned.

7. If you dwell in Me, and My words dwell in you, you shall ask whatever you desire, and it shall come to pass for you.

8. In this is My Father glorified, that you bear much fruit; so shall you be My disciples.

9. As the Father has loved Me, I also have loved you; live in My love.

10. If you keep My commandments, you shall live in My love; just as I have kept My Father's commandments and live in His love.

11. These things I have spoken to you, in order that My joy may dwell in you, and *that* your joy may be full.

12. This is My commandment: that you love one another, as I have loved you.

13. No one has greater love than this: that one lay down his life for his friends.

14. You are My friends, if you do whatever I command you.

15. No longer do I call you servants, because the servant does not know what his master is doing. But I have called you friends because I have made known to you all *the* things that I have heard from My Father.

16. You yourselves did not choose Me, but I have personally chosen you, and ordained you, that you should go *forth* and bear fruit, and that your fruit should remain; so that whatever you shall ask the Father in My name, He may give you.

17. These things I command you, that you love one another.

18. If the world hates you, you know that it hated Me before *it hated* you.

19. If you were of the world, the world would love its own. However, because you are not of the world, but I have personally chosen you out of the world, the world hates you for this.

20. Remember the word that I spoke to you: a servant is not greater than his master. If they persecuted Me, they will persecute you also. If they kept My word, they will keep your *word* also.

21. But they will do all these things to you for My name's sake, because they do not know Him Who sent Me.

22. If I had not come and spoken to them, they would not have had sin; but now they have nothing to cover their sin.

23. The one who hates Me hates My Father also.

24. If I had not done among them the works that no other man has done, they would not have had sin; but now they have both seen and hated both Me and My Father.

25. But this has happened so that the saying might be fulfilled which is written in their law, 'They hated Me without *a* cause.'

26. But when the Comforter has come, which I will send to you from the Father, *even* the Spirit of the truth, which proceeds from the Father, that one shall bear witness of Me.

27. Then you also shall bear witness, because you have been with Me from *the* beginning."

15. FINAL WORDS OF ENCOURAGEMENT

JOHN 16

1. "I have spoken these things to you so that you will not be offended.

2. They shall cast you out of the synagogues; furthermore, the time is coming that everyone who kills you will think that he is rendering service to God.

3. And they shall do these things to you because they do not know the Father, nor Me.

4. But I have told you these things so that when the time comes, you may remember that I said *them* to you. However, I did not say these things to you at *the* beginning because I was with you.

5. But now I am going to Him Who sent Me; and none of you asks Me, 'Where are You going?'

6. But because I have spoken these things to you, grief has filled your hearts.

7. But I am telling you the truth. It is profitable for you that I go away because if I do not go away, the Comforter will not come to you. However, if I go, I will send it to you.

8. And when that one has come, it will convict the world concerning sin, and righteousness, and judgment:

9. Concerning sin, because they do not believe in Me;

10. Concerning righteousness, because I am going to the Father and you no longer will see Me;

11. And concerning judgment, because the ruler of this world has been judged.

12. I have yet many things to tell you, but you are not able to bear them now.

13. However, when that one has come, *even* the Spirit of the truth, it will lead you into all truth because it shall not speak from itself, but whatever it shall hear, it shall speak. And it shall disclose to you the things to come.

14. That one shall glorify Me because it shall disclose to you *the things that* it receives from Me.

15. Everything that the Father has is Mine; for this reason, I said that it shall receive from Me and shall disclose *these things* to you.

16. A little *while*, and you shall not see Me; and again a little *while*, and you shall see Me, because I am going to the Father."

17. Then *some* of His disciples said to one another, "What is this that He is saying to us, 'A little *while*, and you shall not see Me; and again a little *while*, and you shall see Me,' and, 'because I am going to the Father'? "

18. Therefore they said, "What is this that He is saying, the 'little *while*'? We do not understand what He is saying."

19. Then Jesus, knowing that they desired to ask Him, said to them, "*Why* are you inquiring among one another about this that I said, 'A little *while*, and you shall not see Me; and again a little *while*, and you shall see Me'?

20. Truly, truly I tell you, you shall weep and lament, but the world shall rejoice; and you shall be grieved, but your grief shall be turned into joy.

21. A woman when she is giving birth has grief because her time *of travail* has come; but after she gives birth to the child, she no longer remembers the anguish because of the joy that a child has been born into the world.

22. And likewise, you indeed have grief now; but I will see you again, and your heart shall rejoice, and no one shall take your joy from you.

23. And in that day you shall ask Me nothing. Truly, truly I tell you, whatever you shall ask the Father in My name, He will give you.

24. Until this day, you have asked nothing in My name. Ask, and you shall receive, that your joy may be full.

25. These things I have spoken to you in allegories; but the time is coming when I will no longer speak to you in allegories, but I will plainly disclose to you *the things* of the Father.

26. In that day, you shall ask in My name; and I do not tell you that I will beseech the Father for you,

27. For the Father Himself loves you, because you have loved Me, and have believed that I came forth from God.

28. I came forth from the Father and have come into the world; again, I am leaving the world and am going to the Father."

29. *Then* His disciples said to Him, "Behold, now You are speaking plainly and are not speaking *in* an allegory.

30. Now we know that You understand all things, and do not need to have someone ask You. By this we believe that You came forth from God."

31. Jesus answered them, "Do you now believe?"

16. ALL WILL BE SCATTERED. JESUS HAS OVERCOME THE WORLD

JOHN 16

32. "Listen, the time is coming, and has already come, that you shall be scattered each to his own, and you shall leave Me alone; and *yet* I am not alone because the Father is with Me.

33. These things I have spoken to you, so that in Me you may have peace. In the world you shall have tribulation. But be courageous! I have overcome the world."

17. JESUS GOES TO GETHSEMANE

MATTHEW 26

36. Then Jesus came with them to a place called Gethsemane; and He said to His disciples, "Sit here, while I go onward and pray."

37. And He took with *Him* Peter and the two sons of Zebedee, *and* He began to be very melancholy and deeply depressed.

38. Then He said to them, "My soul is deeply grieved, even to death. Stay here and watch with Me."

PASSOVER DAY NISAN 14 - TUESDAY NIGHT; APRIL 4, 30 AD, APPROXIMATELY 10 PM - 1 AM

18. JESUS PRAYS FOR THREE HOURS

LUKE 22

41. And He withdrew from them about a stone's throw; and falling to *His* knees, He prayed,

42. Saying, "Father, if You are willing to take away this cup from Me—; nevertheless, not My will, but Your *will* be done."

43. Then an angel from heaven appeared to Him, strengthening Him.

44. And being in agony, He prayed more earnestly. And His sweat became as great drops of blood falling down to the ground.

45. And after rising up from prayer, He came to *His* disciples *and* found them sleeping for grief.

46. Then He said to them, "Why are you sleeping? Arise and pray, so that you do not enter into temptation."

19. THE LORD'S PRAYER

JOHN 17

1. Jesus spoke these words, and lifted up His eyes to heaven and said, "Father, the hour has come; glorify Your own Son, so that Your Son may also glorify You;

2. Since You have given Him authority over all flesh, in order that He may give eternal life to all whom You have given Him.

3. For this is eternal life, that they may know You, the only true God, and Jesus Christ, Whom You did send.

4. I have glorified You on the earth. I have finished the work that You gave Me to do.

5. And now, Father, glorify Me with Your own self, with the glory that I had with You before the world existed.

6. I have manifested Your name to the men whom You have given Me out of the world. They were Yours, and You have given them to Me, and they have kept Your Word.

7. Now they have known that all things that You have given Me are from You.

8. For I have given them the words that You gave to Me; and they have received *them* and truly have known that I came from You; and they have believed that You did send Me.

9. I am praying for them; I am not praying for the world, but for those whom You have given Me, for they are Yours.

10. All Mine are Yours, and all Yours *are* Mine; and I have been glorified in them.

11. And I am no longer in the world, but these are in the world, and I am coming to You. Holy Father, keep them in Your name, those whom You have given Me, so that they may be one, even as We *are one*.

12. When I was with them in the world, I kept them in Your name. I protected those whom You have given Me, and not one of them has perished except the son of perdition, in order that the Scriptures

might be fulfilled.

13. But now I am coming to You; and these things I am speaking *while yet* in the world, that they may have My joy fulfilled in them.

14. I have given them Your words, and the world has hated them because they are not of the world, just as I am not of the world.

15. I do not pray that You would take them out of the world, but that You would keep them from the evil one.

16. They are not of the world, just as I am not of the world.

17. Sanctify them in Your truth; Your Word is the truth.

18. Even as You did send Me into the world, I also have sent them into the world.

19. And for their sakes I sanctify Myself, so that they also may be sanctified in *Your* truth.

20. I do not pray for these only, but also for those who shall believe in Me through their word;

21. That they all may be one, even as You, Father, *are* in Me, and I in You; that they also may be one in Us, in order that the world may believe that You did send Me.

22. And I have given them the glory that You gave *to* Me, in order that they may be one, in the same way *that* We are one:

23. I in them, and You in Me, that they may be perfected into one; and that the world may know that You did send Me, and have loved them as You have loved Me.

24. Father, I desire that those whom You have given Me may also be with Me where I am, so that they may behold My glory, which You have given Me; because You did love Me before *the* foundation of *the* world.

25. Righteous Father, the world has not known You; but I have known You, and these have known that You did send Me.

26. And I have made known Your name to them, and will make *it* known; so that the love with which You have loved Me may be in them, and I in them."

20. THE TIME OF THE BETRAYAL
APPROXIMATELY 1 AM

MATTHEW 26

45. Then He came to His disciples and said to them, "Sleep on now, and take your rest. Behold, the hour has drawn near, and the Son of man is betrayed into *the* hands of sinners.

46. Arise! Let us be going. Look, the one who is betraying Me is approaching."

PASSOVER DAY NISAN 14 - WEDNESDAY MORNING, APRIL 5, 30 AD

21. JUDAS BETRAYS JESUS WITH A KISS

JOHN 18

1. After saying these things, Jesus went out with His disciples *to a place* beyond the winter stream of Kidron, where *there* was a garden into which He and His disciples entered.
2. And Judas, who was betraying Him, also knew of the place because Jesus had often gathered there with His disciples.
3. Then Judas, after receiving a band and officers from the chief priests and Pharisees, came there with torches and lamps and weapons.
4. Jesus, therefore, knowing all *the* things that were coming upon Him, went forward *and* said to them, "Whom are you seeking?"
5. They answered Him, "Jesus the Nazarean." Jesus said to them, "I AM." And Judas, who was betraying Him, was also standing with them.
6. But when He said to them, "I AM," they went backward and fell to *the* ground.
7. Then He asked them again, "Whom are you seeking?" And they said, "Jesus the Nazarean."
8. Jesus answered, "I told you that I AM. Therefore, if you are seeking Me, allow these to go their way";
9. So that the saying might be fulfilled which He had said, "Of those whom You have given Me, not one of them have I lost."

22. PETER CUTS OFF AN EAR OF THE HIGH PRIEST'S SERVANT - JESUS HEALS HIM

LUKE 22

49. And when those who were with Him saw what was about to happen, they said to Him, "Lord, shall we strike with *the* sword?"
50. Then a certain one of them struck the servant of the high priest and cut off his right ear.
51. But Jesus answered *and* said, "That is enough!" Then He touched his ear *and* healed him.
52. And Jesus said to those who had come out against Him, *the* chief priests and captains of the temple and elders, "Have you come out, as against a thief, with swords and clubs?
53. When I was with you daily in the temple, you did not stretch out *your* hands against Me; but this is your hour, and the power of darkness."

23. ALL WAS DONE TO FULFILL PROPHECY

MATTHEW 26

56. But all this has happened so that the Scriptures of the prophets might be fulfilled. Then all the disciples forsook Him and fled.

MARK 14

50. Then they all forsook Him and fled.
51. Now a certain young man was following Him, having a linen cloth wrapped around *his* naked *body*; and the young men seized him,
52. But he *escaped*, leaving the linen cloth behind, and ran from them naked.

24. JESUS IS LED AWAY TO THE PRIEST'S HOUSE

JOHN 18

13. And they led Him away to Annas first; for he was *the* father-in-law of Caiaphas, who was high priest that year.
14. Now it was Caiaphas who had given counsel to the Jews that it was profitable for one man to perish for the people.

25. PETER FOLLOWS THEM INTO THE COURTYARD

JOHN 18

15. But Simon Peter and the other disciple followed Jesus. And that disciple was known to the high priest, and entered with Jesus into the court of the high priest.
16. But Peter stood outside at the door. Then the other disciple, who was known to the high priest, went out and spoke to the door-keeper, and brought Peter in.
18. Now the servants and the officers had made a fire, for it was cold; and they were standing *there* warming themselves, and Peter was *also* standing and warming himself.

PASSOVER DAY NISAN 14 - WEDNESDAY MORNING, APRIL 5, 30 AD, APPROXIMATELY 2 AM

26. ANNAS QUESTIONS JESUS AND SENDS HIM TO CAIAPHAS

JOHN 18

19. Then the high priest questioned Jesus concerning His disciples

and concerning His teachings.

20. Jesus answered him, "I spoke openly to the world; I always taught in the synagogue and in the temple, where the Jews always assemble, and I spoke nothing in secret.

21. Why do you question Me? Ask those who have heard what I spoke to them; behold, they know what I said."

22. But after He said these things, one of the officers who was standing by struck Jesus on the face, saying, "Do You answer the high priest in that way?"

23. Jesus answered him, "If I have spoken evil, testify of the evil; but if well, why do you strike Me?"

24. *Then* Annas sent Him bound to Caiaphas, the high priest.

27. THE CHIEF PRIESTS ILLEGALLY CONDEMN JESUS

MARK 14

55. And the chief priests and the whole Sanhedrin were trying to find testimony against Jesus, to put Him to death; but they did not find *any*.

56. For many bore false witness against Him, but their testimonies did not agree.

57. And some rose up and bore false witness against Him, saying,

58. "We heard Him say, 'I will destroy this temple made with hands, and in three days I will build another made without hands.' "

59. But neither did their testimonies agree with one another.

60. Then the high priest stood up in the center *and* questioned Jesus, saying, "Have You nothing to *say in* answer *to* what these are testifying against You?"

61. But He remained silent and answered nothing. Again the high priest questioned Him, and said to Him, "Are You the Christ, the Son of the Blessed?"

62. And Jesus said, "I AM. And you shall see the Son of man sitting at *the* right hand of power, and coming with the clouds of heaven."

63. Then the high priest ripped his *own* garments *and* said, "What further need do we have of witnesses?

64. You have heard the blasphemy! What is your verdict?" And they all condemned Him to be deserving of death.

65. Then some began to spit on Him, and to cover His face and strike Him with their fists, saying to Him, "Prophesy!" And the officers struck Him with the palms of their hands.

LUKE 22

63. Then the men who were holding Jesus mocked Him *and* beat *Him*.

64. And after covering His *head,* they *repeatedly* struck His face and asked Him, saying, "Prophesy! Who is it that struck You?"

65. And many other things they blasphemously said against Him.

28. PETER DENIES JESUS THREE TIMES

MARK 14

66. Now Peter was in the court below; *and* one of the maids of the high priest came,

67. And saw Peter warming himself; *and* after looking at him, she said, "Now you were with Jesus the Nazarene."

68. But he denied *it*, saying, "I do not know *Him* or even understand what you are saying." And he went out onto the porch, and a cock crowed.

69. Then the maid saw him again *and* began to say to those who were standing by, "This is *one* of them."

70. And again he denied *it*. And after a little while, those who were standing by again said to Peter, "Truly you are *one* of them, for you are indeed a Galilean, and your speech confirms *it*."

71. Then he began to curse and to swear, *saying*, "I do not know this man of Whom you are speaking."

APPROXIMATELY 3:30 - 4:30 AM

MARK 14

72. And the cock crowed the second time. Then Peter remembered the words that Jesus had spoken to him: "Before the cock crows twice, you shall deny Me three times." And when he thought about this, he wept.

PASSOVER DAY NISAN 14 - WEDNESDAY MORNING, APRIL 5, 30 AD, APPROXIMATELY 5:30 - 6 AM

29. THE SANHEDRIN CONDEMNS JESUS AND SENDS HIM TO PILATE

LUKE 22

66. Now as soon as it was day, the elders of the people assembled together, *with* both *the* chief priests and *the* scribes, and they led Him into their Sanhedrin, saying,

67. "If You are the Christ, tell us." And He said to them, "If I should tell you, you would not believe *Me* at all;

68. And if I should also ask *you*, you would not answer Me at all, nor let *Me* go.
69. Hereafter shall the Son of man be sitting at *the* right hand of the power of God."
70. And they all said, "Then You are the Son of God?" And He said to them, "I am that *one, as* you say."
71. Then they said, "What need do we have of any other witness? For we ourselves have heard from His *own* mouth."

LUKE 23

1. And when the entire assembly of them arose, they led Him to Pilate.

30. JUDAS REPENTS AND HANGS HIMSELF - THE CHIEF PRIESTS BUY POTTER'S FIELD

MATTHEW 27

3. Now when Judas, who had betrayed Him, saw that He was condemned, he changed his mind *and* returned the thirty pieces of silver to the chief priests and the elders, saying,
4. "I have sinned and have betrayed innocent blood." But they said, "What *is that* to us? You see *to it* yourself."
5. And after throwing down the pieces of silver in the temple, he went out and hanged himself.
6. But the chief priests took the pieces of silver *and* said, "It is not lawful to put them into the treasury, since it is *the* price of blood."
7. And after taking counsel, they bought a potter's field with the *pieces of silver*, for a burial ground for strangers.
8. Therefore that field is called The Field of Blood to this day.
9. Then was fulfilled that which was spoken by Jeremiah the prophet, saying, "And I took the thirty pieces of silver, the price of Him on Whom a price was set, Whom they of *the* sons of Israel set a price on,
10. And gave them for the field of the potter, as *the* Lord had directed me."

31. JESUS IS CONDEMNED BEFORE PILATE - HE QUESTIONS JESUS

MATTHEW 27

11. Then Jesus stood before the governor; and the governor questioned Him, saying, "Are You the King of the Jews?" And Jesus said to him, "*It is as* you said."

12. And when He was accused by the chief priests and the elders, He answered nothing.

13. Then Pilate said to Him, "Don't You hear how many things they testify against You?"

14. And He did not answer even one word to him, so that the governor was greatly amazed.

32. PILATE SENDS JESUS TO HEROD

LUKE 23

5. But they were insistent, saying, "He stirs up the people, teaching throughout all of Judea, beginning from Galilee even to here."

6. And when he heard Galilee *named*, Pilate asked whether the man were a Galilean;

7. And after determining that He was from Herod's jurisdiction, he sent Him to Herod, *since* he also was in Jerusalem in those days.

8. And when Herod saw Jesus, he rejoiced greatly; for he had long been desiring to see Him because he had heard many things about Him, and he was hoping to see a miracle done by Him.

9. And he questioned Him with many words; but He answered him nothing.

10. All the while, the chief priests and the scribes stood vehemently accusing Him.

11. Then Herod and his soldiers treated Him with contempt; and after mocking *Him*, he put a splendid robe on Him *and* sent Him back to Pilate.

12. And on that same day, Pilate and Herod became friends with each other, because before there was enmity between them.

33. PILATE FINDS JESUS INNOCENT

LUKE 23

13. And when Pilate had called together the chief priests and the rulers and the people,

14. He said to them, "You brought this man to me as one who was turning away the people; and behold, I have examined *Him* in your presence *and* have found nothing blameworthy in this man concerning *the* accusation which you bring against Him;

15. Nor even *has* Herod; for I sent you to him, and observe, nothing worthy of death was done by Him."

JOHN 18

31. Then Pilate said to them, "You take Him and judge Him ac-

cording to your *own* law." But the Jews said to him, "It is not law-ful for us to put anyone to death";

32. So that the saying of Jesus might be fulfilled, which He had spoken to signify by what death He was about to die.

33. Then Pilate returned to the judgment hall and called Jesus, and said to Him, "Are You the King of the Jews?"

34. Jesus answered him, "Do you ask this of yourself, or did others say *it* to you concerning Me?"

35. Pilate answered Him, "Am I a Jew? The chief priests and your own nation have delivered You up to me. What have You done?"

36. Jesus answered, "My kingdom is not of this world. If My king-dom were of this world, then would My servants fight, so that I might not be delivered up to the Jews. However, My kingdom is not of this world."

37. Pilate therefore answered Him, "Then You are a king?" Jesus answered, "*As* you say, I am a king. For this *purpose* I was born, and for this *reason* I came into the world, that I may bear witness to the truth. Everyone who is of the truth hears My voice."

38. Pilate said to Him, "What is truth?" And after saying this, he went out again to the Jews and said to them, "I do not find any fault in Him."

34. PRIESTS AND PEOPLE DEMAND THAT PILATE RE-LEASE BARABBAS AND CRUCIFY JESUS - 8 AM

MATTHEW 27

15. Now at *the* feast, the governor was accustomed to release one prisoner to the multitude, whomever they wished.

16. And they had at that time a notorious prisoner called Barabbas.

17. Therefore, when they had gathered together, Pilate said to them, "Whom do you desire *that* I release to you? Barabbas, or Jesus Who is called Christ?"

18. For he understood that they had delivered Him up because of envy.

19. Now as he sat on the judgment seat, his wife sent *a message* to him, saying, "*Let there be* nothing between you and that righteous *man*, for I have suffered many things today in a dream because of Him."

20. But the chief priests and the elders persuaded the multitudes to demand Barabbas, and to destroy Jesus.

21. Then the governor answered *and* said to them, "Which of the two do you desire *that* I release to you?" And they said, "Barabbas."

22. Pilate said to them, "What then shall I do with Jesus Who is

called Christ?" They all said to him, "Let *Him* be crucified!"
23. And the governor said, "Why? What evil did He commit?"
But they shouted *all* the more, saying, "Let *Him* be crucified!"

35. PILATE WASHES HIS HANDS IN
A SHOW OF INNOCENCY

MATTHEW 27

24. Now Pilate, seeing that he was accomplishing nothing, but *that* a riot was developing instead, took water *and* washed *his* hands before the multitude, saying, "I am guiltless of the blood of this righteous *man*. You see *to it*."
25. And all the people answered *and* said, "His blood *be* on us and on our children."

36. PILATE RELEASES BARABBAS -
JESUS IS BEATEN AND SCOURGED

MATTHEW 27

26. Then he released Barabbas to them; but after scourging Jesus, he delivered *Him* up so that He might be crucified.
27. Then the governor's soldiers, after taking Jesus with *them* into the Praetorium, gathered the entire band against Him;
28. And they stripped Him *and* put a scarlet cloak around Him.
29. And after platting a crown of thorns, they put *it* on His head, and a rod in His right hand; and bowing *on* their knees before Him, they mocked Him, and *kept on* saying, "Hail, King of the Jews!"
30. Then, after spitting on Him, they took the rod and struck *Him* on the head.
31. When they were done mocking Him, they took the cloak off Him; and they put His own garments on Him and led Him away to crucify Him.

37. PILATE HAS SECOND THOUGHTS
ABOUT CRUCIFYING JESUS

JOHN 19

6. But when the chief priests and the officers saw Him, they cried aloud, saying, "Crucify *Him*, crucify *Him*!" Pilate said to them, "You take Him and crucify *Him* because I do not find any fault in Him."
7. The Jews answered him, "We have a law, and according to our law it is mandatory that He die, because He made Himself *the* Son

of God."

8. Therefore, when Pilate heard this saying, he was even more afraid.

9. And he went into the judgment hall again, and said to Jesus, "Where have You come from?" But Jesus did not give him an answer.

10. Then Pilate said to Him, "Why don't You speak to me? Don't You know that I have authority to crucify You, and authority to release You?"

11. Jesus answered, "You would not have any authority against Me if it were not given to you from above. For this reason, the one who delivered Me to you has *the* greater sin."

12. Because of this *saying*, Pilate sought to release Him; but the Jews cried out, saying, "If you release this *man*, you are not a friend of Caesar. Everyone who makes himself a king speaks against Caesar."

13. Therefore, after hearing this saying, Pilate *had* Jesus led out, and sat down on the judgment seat at a place called *the* Pavement; but in Hebrew, Gabbatha.

14. (Now it was *the* preparation of the Passover, and about the sixth hour.) And he said to the Jews, "Behold your King!"

15. But they cried aloud, "Away, away *with Him*! Crucify Him!" Pilate said to them, "Shall I crucify your King?" The chief priests answered, "We have no king but Caesar."

38. THE SOLDIERS LEAD JESUS AWAY TO BE CRUCIFIED, AND MAKE SIMON OF CYRENE CARRY HIS CROSS

LUKE 23

26. And as they led Him away, they laid hold on a certain Cyrenian *named* Simon, who was coming from a field; *and* they put the cross on him, that he might carry *it* behind Jesus.

27. And following Him was a great multitude of people with *many* women, who also were bewailing and lamenting Him.

28. But Jesus turned to them *and* said, "Daughters of Jerusalem, do not weep for Me, but weep for yourselves and for your children.

29. For behold, *the* days are coming in which they shall say, 'Blessed *are* the barren, and *the* wombs that did not bear, and *the* breasts that did not give suck.'

30. Then shall they begin to say to the mountains, 'Fall on us'; and to the hills, 'Cover us.'

31. For if they do these things in the green tree, what shall take place in the dry?"

39. JESUS REFUSES WINE AND MYRRH (VINEGAR AND GALL) - THEY CRUCIFY HIM APPROXIMATELY 9 AM - 12 NOON

MATTHEW 27

34. They gave Him vinegar mingled with gall to drink; but after tasting it, He would not drink.

40. THE SOLDIERS CAST LOTS FOR HIS GARMENTS - JESUS ASKS THE FATHER TO FORGIVE THEM FOR CRUCIFYING HIM

LUKE 23

34. Then Jesus said, "Father, forgive them, for they do not know what they are doing." And as they divided His garments, they cast lots.

JOHN 19

23. Now the soldiers, after they had crucified Jesus, took His garments and made four parts, a part for each soldier, and the coat *also*. But the coat was seamless, woven *in one piece* from the top all the way throughout.
24. For this reason, they said to one another, "Let us not tear it, but let us cast lots for it *to determine* whose it shall be"; that the scripture might be fulfilled which says, "They divided My garments among them, and they cast lots for My vesture." The soldiers therefore did these things.

41. PILATE HAS A TITLE AND ACCUSATION WRITTEN AND PUT ON THE CROSS

JOHN 19

19. And Pilate also wrote a title and put *it* on the cross; and it was written, "Jesus the Nazarean, the King of the Jews."
20. As a result, many of the Jews read this title, for the place where Jesus was crucified was near the city; and it was written in Hebrew, in Greek *and* in Latin.
21. Then the chief priests of the Jews said to Pilate, "Do not write, 'The King of the Jews'; but that He said, 'I am King of the Jews.' "
22. Pilate answered, "What I have written, I have written."

42. TWO MALEFACTORS (THIEVES) CRUCIFIED WITH JESUS

MARK 15

27. And with Him they crucified two robbers, one at *His* right hand and one at His left.
28. Then the scripture was fulfilled which says, "And He was numbered among lawbreakers."

43. THE PEOPLE, PRIESTS AND TWO THIEVES MOCK AND REVILE HIM. DARKNESS FROM THE SIXTH HOUR TO THE NINTH HOUR (APPROXIMATELY NOON TO 3 PM)

LUKE 23

35. Now the people stood *by* observing, and the rulers among them were also deriding *Him*, saying, "He saved others; let Him save Himself, if this is the Christ, the chosen of God."
36. And the soldiers also mocked Him, coming near and offering Him vinegar,
37. And saying, "If You are the King of the Jews, save Yourself."
38. And there also was an inscription over Him written in Greek and Latin and Hebrew: "This is the King of the Jews."
39. Then one of the malefactors who was hanging *there* railed at Him, saying, "If You are the Christ, save Yourself and us."
40. But the other *one* answered *and* rebuked him, saying, "Do not even you fear God, you who are under the same condemnation?
41. And we indeed justly, for we are receiving due payment for what we did; but this *man* did nothing wrong."
42. Then he said to Jesus, "Remember me, Lord, when You come into Your kingdom."
43. And Jesus said to him, "Truly, I tell you today, you shall be with Me in paradise."
44. Now it was about *the* sixth hour, and darkness came over the whole land until *the* ninth hour.

44. JESUS MAKES JOHN RESPONSIBLE FOR HIS MOTHER, MARY

JOHN 19

25. And Jesus' mother stood by the cross, and His mother's sister, Mary the *wife* of Cleopas, and Mary Magdalene.
26. When Jesus saw *His* mother, and the disciple whom He loved

standing by, He said to His mother, "Woman, behold your son."
27. Then He said to the disciple, "Behold your mother." And from that time, the disciple took her into his own *home*.

45. AT THE NINTH HOUR JESUS IS FORSAKEN AND OFFERED VINEGAR - A SPEAR IS THRUST INTO HIS SIDE AND HE DIES - THE TEMPLE VEIL IS TORN IN TWO (APPROXIMATELY 3 PM)

MATTHEW 27

46. And about the ninth hour, Jesus cried out with a loud voice, saying, "Eli, Eli, lama sabachthani?" That is, "My God, My God, why have You forsaken Me?"
47. And some of those who were standing there heard *and* said, "This *one* is calling for Elijah."
48. And immediately one of them ran and, taking a sponge, filled *it* with vinegar and put *it* on a stick, *and* gave *it to* Him to drink.
49. But the rest said, "Let Him alone! Let us see if Elijah comes to save Him." *Then another took a spear and thrust it into His side, and out came water and blood.* *
50. And after crying out again with a loud voice, Jesus yielded up *His* spirit.
51. And suddenly the veil of the temple was ripped in two from top to bottom...

46. AN EARTHQUAKE OPENS SOME GRAVES; RESURRECTION OF SOME OF THE SAINTS TO ANOTHER PHYSICAL LIFE AS A SIGN AND A WITNESS

MATTHEW 27

51. ...and the earth shook, and the rocks were split,
52. And the tombs were opened, and many bodies of the saints who had died arose.

The latter half of this verse, which includes the words "...Then another took a spear and ...out came water and blood," has been omitted from the King James Version. However, some ancient manuscripts contain this part of the verse. The latter part of the verse is also found in other manuscripts that are designated by letter (L, T, Z) and by number (33, 49, 892 and 1241). Older translations which contain the complete verse are the Moffatt translation and the Fenton translation. Newer translations generally footnote this portion of Matthew 27:49 rather than including it in the text. The weight of evidence indicates that the latter half of the verse is an authentic part of the Greek text and should be included in translations of the New Testament. The veracity of this portion of Matthew 27:49 is substantiated by the records in John 19:34 and 20:27.

53. And after His resurrection, they came out of the tombs *and* entered into the holy city, and appeared to many.

47. THE CENTURION ACKNOWLEDGES THAT JESUS WAS THE SON OF GOD

MATTHEW 27

54. Then the centurion and those with him who had been keeping guard over Jesus, after seeing the earthquake and the things that took place, were filled with fear, *and* said, "Truly this was the Son of God!"

48. THE JEWS WANT JESUS' BODY OFF THE CROSS BEFORE THE HOLY DAY BEGINS AT SUNSET

JOHN 19

31. The Jews therefore, so that the bodies might not remain on the cross on the Sabbath, because it was a preparation *day* (for that Sabbath was a high day), requested of Pilate that their legs might be broken and *the bodies* be taken away.
32. Then the soldiers came and broke the legs of the first *one*, and *the legs* of the other who was crucified with Him.
33. But when they came to Jesus *and* saw that He was already dead, they did not break His legs;
34. But one of the soldiers had pierced His side with a spear, and immediately blood and water had come out.
35. And he who saw *this* has testified, and his testimony is true; and he knows that *what* he says *is* true, so that you may believe.
36. For these things took place so that the scripture might be fulfilled, "Not a bone of Him shall be broken."
37. And again another scripture says, "They shall look upon Him Whom they pierced."

49. MANY OF THE WOMEN WATCH TO THE END

MATTHEW 27

55. Now there were many women who were watching from a distance, who had followed Jesus from Galilee, ministering to Him;
56. With whom were Mary Magdalene, and Mary the mother of James and Joses, and the mother of the sons of Zebedee.

50. JUST BEFORE SUNSET, JOSEPH OF ARIMATHEA GETS THE BODY OF JESUS AND LAYS IT IN THE TOMB (APPROXIMATELY 4:30 - 6 PM)

JOHN 19

38. Now after these things, Joseph (the one from Arimathea, being a disciple of Jesus, but having concealed it for fear of the Jews) asked Pilate that he might take Jesus' body away; and Pilate gave *him* permission. Then he came and took away the body of Jesus.
39. And Nicodemus, who had come to Jesus by night at *the* first, also came, bearing a mixture of myrrh and aloes, about a hundred pounds.
40. Then they took Jesus' body and wound it in linen cloths with the aromatics, as is the custom among the Jews to prepare for burial.
41. Now there was a garden in the place where He was crucified, and in the garden a new tomb, in which no one had ever been laid.
42. Because of the preparation of the Jews, they laid Jesus there; for the tomb was near.

THIS ENDS THE EVENTS OF THE PASSOVER DAY - NISAN 14 FROM SUNSET APRIL 4 TO SUNSET APRIL 5, 30 AD, THE DAY JESUS THE CHRIST DIED!

CHAPTER SIX

Jesus in the Tomb
Three Days and Three Nights
And the Resurrection

The Exact Length Of Time That Jesus Was In the Tomb

Many prophecies in the Old Testament foretold the death and resurrection of Jesus the Christ. The prophet Daniel foresaw that His life would be taken (Dan. 9:26), and both David and Isaiah described the suffering and humiliation that He would endure before His death (Psa. 22, Isa. 53). Other prophecies pointed to His resurrection to immortality (Psa. 16:10-11, Dan. 7:13-14, Isa. 9:6-7). However, there is no scripture in the Old Testament that foretold the length of time that the Messiah would be in the tomb before He was resurrected from the dead. This prophecy is found only in the Gospel accounts, spoken by Jesus Himself: "Then some of the scribes and Pharisees answered, saying, 'Master, we desire to see a sign from You.' And He answered *and* said to them, '**A wicked and adulterous generation seeks after a sign, but no sign shall be given to it except the sign of Jonah the prophet. For just as Jonah was in the belly of the whale three days and three nights, in like manner the Son of man shall be in the heart of the earth three days and three nights**' " (Matt. 12:38-40).

Jesus spoke these words because the scribes and Pharisees did not believe in Him, nor did they believe that His works of healing were done by the power of God. When they challenged Him to perform a miraculous sign in their presence, Jesus did not do so. Instead, the only sign He gave them was the sign of Jonah the prophet. The fulfillment of this sign was a testimony not only to that generation but to all future generations that He was the Messiah.

The vast majority of Christians today believe that Jesus was crucified and laid in the tomb on a Friday, and He was resurrected on Sunday morning. Thus, He was not in the tomb for three days and three nights, as He had prophesied, but for two nights and one full day. This traditional interpretation of Jesus' death and resurrection is completely contrary to the Gospel accounts.

Nearly all churches within Christendom have misinterpreted or rejected the scriptural record. In its place, they have adopted an ancient Babylonian religious tradition that predates the ministry, death and resurrection of Jesus the Christ by thousands of years.* Various theories have been ad-

---

*For historical evidence of the Babylonian practices, see *The Two Babylons* by Alexander Hislop and *The Golden Bough* by Sir James George Frazer.

vanced in an attempt to reconcile this ancient religious tradition with the scriptural accounts, but the error is clearly exposed by examining the accounts that have been accurately recorded and faithfully preserved in the Gospels of Matthew, Mark, Luke and John.

The Gospel accounts do not support the traditional belief in a Good Friday crucifixion and an Easter Sunday resurrection. The facts that are recorded by the Gospel writers reveal a profoundly different time frame for the death and resurrection of Jesus the Christ.

The Scriptural Definition of a Day

Some have claimed that Jesus was using an idiomatic expression when He declared that He would remain in the tomb for three days and three nights. They teach that His words should be interpreted as referring to parts of days rather than to whole days. But when the scriptural use of the term "day" is examined one finds that it is very specific. The Scriptures of the Old Testament show that a day consists of an evening and a morning (Gen. 1). An entire day has two portions: the night portion, which begins at evening, or sunset; and the day portion, which begins at sunrise, or morning. These two consecutive periods are identified as one complete day, reckoned from sunset to sunset, or evening to evening (Lev. 23:32, *KJV*).

According to Scripture, each day has an average of twelve hours in the night portion and twelve hours in the day portion, making a complete day of twenty-four hours. Jesus Himself verified that the day portion is about twelve hours long when He said, "Are there not twelve hours in the day?" (John 11:9.) Jesus also spoke of the three watches of the night, which extended from sunset to sunrise and were each four hours long, making a total of twelve hours (Luke 12:36-38). There is no question that Jesus included a full twelve hours of daylight and a full twelve hours of night in reckoning the length of each calendar day. This scriptural method of reckoning time had been used by the Hebrews for centuries. Moreover, it is clear that Jesus and His disciples observed the Passover and the holy days of God each year according to the determination of the Hebrew Calendar, as God had ordained. This is a key fact in understanding the exact length of time that Jesus was in the tomb.

When the four Gospel accounts are examined, it is clear that the Gospel writers used the scriptural method of reckoning each day from sunset to sunset, or evening to evening. Beginning six days before Jesus' last Passover until the day after His resurrection, the Gospel writers accurately recorded all the events day by day. They took careful note of the mornings and evenings, making it possible to determine the beginning and end of each day. The fact that they meticulously noted the mornings and evenings demonstrates that these days were whole days composed of twenty-four hours. Nowhere do the scriptural records leave room for an interpretation of partial days or partial nights.

An Analysis of the Phrase "Three Days and Three Nights" in the Book of Jonah

Jesus' prophecy that He would be in the grave for three days and three nights is a direct reference to Jonah 1:17, which speaks of Jonah's symbolic entombment in the belly of a great fish: "Now the LORD had prepared a great fish to swallow up Jonah. **And Jonah was in the belly of the fish three days and three nights**" (*KJV*).

The word "days" in this verse is translated from the Hebrew *yom*, and the word "night" is translated from the Hebrew *lailah*. Both of these words are preceded by the cardinal number "three," which is translated from the Hebrew *shalosh*. This cardinal number is used as an adjective before the nouns "days" and "nights" to express a specific period of time. Other scriptural references confirm the use of cardinal numbers to record the exact duration of a condition or event:

Gen. 7:4	"seven days"
Gen. 7:12	"forty days and forty nights"
Ex. 10:23	"three days"
Ex. 24:18	"forty days and forty nights"
Lev. 12:4	"three and thirty days"
I Sam. 30:12	"three days and three nights"
I Kings 19:8	"forty days and forty nights"

The use of a cardinal number with the terms "days" and "nights" shows that these terms are being used in a very specific sense. The presence of the Hebrew *waw* (the conjunction "and") between "days" and "nights" makes the meaning of the text even more emphatic, limiting the duration of time to the exact number of days and nights that are specified. By the Scriptural method of reckoning time, it takes an "evening" and a "morning" to complete one full day (Gen. 1:5). Just as "the evening and the morning" in Genesis 1 denote a whole day of twenty-four hours, so the term "a day and a night" denotes a full day of twenty-four hours. In the same way also, the expression "three days and three nights" denotes three whole days of twenty-four hours each.

The Hebrew text leaves no room to interpret the expression "three days and three nights" in Jonah 1:17 in a broad or general sense. The use of this same Hebrew expression in I Samuel 30:12 demonstrates that it is a literal period of three 24-hour days: "... for he had eaten no bread, nor drunk water, three days and three nights" (*KJV*). The following verse in I Samuel 30 uses the expression "three days agone" in reference to the period of three days and three nights. These were the words of an Egyptian who was accustomed to reckoning days from sunrise to sunrise. The use of the expression "three days agone" by the Egyptian confirms that he had completed a full three days and three nights of fasting from sunrise on the first day until sunrise on the fourth day. The literal meaning of "three days" in I Samuel

30:13 is confirmed by the use of the same Hebrew expression in II Samuel 24:13 to describe a specific duration of time: "three days' pestilence."

The construction of the Hebrew text does not allow the expression "three days and three nights" in Jonah 1:17 to be interpreted in any manner except the literal sense of three 24-hour days. The Hebrew terminology cannot be interpreted as an idiomatic expression that is describing incomplete units of time, such as part of a day and part of a night. To denote incomplete units of time, the Hebrew text uses a word that means "to divide." This word is not found in the expression "three days and three nights," either in Jonah 1:17 or in I Samuel 30:12. However, this word is found in reference to a duration of time in Daniel 12:7: "... a time, times, and half a time." The word "half" is translated from the Hebrew word meaning "to divide." Since this word is not used to describe the duration of time in Jonah 1:17 and I Samuel 30:12, it is evident that the Hebrew text is describing complete units of time—three 12-hour days and three 12-hour nights. By testifying that Jonah was in the belly of the fish "three days and three nights," the Scriptures reveal that a full 72 hours had elapsed before Jonah was cast out on the shore.

The New Testament reveals that Jesus the Christ was the Lord God of the Old Testament before He became a man. He was the one Who caused the great fish to swallow Jonah and descend to the bottom of the sea for a period of time before swimming to the shore and depositing Jonah on the land. As the Lord God, He knew exactly how long Jonah had remained in the belly of the fish, and He inspired Jonah to record this duration of time, which was a foretelling of His future burial. There is no question concerning the length of time that passed as Jonah lay in the belly of the fish, because this fact is preserved in the Scriptures of the Old Testament. Since the Hebrew text cannot be interpreted in an idiomatic sense, but must be interpreted literally, it is clear that three whole days and three whole nights passed while Jonah lay in the fish's belly. Jesus was fully aware of this fact of Scripture when He declared to the Jews, "... **in like manner the Son of man shall be in the heart of the earth three days and three nights**" (Matt. 12:40).

Jesus Said That He Would Rise Three Days After His Death

The Gospel writers record that Jesus made specific statements to His disciples concerning the length of time that He would be in the tomb and when He would be resurrected: "And He began to teach them that it was necessary for the Son of man to suffer many things, and to be rejected by the elders and chief priests and scribes, and **to be killed, but after three days to rise** *from the dead*" (Mark 8:31; see also Matt. 16:21 and Mark 9:31). Jesus proclaimed to His disciples that He would not rise from the dead until **three days after He had been killed**. Jesus' statement that **He would rise three days after He had died** is most significant. According to Jewish law, to be declared legally dead, a person had to be dead for more than three full days. If someone who appeared to be dead revived and came back to life prior to three full days, he or she was not legally deemed to have been dead. Therefore, if Jesus had risen from the dead before 3 PM on the afternoon of Nisan 17, a weekly Sabbath, He would not have been considered legally dead. As a result, His return to life would not have been considered a true resurrection from the dead.

Knowing this fact, one can understand why Jesus delayed going to Lazarus in the account in John 11. Jesus knew that Lazarus was sick unto death, but He deliberately remained where He was for two more days (John 11:6). He knew that Lazarus would not be considered legally dead until he had been dead for four days. When Lazarus was legally dead, Jesus went to resurrect him from the grave: "Jesus said, **'Take away the stone.' Martha, the sister of him who had died, said to Him, 'Lord, he already stinks, for it has been four days**.' Jesus said to her, 'Did I not say to you that if you will believe, you shall see the glory of God?' Then they removed the stone *from the tomb* where the dead man had been laid. And Jesus lifted *His* eyes upward and said, 'Father, I thank You that You have heard Me. And I know that You hear Me always; but because of the people who stand around I say *this*, so that they may believe that You did send Me.' And after He had spoken these things, He cried with a loud voice, **'Lazarus, come forth.' And he who had been dead came forth, his feet and hands bound with grave clothes, and his face bound up with a napkin**. Jesus said to them, 'Loose him and let *him* go' " (John 11:39-44).

Like Lazarus, Jesus had to remain dead for a minimum of three full days in order to be declared officially dead. If He had been crucified on a Friday and restored to life on Sunday morning at sunrise, His death would not have been "valid" since only two nights and one day would have passed between Friday sunset and Sunday morning. In order for His death to be publicly recognized and acknowledged, it was necessary for Jesus to remain in the grave for three nights and three days before He was raised from the dead. The Scriptures reveal that Jesus died at the ninth hour, or 3 PM, on the Passover day, Nisan 14, which fell on Wednesday, April 5, in 30 AD (Matt. 27:46 and Mark 15:34), and He was placed in the tomb just before sunset at approximately 6 PM. The Gospel of Matthew describes His burial by Joseph of Arimathea: "And **when evening was coming on**, a rich man of Arimathea came, named Joseph, who was himself a disciple of Jesus. After going to Pilate, he begged *to have* the body of Jesus. Then Pilate commanded the body to be given over *to him.* And after taking the body, Joseph [with the help of Nicodemus (John 19:39)] wrapped it in clean linen cloth, and placed it in his new tomb, which he had hewn in the rock; and after rolling a great stone to the door of the tomb, he went away" (Matt. 27:57-60). Luke records that "a Sabbath was coming on" (Luke 23:54), which means that by the time they had closed the entrance of the tomb with a huge stone, the Sabbath was nearly upon them. Since all Sabbaths were reckoned from sunset to sunset, it is clear that the sun was about to set.

Both Matthew and Mark testify that Jesus died at the ninth hour, or 3 PM. Luke's account shows that they closed the entrance to the tomb with a huge stone just before sunset. Because the Passover is in the spring of the year when the days are twelve hours in length, we know that the tomb was closed at about 6 PM. Since He died about 3 PM, Jesus was dead for approximately 75 hours before He was resurrected. The total length of time included three days (from sunrise to sunset) and three nights (from sunset to sunrise) plus approximately three hours. Because He had been dead for more than three days, His death was legally established. When He appeared to His disciples three days after He had been placed in the tomb, the reality of His resurrection was beyond question.

Additional Statements of Jesus Confirm That He Was in the Tomb for Three Days and Three Nights

While Matthew and Mark record Jesus saying that He would be raised "after three days," Luke records that He would be raised "on the third day." Luke wrote: "For He shall be delivered up to the Gentiles, and shall be mocked and insulted and spit upon. And after scourging *Him*, they shall kill Him; **but on the third day, He shall rise again**" (Luke 18:32-33).

The apostle John records another statement by Jesus that He would be raised up "in three days." Jesus made this statement when the Jews confronted Him for casting the money exchangers out of the temple and driving out the animals they were selling: "... The Jews answered and said to Him, 'What sign do You show to us, seeing that You do these things?' Jesus answered and said to them, '**Destroy this temple, and in three days I will raise it up.**' Then the Jews said, 'This temple was forty-six years in building, and You will raise it up in three days?' **But He spoke concerning the temple of His body**. Therefore, when He was raised from *the* dead, His disciples remembered that He had said this to them; and they believed the Scriptures, and the word that Jesus had spoken" (John 2:18-22).

The phrase "in three days" contains the Greek preposition *en*. This Greek preposition, which is translated "in" in John 2:19-20, can also mean "within." At first glance, the statements "**in three days**" and "**on the third day**" appear to conflict with the statement that He would be raised "**after three days**." How is it possible for all three of Jesus' statements to be correct?

When we understand Jesus' statements, we find that instead of being contradictory, they reveal the exact time that He was raised from the dead. Jesus made it clear that He would be raised after He had been dead for three days. The other statements, "**in three days**" and "**on the third day**," do not include the total time that He was dead but only the time that He was buried in the tomb. The Gospel accounts show that Joseph of Arimathea and Nicodemus closed the tomb just before sunset, three hours after Jesus died on the cross. Although He was in the tomb for exactly three days and three nights, He was dead for a longer period than that. Thus He rose from the dead "**after three days**." The difference between this statement and the statements "**in three days**" and "**on the third day**" is that these two statements refer to His burial "**in the heart of the earth three days and three nights**."

When one compares all of Jesus' statements, it is evident that they place specific limits on the time frame between His death and resurrection. Of itself, "**in three days**" could mean any time on the third day, even the first minute of the third day. "**On the third day**" could mean any time on the third day up to the last minute on the third day. But the statement that He would "**be in the heart of the earth three days and three nights**" shows that three whole days and three whole nights would pass while He lay in the tomb.

When all of Jesus' statements are taken into consideration, there is only one moment of time to which all can apply. Here is the explanation: The end of the third day is still "on" and "in" the third day. At the end of the third day, precisely at sunset, Jesus was resurrected. This was the only moment of time that could fulfill all of Jesus' prophecies concerning the time of His death, the length of time that He would be in the tomb, and the time of His resurrection.

The Gospels record that Jesus died on the Passover day, Nisan 14, which fell on a Wednesday in 30 AD. Joseph of Arimathea and Nicodemus placed Jesus' body in the tomb and closed the entrance with a huge stone when the sun was setting at approximately 6 PM, ending Nisan 14. Jesus was resurrected from the dead precisely three days and three nights later, when the sun was setting at the end of the weekly Sabbath, or Saturday, Nisan 17, 30 AD. As He had prophesied, He remained in the tomb for three full days and three full nights. **Jesus the Christ was raised from the dead at sunset on the weekly Sabbath, the seventh day of the week. He had already been resurrected when the sun rose on Sunday, the first day of the week**. *(Please see the chart on pages 80-81)*

Scriptural Evidence of Two Sabbaths During the Three Days and Three Nights

According to religious tradition, Jesus was crucified on a Friday. This religious tradition appears to be supported by the statement in John 19:31 that the day of His death "was the preparation." Most have assumed that this statement refers to the Jews' preparation for the weekly Sabbath. They fail to realize that the Passover day, on which Jesus died, has always been a preparation day for the Feast of Unleavened Bread, which immediately follows (Lev. 23:4-6). The first day of this feast, Nisan 15, is observed as an annual holy day, or "high day." Like the Passover day, it may fall on different days of the week. Regardless of which day of the week it falls on, it is always observed as an annual Sabbath, and the day portion of the Passover is always used as a day of preparation. It is erroneous to interpret "the preparation" in John 19:31 as evidence that the day of the crucifixion was a Friday.

The mistaken belief in a Friday crucifixion is based on the assumption that there was only one Sabbath during the crucifixion week. However, the Scriptures clearly reveal that during that week there were two Sabbaths. The first Sabbath was an annual holy day, the first day of the Feast of Unleavened Bread. The second Sabbath was the weekly Sabbath, the seventh day of the week. Consequently, during the week of Jesus' crucifixion there were two preparation days. The day portion of Nisan 14, the Passover day, was the preparation day for the first day of the Feast of Unleavened Bread, the 15th, which was an annual Sabbath. The following day, the 16th, which was a Friday, was the preparation day for the weekly Sabbath.

When the Gospel of John is examined, it is evident that the Sabbath immediately following the day Jesus died was an annual Sabbath: "The Jews therefore, so that the bodies might not remain on the cross on the Sabbath, because it was **a preparation *day* (for that Sabbath was a high day**) ..." (John 19:31). The term "high day" was never used to refer to the weekly Sabbath, but only to annual Sabbaths. John's use of this term makes it clear that the Sabbath that was about to begin was the first day of the Feast of Unleavened Bread, Nisan 15. Mark's account makes reference to the coming of sunset, which would bring the end of the preparation and the beginning of the annual Sabbath, or high day: "**Now evening was coming, *and* since it was *a* preparation, (that is, *the day* before a Sabbath) ...**" (Mark 15:42).

As the Gospel of Luke shows, this Sabbath was about to begin when Jesus was put into the tomb: "Now it was *a* **preparation day, and *a* Sabbath was coming on**. And *the* women also, who had come with Him from Galilee, followed *and* saw the tomb, and how His body was laid" (Luke 23:54-55).

The Gospels record the events that followed Jesus' burial. On Nisan 15, the day after the crucifixion, the chief priests and the Pharisees went to Pilate to request that guards be assigned to watch Jesus' tomb. Because they were afraid that the disciples would come and steal away His body, they did not hesitate to take care of their business on the holy day (Matt. 27:62-66). While the priests and Pharisees went to Pilate, the women who followed Jesus were observing the annual Sabbath, as commanded by God. They could not buy spices on that day because all the businesses were closed in observance of the command to rest (Lev. 23:6-7). After the end of that Sabbath, or high day, they bought spices and aromatic oils to anoint Jesus. Mark relates this event: "**Now when the Sabbath had passed**, Mary Magdalene and Mary, the *mother* of James, and Salome bought aromatic oils, so that they might come and anoint Him" (Mark 16:1).

It is quite evident that the women could not have purchased the spices until after the high day, or annual Sabbath, had ended. The high day began when the Passover day, Nisan 14, ended at sunset. The observance of the high day, Nisan 15, lasted until the following sunset, which began Nisan 16. The women bought the spices **"when the Sabbath had passed"** and prepared them on the same day. When they had finished, they observed **a second Sabbath:** "And they returned *to the city, and* prepared spices and ointments, and *then* **rested on the Sabbath** according to the commandment" (Luke 23:56). The Gospel records concerning the buying and preparation of the spices by the women clearly reveal the observance of two Sabbaths during the crucifixion week.

Two Women View the Tomb
Late on the Weekly Sabbath

Before the weekly Sabbath came to an end, Matthew records that Mary Magdalene and the other Mary went to observe the tomb: "Now late on the Sabbath, as *the* first *day* of *the* weeks was drawing near, Mary Magdalene and the other Mary went to observe the sepulcher" (Matt. 28:1). Because it was still the Sabbath day, the women did not come to anoint His body with the spices they had prepared. Perhaps they went to observe the tomb because they remembered Jesus' words that after three days and three nights in the grave, He would rise from the dead.

After the two women viewed the tomb and saw that the stone covering the entrance was still in place with the soldiers standing guard, they returned home for the night. The next morning, as they were coming back to the tomb, they were wondering who might roll back the stone so that they could anoint Jesus' body: "And very early on the first *day* of the weeks, at the rising of the sun, they were coming to the tomb; and they were asking themselves, 'Who will roll away the stone for us from the entrance to the tomb?' " (Mark 16:2-3) But when the women arrived, they found that the stone had already been removed and the tomb was empty. The three days and three nights had ended at sunset on the weekly Sabbath, and Jesus had risen from the dead! (For further discussion of the third day see Appendix B, page 145.)

See Chart on pages 80-81 for The Three Days and Three Nights in the Tomb and the Resurrection After Three Days and Three Nights

The Three Days and Three Nights In After Three Days

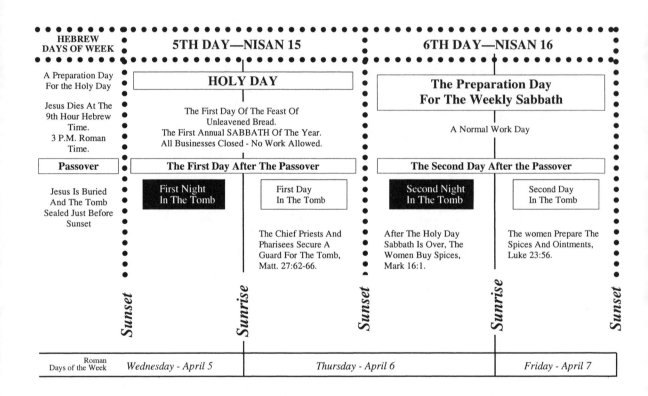

HEBREW DAYS OF WEEK	5TH DAY—NISAN 15	6TH DAY—NISAN 16
A Preparation Day For the Holy Day	**HOLY DAY**	**The Preparation Day For The Weekly Sabbath**
Jesus Dies At The 9th Hour Hebrew Time. 3 P.M. Roman Time.	The First Day Of The Feast Of Unleavened Bread. The First Annual SABBATH Of The Year. All Businesses Closed - No Work Allowed.	A Normal Work Day
Passover	**The First Day After The Passover**	**The Second Day After the Passover**
Jesus Is Buried And The Tomb Sealed Just Before Sunset	First Night In The Tomb / First Day In The Tomb	Second Night In The Tomb / Second Day In The Tomb
	The Chief Priests And Pharisees Secure A Guard For The Tomb, Matt. 27:62-66.	After The Holy Day Sabbath Is Over, The Women Buy Spices, Mark 16:1. / The women Prepare The Spices And Ointments, Luke 23:56.

Sunset — *Sunrise* — *Sunset* — *Sunrise* — *Sunset*

Roman Days of the Week	*Wednesday - April 5*	*Thursday - April 6*	*Friday - April 7*

The Key To The Time Period From The Burial To The Resurrection:
Jesus Said He Would Be In The Heart Of The Earth (The Tomb)
Three Days And Three Nights, A Complete 72-Hour Period.

Matt. 12:38-40; 27:63	John 2:18-22
Mark 8:31; 9:31	Acts 10:40
Luke 13:32; 18:33; 24:7, 46	1 Cor. 15:4

the Tomb and the Resurrection
and Three Nights

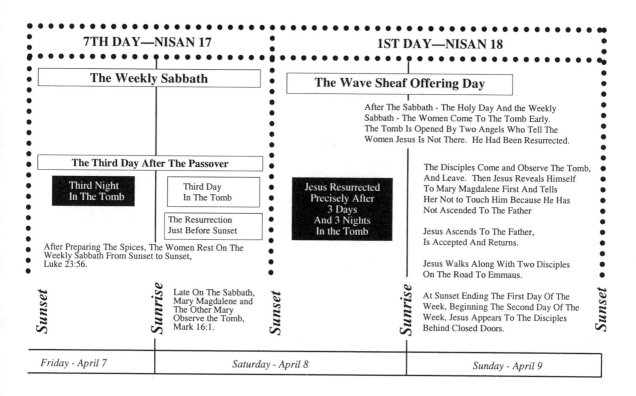

Knowledge of a Wednesday crucifixion was passed down for at least three centuries after the founding of the apostolic church. The *Didascalia*, which dates from the third century, offers historical evidence that the belief in a Friday crucifixion was a change from the original teaching. The following description of the day of Jesus' crucifixion appears in Book V of the *Apostolic Constitutions*, which contains the original words of the *Didascalia*:

"**For they began to hold a council against the Lord on the second day of the week**, in the first month, which is Xanthicus; and the deliberation continued on the third day of the week; **but on the fourth day [Wednesday] they determined to take away His life by crucifixion**" (*Apostolic Constitutions—Didascalia Apostolorum*, book V, section I, paragraph xiv). A church historian explains the significance of this record in the *Didascalia*: "…the only reason can have been that **Jesus' passion began on a Wednesday, i.e., the day when He was arrested [and crucified]**" (Lietzmann, *A History of the Early Church*, p. 69).

Scriptures: Jesus the Christ's Three Days and Three Nights In the Tomb

THE FIRST DAY OF UNLEAVENED BREAD NISAN 15 - THURSDAY, APRIL 6, 30 AD

51. ON THE HOLY DAY, GUARDS ARE PLACED AT THE TOMB

MATTHEW 27

62. Now on the next day, which followed the preparation *day*, the chief priests and the Pharisees came together to Pilate,
63. Saying, "Sir, we remember that that deceiver said while *He was* living, 'After three days I *will* rise.'
64. Therefore, command *that* the sepulcher be secured until the third day; lest His disciples come by night and steal Him away, and say to the people, 'He is risen from the dead'; and the last deception shall be worse than the first."
65. Then Pilate said to them, "You have a guard. Go, make *it as* secure as you know *how*."
66. And they went *and* made the sepulcher secure, sealing the stone *and* setting the guard.

THE WEEKLY SABBATH NISAN 17 - SATURDAY, APRIL 8, 30 AD

53. THE WOMEN REST ON THE WEEKLY SABBATH

LUKE 23

56. And they returned *to the city, and* prepared spices and ointments, and *then* rested on the Sabbath according to the commandment.

54. TOWARD THE END OF THE WEEKLY SABBATH, MARY MAGDALENE AND MARY GO TO OBSERVE THE TOMB

MATTHEW 28

1. Now late on the Sabbath, as *the* first *day* of *the* weeks* was drawing near, Mary Magdalene and the other Mary came to observe the sepulcher.

---

*See Appendix C, page 147

CHAPTER SEVEN

The Events on the First Day of
the Week to Jesus'
Final Ascension

The scriptural records and the calculations of the Hebrew calendar prove conclusively that Jesus was resurrected when the sun set at the end of the weekly Sabbath. The Gospel accounts do not directly reveal what Jesus did between the time that He was resurrected and the time that He was seen by Mary Magdalene the next morning. However, from the scriptural records we can piece together what Jesus did from the time that He was resurrected until He ascended to be accepted by God the Father in the morning as the true Wave Sheaf. The account in the Gospel of John gives us an understanding of what Jesus did first when He came back to life in the tomb: "Then Simon Peter came following him, and he went into the tomb and **saw the linen cloths lying, and the napkin that had been on His head, not lying with the linen cloths but folded up in a place by itself**" (John 20:6-7).

The record of John shows that when Jesus came back to life, He rose straight out of the burial wrappings without disturbing them. When Peter entered the tomb, he saw Jesus' burial wrappings still in the form of His body. This was absolute proof that Jesus had risen from the dead, and no one had taken His body. If someone had taken away His body, it would still have been wrapped with the linen burial cloths.

After rising out of the burial wrappings, Jesus took off the napkin that covered His head and neatly folded it and placed it close by, separate from the other burial cloths. This was an additional proof that He was alive. If anyone had taken His body, the napkin would have either remained on His head or fallen to the ground. It would not have been folded and placed neatly by itself. The apostle John, who was with Peter, saw these things and believed (verse 8).

After folding the napkin, Jesus undoubtedly offered a prayer of thanksgiving to God the Father for raising Him back to life. Perhaps Jesus thought of the prophecy of His resurrection in Psalm 16: "The LORD *is* the portion of mine inheritance and of my cup: *Thou* maintainest my lot. The lines are fallen unto me in pleasant *places*; yea, I have a goodly heritage....Therefore my heart is glad, and my glory rejoiceth: **my flesh also shall rest in hope. For Thou wilt not leave my soul in hell; neither wilt Thou suffer Thine Holy One to see corruption**. Thou wilt show me the path of life: in Thy presence is fullness of joy; at Thy right hand there are pleasures for evermore" (verses 5-6, 9-11, *KJV*).

After offering His prayer of thanksgiving, Jesus must have left the tomb. He did not need to have the stone removed from the entrance of the tomb because He was now spirit and had the ability to pass through matter. The Gospel of Luke confirms this fact. Luke records that approximately twenty-four hours after His resurrection, Jesus suddenly appeared in a closed room where the disciples were assembled. This took place late on the first day of the week, after He had walked with the two disciples to the village of Emmaus: "And they [the two disciples] rose up that very hour *and* returned to Jerusalem; and they found the eleven and those with them assembled together, saying, 'In truth, the Lord has risen! And He has appeared to Simon.' Then they related the things that had happened *to them* on the road, and how He was known to them in the breaking of the bread. Now as they were telling these things, **Jesus Himself stood in their midst** and said to them, 'Peace *be* to you' "(Luke 24:33-36).

The apostle John also wrote of Jesus' sudden appearance: "Afterwards, as evening was drawing near that day, the first *day* of the weeks, and **the doors were shut where the disciples had assembled for fear of the Jews, Jesus came and stood in the midst**, and said to them, 'Peace *be* to you.' And after saying this, He showed them His hands and His side. Then the disciples rejoiced, *because* they had seen the Lord" (John 20:19-20).

Because the resurrected Jesus had the ability to pass through matter, He was able to leave the tomb before the stone was rolled away from the entrance. It is certain that He left the tomb almost immediately after He was resurrected. Remember, Jesus had said, "...the Son of man shall be in the heart of the earth three days and three nights." If He had remained in the tomb for any length of time after His resurrection, He would have been in the heart of the earth for more than three days and three nights.

Where did Jesus go after He left the tomb? The Scriptures do not specify. However, it is probable that He went to a place on the Mount of Olives. Luke records that Jesus was accustomed to going there, where He had a special place of prayer. On the Passover night, after Jesus instituted the New Covenant ceremony, He and the disciples had gone to the Mount of Olives: **"Then He left *the house and* went, as He was accustomed, to the Mount of Olives**; and His disciples also followed Him. And when He arrived at the place, He said to them, 'Pray *that you* do not enter into temptation.' **And He withdrew from them about a stone's throw; and falling to *His* knees, He prayed"** (Luke 22:39-41).

In his account, Matthew identifies the place of prayer as Gethsemane: "Then Jesus came with them to a place called Gethsemane; and He said to His disciples, 'Sit here, while I go onward and pray' " (Matt. 26:36). This is the place where Jesus prayed for nearly three hours before He was arrested (verses 37-44).

Since Jesus did not ascend to the Father until the morning after His resurrection, it is very probable that He went to the Mount of Olives to His special place of prayer in the Garden of Gethsemane. Once there, Jesus most certainly would have offered up prayers of praise and thanksgiving to God the Father the entire night for having raised Him from the dead. We are able get a glimpse of what Jesus might have prayed from the prophecies in the book of Psalms that foretold Jesus' death and resurrection.

Jesus Christ had complete faith that God the Father would raise Him from the dead. Psalm 108 reveals Jesus' faith for that deliverance: "O God, my heart is fixed; I will sing and give praise, even with my glory. Awake, psaltery and harp: I *myself* will awake early. **I will praise Thee, O LORD, among the people: and I will sing praises unto Thee among the nations**. For Thy mercy *is* great above the heavens: and Thy truth *reacheth* unto the clouds.

"**Be Thou exalted, O God, above the heavens: and Thy glory above all the earth; that Thy beloved** [Jesus Christ, the Father's beloved Son] **may be delivered** [from the power of death]: **save** *with* **Thy right hand**, and answer me. God hath spoken in His holiness [to raise Jesus from the dead]; I will rejoice..." (Psa. 108:1-7, *KJV*).

Paul's epistle to the Hebrews confirms that while Jesus was still in the flesh, He cried out to the Father to save Him from death: "Who, in the days of His flesh, **offered up both prayers and supplications with strong crying and tears to Him Who was able to save Him from death, and was heard because *He* feared *God***. Although He was a Son, *yet* He learned obedience from the things that He suffered; and having been perfected, He became *the* Author of eternal salvation to all those who obey Him..." (Heb. 5:7-9). During His life in the flesh, Jesus had prayed fervently to the Father for strength to resist temptation, so that He would not incur the death penalty for sin, but might lay down His life as the perfect sacrifice for the sins of the world. Since He prayed so fervently before He died, He must have been equally fervent in thanking and praising the Father for having raised Him from the dead.

We know that the words of Psalm 22 were uttered by Jesus as He was dying on the cross. Just before He died, He uttered the last words of Psalm 22, "It is finished." The following psalm, Psalm 23, has far more meaning when viewed in the context of His crucifixion and resurrection. Could He not also have uttered these words in His prayers to God the Father after He was resurrected?

"The LORD *is* my shepherd; I shall not want [lack any thing]. He maketh me to lie down in green pastures: He leadeth me beside the still waters. He restoreth my soul [by the resurrection]: he leadeth me in the paths of righteousness for His name's sake. Yea, though I walk through the valley of the shadow of death [the crucifixion], I will fear no evil: for *Thou art* with me; Thy rod and Thy staff *they* comfort me. Thou preparest a table before me in the presence of mine enemies: Thou anointest my head with oil; my cup runneth over. Surely goodness and mercy shall follow me all the days of my life: and I will dwell in the house of the LORD for ever [into the ages of eternity]" (*KJV*).

The Events on the Morning
After Jesus' Resurrection

The Gospel accounts show that as the sun was rising, early in the morning on the first day of the week, the women came bringing spices to anoint Jesus' body. Although Mary Magdalene left home while it was still dark, by the time she arrived at the tomb it was light enough for her to see that the stone had been removed (John 20:1). Apparently, just before she and the other women arrived, an angel had opened the tomb. If it had been opened for any length of time before the women arrived, the soldiers would not have been standing guard. "And *in the morning* suddenly there was a great earthquake; for an angel of *the* Lord descended from heaven, and came and rolled away the stone from the door, and sat upon it. Now his appearance was as lightning, and his raiment white as snow. And for fear of him, those who were keeping guard trembled, and became as dead *men*" (Matt. 28:2-4).

As the women were approaching the tomb, they were wondering who would roll away the huge stone from the entrance of the tomb in order for them to anoint Jesus' body with the spices. But when they arrived, they saw that the stone had already been removed and the tomb was open. Mark gives this account: "And very early on the first *day* of the weeks, at the rising of the sun, they were coming to the tomb; and they were asking themselves, 'Who will roll away the stone for us from the entrance to the tomb?' For it was a massive *stone*. **But when they looked up, they saw that the stone had been rolled away**. And after entering the tomb, they saw a young man [the angel who had rolled away the stone] sitting on the right, clothed in a white robe; and they were very frightened. But he said to them, '**Do not be afraid. You are seeking Jesus the Nazarene, Who was crucified. He has risen; He is not here. Look,** *there is* **the place where they laid Him**. But go, tell His disciples and Peter that He goes before you into Galilee; there you shall see Him, as He said to you.' And they went out quickly and fled from the tomb, for trembling and astonishment had seized them; and they did not say anything to anyone because they were afraid" (Mark 16:2-8).

The Gospel accounts clearly record that the angel told the women, **"He is risen. He is not here." Jesus was not in the tomb**! Jesus was not there because He had been resurrected from the dead as the weekly Sabbath ended over twelve hours earlier. He did not need the stone to be rolled away to leave the tomb, because He had the power to pass through matter. However, it was necessary for the stone to be removed in order for the women to see that He was not there. They found the tomb empty except for the grave cloths that had been wound around His body.

When the other women left to tell the disciples, Mary Magdalene went to tell Peter and John: "Then she ran and came to Simon Peter and to the other disciple whom Jesus loved, and said to them, 'They have taken away the Lord from the tomb, and we do not know where they have laid Him.' As a result, Peter and the other disciple went out and came to the tomb. Now the two ran together, but the other disciple ran faster than Peter and came to the tomb first; and he stooped down *and* saw the linen cloths lying *there*, but he did not enter.

"Then Simon Peter came following him, and he went into the tomb and saw the linen cloths lying, and the napkin that had been on His head, not lying with the linen cloths but folded up in a place by itself. Then the other disciple, who had come to the tomb first, also went in and saw *these things*; and he believed. For they did not yet understand the scripture *which decreed* that He must rise from *the* dead. Then the disciples went away again to their *home*" (John 20:2-10).

After Peter and John left, Mary Magdalene remained at the tomb because she thought that "they had taken away the Lord," and she did not know where He was. "But Mary stood outside the tomb weeping; and as she wept, she stooped down *and looked* into the tomb. And she saw two angels in white who were sitting, one at the head and the other at the feet, where the body of Jesus had been laid. And they said to her, 'Woman, why are you weeping?' She said to them, 'Because they have taken away my Lord, and I do not know where they have laid Him' " (John 20:11-13).

After all those things transpired, Jesus returned to the tomb and appeared to Mary Magdalene: "And after saying these things, she turned around and saw Jesus standing, but did not know that it was Jesus. Jesus said to her, 'Woman, why are you weeping? Whom are you seeking?' Thinking that He was the gardener, she said to Him, 'Sir, if you have carried Him off, tell me where you have laid Him, and I will take Him away.' Jesus said to her, 'Mary.' Turning around, she said to Him, 'Rabboni'; that is to say, 'Teacher.' Jesus said to her, 'Do not touch Me, because I have not yet ascended to My Father. But go to My brethren and tell them that I am ascending to My Father and your Father, and My God and your God.' Mary Magdalene came to the disciples, bringing word that she had seen the Lord, and that He had said these things to her" (verses 14-18).

Correcting the Misinterpretation of Mark 16:9

In the King James Version, Mark 16:9 reads as follows: "**Now when Jesus was risen early the first day of the week,** He appeared first to Mary Magdalene...." This translation makes it appear that Jesus was resurrected early in the morning on the first day of the week. However, the Gospel accounts show that Jesus was raised at the close of the weekly Sabbath, approximately twelve hours before the women came to the tomb. The erroneous impression that the KJV translation gives can be corrected simply by the addition of a comma in the proper place: "**Now when Jesus was risen,** early *the* first *day* of the week He appeared first to Mary Magdalene...." A more accurate translation, as well as the proper placement of the comma, clears up any misunderstanding or misinterpretation. It reads as follows: "**Now after Jesus had risen**, early *the* first *day* of the week He appeared first to Mary Magdalene...." With the proper translation and placement of the comma, this verse harmonizes with the rest of the scriptural facts as found in the other Gospel accounts.

Jesus Fulfilled the Wave Sheaf Offering

In John's Gospel we find this post-resurrection account: "Jesus said to her [Mary Magdalene], '**Do not touch Me, because I have not yet ascended to My Father**. But go to My brethren and **tell them that I am ascending to My Father and your Father, and My God and your God**' " (John 20:17).

When Jesus appeared to Mary Magdalene, He did not allow her to touch Him because He had not yet ascended to God the Father. The words that He spoke to her show that He was about to ascend. We can conclude that He ascended to the Father soon after she left to tell the disciples. When Jesus ascended, He fulfilled a very special temple ceremony that God had commanded for this day. This ceremony was the presentation of the wave sheaf offering of the first of the firstfruits of the grain harvest, which was performed at approximately 9 AM in the morning, after the morning burnt offering had been made. It was at this time that Jesus ascended to God the Father.

The wave sheaf was offered each year on the first day of the week during the Feast of Unleavened Bread. As the sacrifice of the Passover lamb was a foretype of the crucifixion and death of Jesus Christ, so the offering of the wave sheaf was a foretype of Jesus' ascension to the Father. This day was a special day, but not a holy day. At the temple, on the first day of the week during the Feast of Unleavened Bread, the priest would perform the wave sheaf ritual. We find God's command for the wave sheaf offering in the book of Leviticus: "And the LORD spake unto Moses, saying, 'Speak unto the children of Israel, and say unto them, When ye be come into the land which *I* give unto you, and shall reap the harvest thereof, then ye shall bring a sheaf of the firstfruits of your harvest unto the priest: and he shall wave the sheaf before the LORD, to be accepted for you: on the morrow after the sabbath [the first day of the week during the Feast of Unleavened Bread] the priest shall wave it' " (Lev. 23:9-11, *KJV*).

Messianic Rabbi Alfred Edersheim records the details of the harvesting of the wave sheaf in his book *The Life and Times of Jesus the Messiah:*

"This Passover-sheaf was reaped in public the evening before it was offered, and it was to witness this ceremony that the crowd had gathered around the elders. Already on the 14th [of] Nisan the spot whence the first sheaf was to be reaped had been marked out, by tying together in bundles, while still standing, the barley that was to be cut down, according to custom, in the sheltered Ashes-Valley across Kidron. When the time for cutting the sheaf had arrived—that is, on the evening of the 15th [of] Nisan [by Pharisaic reckoning], even though it were a Sabbath [the journey to harvest was undertaken before the end of the Sabbath, but was within the prescribed traditional "Sabbath day's journey"], just as the sun went down, three men, each with a sickle and basket, set to work.

"Clearly to bring out what was distinctive in the ceremony, they first asked of the bystanders three times each of these questions: 'HAS THE SUN GONE DOWN?' 'With this sickle?' 'Into this basket?' 'On this Sabbath? (or first Passover-day)'—and lastly, 'Shall I reap?' Having each time been answered in the affirmative, they cut down barley to the amount of one ephah, or about three pecks and three pints of our English measure" (*The Life and Times of Jesus the Messiah*, p. 619).

Note: There was a dispute between the Pharisees and the Sadducees as to which Sabbath this verse is designating. The Pharisees applied this command to the first holy day of the Feast of Unleavened Bread, which was the 15th day of the first month, or Nisan. In their view, the "morrow after the Sabbath"—the day for harvesting the wave sheaf—was always the 16th of Nisan. On the other hand, the Sadducees, who were in charge of the temple during the days of Jesus Christ, understood that God's command in Leviticus 23:11 was referring to the weekly Sabbath which occurred in conjunction with the Feast of Unleavened Bread. In years when the first day of the Feast of Unleavened Bread fell on the weekly Sabbath, both the Sadducees and the Pharisees would observe the 16th of Nisan as the day for the wave sheaf offering. Although the Sadducees and the Pharisees generally disagreed over the correct DAY for the wave sheaf offering, there was never any question about the correct TIME of the day for harvesting it.

After it was cut, the bundled sheaf was brought to the temple and placed alongside the altar of burnt offering. Then in the morning, after the daily burnt offering of a lamb, the priest would "wave" or elevate the sheaf to be accepted of the Lord. This was a special ceremonial sheaf. In The Shocken Bible, Volume I, The Five Books of Moses, Everett Fox translates Leviticus 23:10-11 in this manner: "Speak to the children of Israel and say to them; When you enter the land that I am giving you, and you harvest its harvest, you are to bring **the premier sheaf** of your harvest to the priest. He is to elevate the sheaf before the presence of YHWH for acceptance for you; on the morrow of the Sabbath the priest shall elevate it."

Note the key words in God's instructions for the wave sheaf offering: "for acceptance for you," meaning "on your behalf." When Jesus Christ ascended to the Father on the Wave Sheaf Day, as the first of the firstfruits, His sacrifice for our sins was accepted by the Father on our behalf. Jesus, as the Lamb of God, was accepted as the sin offering not only for our sins but for the sins of all mankind: "...The lamb of God, Who takes away the sin of the world" (John 1:29).

Jesus fulfilled the wave sheaf offering as the first of the firstfruits to be resurrected from the dead. The premier sheaf symbolized the risen

Christ. When the priest elevated the sheaf to be accepted by the Lord, it represented Jesus Christ ascending to the Father to be accepted as the first of the firstfruits. The apostle Paul makes it clear that this premier sheaf of the firstfruits was a type of Jesus Christ after He rose from the dead and ascended into heaven to present Himself to God the Father: "But now Christ has been raised from *the* dead; **He has become the firstfruit of those who have fallen asleep**. For since by man *came* death, by man also *came the* resurrection of *the* dead. For as in Adam all die, so also in Christ shall all be made alive. But each one in his own order: **Christ *the* firstfruit;** then, those who are Christ's at His coming" (I Cor. 15:20-23).

Because Jesus is the first of many who will be resurrected from the dead as immortal children of God, He is also called "the firstborn from among the dead," as Paul writes to the Colossians: "Because by Him were all things created, the things in heaven and the things on earth, the visible and the invisible, whether *they be* thrones, or lordships, or principalities, or powers: all things were created by Him and for Him. And He is before all, and by Him all things subsist. **And He is the Head of the body, the church; Who is *the* beginning, *the* firstborn from among the dead, so that in all things He Himself might hold the preeminence**" (Col. 1:16-18).

In his epistle to the Romans, Paul makes it clear that many will be resurrected from the grave and be added to the Family of God as immortal brethren of Jesus Christ: "Because those whom He did foreknow, He also predestinated *to be* conformed to the image of His own Son, **that He might be *the* firstborn among many brethren**" (Rom. 8:29). Paul also tells the Corinthians that those who die in the faith will be resurrected at His coming. The resurrection of the saints of God to immortality and glory will mark the end of the firstfruits harvest, just as the resurrection of Jesus signaled its beginning. As He ascended to heaven in the clouds, so He will return, and all the transformed saints will rise into the air to meet Him. The entrance of the saints into the Family of God has been made possible through the sacrifice of Jesus Christ, which was accepted by God the Father on the Wave Sheaf Day.

Jesus Christ Accepted by God the Father

The ascension of Jesus to God the Father was an awesome event. Jesus Christ had finished the work that the Father had given Him to do. As God manifest in the flesh, He had lived a perfect, sinless life and had died by crucifixion to become the perfect sacrifice for the sins of all mankind. God the Father had raised Jesus back to life, and on the Wave Sheaf Day He was ready to ascend to the throne of God the Father to be accepted as the first of the firstfruits, the firstborn among many brethren, and the perfect sacrifice to propitiate the sins of the world.

As He was ascending to the Father, Jesus must have been filled with great joy and anticipation. He would see the Father face to face for the first time since He had become a pinpoint of life when He divested Himself of His power and glory as God to be born of the virgin Mary. Again, the Psalms help us comprehend some of the thoughts and feelings that Jesus might have experienced as He looked forward to being reunited with the Father: "**O God, *Thou art* my God**; early will I seek Thee: my soul thirsteth for Thee, my flesh longeth for Thee in a dry and thirsty land, where no water is; **to see Thy power and Thy glory, so *as* I have seen Thee in the sanctuary**. Because Thy lovingkindness is better than life, my lips shall praise Thee" (Psa. 63:1-3, *KJV*).

As previously noted, Psalm 23 foreshadowed the prayers of Jesus after He was resurrected from the dead. The psalm to follow, Psalm 24, is in prophetic sequence and depicts Jesus' ascension to be received of God the Father. When He arrived in heaven, the angels sang and shouted for joy. Perhaps this psalm was sung by the angels as they opened the everlasting doors and announced that the King of glory was entering into the presence of God the Father: "The earth is the LORD'S, and the fullness thereof; the world, and they that dwell therein. For *He* hath founded it upon the seas, and established it upon the floods. **Who shall ascend into the hill of the LORD? Or who shall stand in His holy place? He that hath clean hands, and a pure heart; who hath not lifted up his soul unto vanity, nor sworn deceitfully** [the perfect life of Jesus Christ]. **He shall receive the blessing from the LORD, and righteousness from the God of his salvation.**"

"**Lift up your heads, O ye gates; and be ye lifted up, ye everlasting doors; and the King of glory shall come in. Who *is* this King of glory? The LORD strong and mighty, the LORD mighty in battle** [He was victorious over human nature, sin, Satan the devil and death]. **Lift up your heads, O ye gates; even lift *them* up, ye everlasting doors; and the King of glory shall come in. Who is *this* King of glory? The LORD of hosts, *He is* the King of glory**" (Psa. 24:1-5, 7-10, *KJV*).

What a magnificent scene of splendor and glory Jesus would have seen when He entered through the everlasting gates of heaven! Standing on the sea of glass, He would have seen the resplendent glory and awesome majesty of God the Father seated on His throne with the heavenly host round about. The apostle John, the one whom Jesus loved, saw a vision of God's throne and recorded it in the book of Revelation. What John recorded is what Jesus would have seen when He ascended to the Father.

"After these things I looked, and behold, **a door opened in heaven**, and the first voice that I heard *was* as if a trumpet were speaking with me, saying, 'Come up here, and I will show you *the* things that must take place after these things.' And immediately I was in *the* Spirit; and **behold, a throne was set in heaven, and *one was* sitting on the throne**. And He Who *was* sitting was in appearance like a jasper stone and a sardius stone: and a rainbow *was* around the throne, like an emerald in its appearance.

"And around the throne *were* twenty-four thrones, and on the thrones

I saw twenty-four elders sitting, clothed in white garments; and they had on their heads golden crowns. **And proceeding from the throne were lightnings and thunders and voices**; and seven lamps of fire, which are the seven Spirits of God, *were* burning before the throne. **And before the throne** *was* **a sea of glass, like crystal. And around the throne and over the throne** *were* **four living creatures, full of eyes before and behind**; and the first living creature *was* like a lion, and the second living creature *was* like a calf, and the third living creature had the face of a man, and the fourth living creature *was* like a flying eagle. And each of *the* four living creatures had six wings respectively; *and* around and within *they were* full of eyes; **and day and night they ceased not saying, 'Holy, holy, holy, Lord God Almighty, Who was, and Who is, and Who** *is* **to come.'**

"And when the living creatures give glory and honor and thanksgiving to Him Who sits on the throne, Who lives into the ages of eternity, the twenty-four elders fall down before Him Who sits on the throne; and they worship Him Who lives into the ages of eternity, and cast their crowns before the throne, saying, '**Worthy are You, O Lord, to receive glory and honor and power because You did create all things, and for Your will they were created and exist**' " (Rev. 4:1-11).

This was the scene that Jesus would have seen as He walked forward to present Himself to the Father as the perfect sacrifice for sin. He was the first of the firstfruits and the firstborn from the dead. As He walked on the sea of glass toward the Father sitting on His throne, the angels, the twenty-four elders and God the Father would see on His body the scars of the lashes that He had received when He was beaten with the cat-of-nine-tails which tore open His flesh. They would see the scars in His hands and feet where the soldiers had nailed Him to the cross. When the Father's beloved Son greeted His Father, They must have opened their arms and embraced each other in profound love and tears of joy. Thus Jesus Christ, the Lamb of God, was accepted by God the Father on the Wave Sheaf Day.

After He was accepted of the Father, Jesus was selected to open the seven seals. He and He alone was qualified, because He had overcome all. The apostle John saw this tremendous scene in the vision and recorded it:

"And in the right hand of Him Who sits on the throne I saw a book, written within and on *the* back, which had been sealed with seven seals. And I saw a strong angel proclaiming with a loud voice, '**Who is worthy to open the book and to loose its seals**?' But no one in heaven, or on the earth, or under the earth was able to open the book, or to look inside it. And I [John] was weeping greatly because no one was found worthy to open and to read the book, or to look into it.

"Then one of the elders said to me, 'Do not weep. Behold, the Lion Who is of the tribe of Judah, the Root of David, has overcome to open the book, and to loose its seven seals.' **Then I saw, and behold, before the throne and the four living creatures, and before the elders,** *was* **standing a Lamb as having been slain**, having seven horns and seven eyes, which are the seven Spirits of God that are sent into all the earth; and **He came and took the book out of the right hand of Him Who sits on the throne**.

"And when He took the book, the four living creatures and the twenty-four elders fell down before the Lamb, each having harps and golden bowls full of incense, which are the prayers of the saints. And they sang a new song, saying, '**Worthy are You to take the book, and to open its seals because You were slain, and did redeem us to God by Your own blood, out of every tribe and language and people and nation,** and did make us unto our God kings and priests; and we shall reign on the earth.'

"**And I saw, and I heard** *the* **voices of many angels around the throne, and** *the voices* **of the living creatures and the elders, and thousands of thousands, saying with a loud voice, 'Worthy is the Lamb Who was slain to receive power, and riches, and wisdom, and strength, and honor, and glory and blessing.' And every creature that is in heaven, and on the earth, and under the earth, and those that are on the sea, and all the things in them, I heard saying, 'To Him Who sits on the throne, and to the Lamb,** *be* **blessing, and honor, and glory, and sovereignty into the ages of eternity.' And the four living creatures said, 'Amen.'** And the twenty-four elders fell down and worshiped *Him Who* lives into the ages of eternity" (Rev. 5:1-12).

This is the glory and majesty that Jesus Christ received when He was accepted by God the Father as the Savior and Redeemer of mankind on the Wave Sheaf Day. Jesus had overcome sin in the flesh and gained complete victory over death, opening the way for the redemption and salvation of all mankind through faith in Him. Now He lives in eternal glory, as the first of many sons of God who will be resurrected at His second coming to share His eternal glory and immortality. Those who are Jesus Christ's are now being perfected through the love, grace and power of God the Father. They will be granted the identical spiritual existence that the Father and the Son have. They will be the sons and daughters of God the Father, and the brethren of Jesus Christ. Jesus shared human existence with mankind in order to become the sin offering for the world so that all who believe in Him may ultimately share His eternal existence and glory in the Family of God throughout the ages of eternity.

Scriptures: From the Day After Jesus' Resurrection To His Ascension

NISAN 18 - SUNDAY MORNING, APRIL 9, 30 AD

55. EARLY THE FIRST DAY OF THE WEEK, JUST BEFORE WOMEN ARRIVE AT THE TOMB, AN ANGEL OPENS THE TOMB

MATTHEW 28

2. And *in the morning* suddenly there was a great earthquake; for an angel of *the* Lord descended from heaven, and came and rolled away the stone from the door, and sat upon it.
3. Now his appearance was as lightning, and his raiment white as snow.
4. And for fear of him, those who were keeping guard trembled, and became as dead *men.*

56. EARLY THE FIRST DAY OF THE WEEK, WOMEN COME TO THE TOMB, BUT JESUS HAS ALREADY BEEN RESURRECTED

JOHN 20

1. Now on the first *day* of the weeks,* while it was still dark, Mary Magdalene came early to the tomb; and she saw *that* the stone had been taken away from the tomb.
2. Then she ran and came to Simon Peter and to the other disciple whom Jesus loved, and said to them, "They have taken away the Lord from the tomb, and we do not know where they have laid Him."
3. As a result, Peter and the other disciple went out and came to the tomb.
4. Now the two ran together, but the other disciple ran faster than Peter and came to the tomb first;
5. And he stooped down *and* saw the linen cloths lying *there*, but he did not enter.
6. Then Simon Peter came following him, and he went into the tomb and saw the linen cloths lying,
7. And the napkin that had been on His head, not lying with the linen cloths but folded up in a place by itself.
8. Then the other disciple, who had come to the tomb first, also went in and saw *these things*; and he believed.
9. For they did not yet understand the scripture *which decreed* that He must rise from *the* dead.
10. Then the disciples went away again to their *home.*

---

*See Appendix C, page 147.

57. JESUS APPEARS FIRST TO MARY MAGDALENE

MARK 16

9. Now after *Jesus* had risen, early *the* first *day* of the weeks He appeared first to Mary Magdalene, from whom He had cast out seven demons.
10. She went *and* told *it* to those who had been with Him, *who* were grieving and weeping.
11. And when they heard that He was alive and had been seen by her, they did not believe *it*.

JOHN 20

11. But Mary stood outside the tomb weeping; and as she wept, she stooped down *and looked* into the tomb.
12. And she saw two angels in white who were sitting, one at the head and the other at the feet, where the body of Jesus had been laid.
13. And they said to her, "Woman, why are you weeping?" She said to them, "Because they have taken away my Lord, and I do not know where they have laid Him."
14. And after saying these things, she turned around and saw Jesus standing, but did not know that it was Jesus.
15. Jesus said to her, "Woman, why are you weeping? Whom are you seeking?" Thinking that He was the gardener, she said to Him, "Sir, if you have carried Him off, tell me where you have laid Him, and I will take Him away."
16. Jesus said to her, "Mary." Turning around, she said to Him, "Rabboni"; that is to say, "Teacher."
17. Jesus said to her, "Do not touch Me, because I have not yet ascended to My Father. But go to My brethren and tell them that I am ascending to My Father and your Father, and My God and your God."
18. Mary Magdalene came to the disciples, bringing word that she had seen the Lord, and that He had said these things to her.

58. SOLDIERS BRIBED TO LIE

MATTHEW 28

11. And as they were going, behold, some of the guard went into the city *and* reported to the chief priests all the things that were done.
12. Then, after gathering together with the elders and taking counsel, they gave a large sum of money to the soldiers,
13. Saying, "Tell *everyone* that His disciples came by night and stole Him while you were sleeping.
14. And if the governor hears *of* this, we will persuade him to release you

from responsibility."

15. And they took the money *and* did as they were instructed; and this report has been spread abroad among the Jews to this day.

59. JESUS APPEARS TO TWO DISCIPLES ON A JOURNEY TO EMMAUS

LUKE 24

13. And behold, on the same day, two of them were going to a village called Emmaus, which was about sixty furlongs from Jerusalem.

14. And they were talking with one another about all the things that had taken place.

15. And it came to pass, as they were talking and reasoning, that Jesus Himself drew near *and* went with them;

16. But their eyes were restrained, *so that* they did not know Him.

17. And He said to them, "What *are* these words that you are exchanging with one another as you walk, and *why* are you downcast in countenance?"

18. Then the one named Cleopas answered *and* said to Him, "Are You only traveling through Jerusalem, and have not known of the things that have happened in these days?"

19. And He said to them, "What things?" And they said to Him, "The things concerning Jesus the Nazarean, a man Who was a prophet, Who was mighty in deed and word before God and all the people;

20. And how the chief priests and our rulers delivered Him up to *the* judgment of death, and crucified Him.

21. And we were hoping that He was the one Who would redeem Israel. But besides all these things, as of today, the third day has already passed since these things took place.

22. And also, certain women from among us astonished us, after they went to the tomb early;

23. For when they did not find His body, they came *to us*, declaring that they had indeed seen a vision of angels, who said, 'He is living.'

24. And some of those with us went to the tomb and found *it* exactly as the women had said, but they did not see Him."

25. Then He said to them, "O foolish and slow of heart to believe in all that the prophets have spoken!

26. Was it not necessary for the Christ to suffer these things, and to enter into His glory?"

27. And beginning with Moses, and from all the prophets, He interpreted to them the things concerning Himself in all the Scriptures.

28. And *as* they approached the village where they were going, He appeared to be going on farther.

29. But they constrained Him, saying, "Stay with us, for it is toward eve-

ning, and the day is declining." And He entered in *as if* to stay with them.

30. And it came to pass, as He sat *at the table* with them, He took the bread *and* blessed *it*; and after breaking *it*, He gave *it* to them.

31. Then their eyes were opened, and they knew Him; and He disappeared from them.

32. And they said to one another, "Did not our hearts burn within us as He was speaking to us on the road, while He was opening the Scriptures to us?"

33. And they rose up that very hour *and* returned to Jerusalem; and they found the eleven and those with them assembled together,

34. Saying, "In truth, the Lord has risen! And He has appeared to Simon."

35. Then they related the things that had happened *to them* on the road, and how He was known to them in the breaking of the bread.

60. AT SUNSET, AS THE FIRST DAY OF THE WEEK IS ENDING, JESUS APPEARS TO THE DISCIPLES BEHIND CLOSED DOORS

LUKE 24

36. Now as they were telling these things, Jesus Himself stood in their midst and said to them, "Peace *be* to you."

37. But they were terrified and filled with fear, thinking *that* they beheld a spirit.

38. Then He said to them, "Why are you troubled? And why do doubts come up in your hearts?

39. See My hands and My feet, that it is I. Touch Me and see *for your-selves*; for a spirit does not have flesh and bones, as you see Me having."

40. And after saying this, He showed them *His* hands and *His* feet.

41. But while they were still disbelieving and wondering for joy, He said to them, "Do you have anything here to eat?"

42. Then they gave Him part of a broiled fish and a *piece* of honeycomb.

43. And He took these *and* ate in their presence.

44. And He said to them, "These *are* the words that I spoke to you when I was yet with you, that all *the* things which were written concerning Me in the Law of Moses and *in the* Prophets and *in the* Psalms must be fulfilled."

45. Then He opened their minds to understand the Scriptures,

46. And said to them, "According as it is written, it was necessary for the Christ to suffer, and to rise from *the* dead the third day.

47. And in His name, repentance and remission of sins should be preached to all nations, beginning at Jerusalem.

48. For you are witnesses of these things.

61. EIGHT DAYS LATER, JESUS APPEARS
TO HIS DISCIPLES AGAIN

JOHN 20

26. Now after eight days, His disciples again were within, and Thomas with them. Jesus came after the doors were shut, and stood in the midst and said, "Peace *be* to you."
27. Then He said to Thomas, "Put forth your finger, and see My hands; and reach *out* your hand, and put *it* into My side; and be not unbelieving, but believing."
28. And Thomas answered and said to Him, "My Lord and My God."
29. Jesus said to him, "Because you have seen Me, Thomas, you have believed; blessed are the ones who have not seen, but have believed."

62. JESUS DOES MANY MIRACLES IN THE PRESENCE
OF THE DISCIPLES

JOHN 20

30. Now then, Jesus did many other miracles in *the* presence of His disciples, which are not written in this book.
31. But these have been written, so that you may believe that Jesus is the Christ, the Son of God; and that believing, you may have life through His name.

63. SOME TIME LATER, JESUS IS SEEN BY
500 OF THE BRETHREN

1 CORINTHIANS 15

4. And that He was buried; and that He was raised the third day, according to the Scriptures;
5. And that He appeared to Cephas, *and* then to the twelve.
6. Then He appeared to over five hundred brethren at one time, of whom the greater part are alive until now, but some have fallen sleep.
7. Next He appeared to James; then to all the apostles;

64. JESUS MEETS THE APOSTLES AT THE
APPOINTED MOUNTAIN

MATTHEW 28

16. Now the eleven disciples went into Galilee, to the mountain which Jesus had appointed *for* them *to meet Him.*
17. And when they saw Him, they worshiped Him; but some doubted.

65. LATER, JESUS APPEARS TO HIS
DISCIPLES IN GALILEE

JOHN 21

1. After these things, Jesus again revealed Himself to the disciples at the Sea of Tiberias. And this *is how* He revealed *Himself*:
2. Simon Peter, and Thomas (called Didymus), and Nathanael from Cana of Galilee were there together, and the *sons* of Zebedee and two of His other disciples.
3. Simon Peter said to them, "I am going fishing." They said to him, "We also will come with you." They left immediately and got into the ship, but during that night they took nothing.
4. And when morning had now come, Jesus stood on the shore. However, none of the disciples realized that it was Jesus.
5. Then Jesus said to them, "Children, do you have any food?" They answered Him, "No."
6. And He said to them, "Cast the net to the right side of the ship, and you shall find *some*." Then they cast *the net*, but they did not have the strength to draw *it in* because of the multitude of fish.
7. Then that disciple whom Jesus loved said to Peter, "It is the Lord." And after hearing that it was the Lord, Peter put on *his* outer garment, because he was naked, and threw himself into the sea.
8. But the other disciples came in a small ship, dragging the net *full* of fish; for they were not far from land, but about two hundred cubits *away*.
9. Now then, when they came up to the land, they saw a fire of coals spread, and fish lying on *it*, and bread.
10. Jesus said to them, "Bring some of the fish that you have just caught."
11. Simon Peter went up *to the shore* and drew the net to the land, full of large fish, one hundred *and* fifty-three; and *although* there were so many, the net was not torn.
12. Jesus said to them, "Come *and* dine." But none of the disciples dared to ask Him, "Who are You?" *For* they knew that it was the Lord.
13. Then Jesus came and took the bread, and gave *it* to them, and likewise the fish.
14. This *was* now the third time *that* Jesus revealed Himself to His disciples after being raised from *the* dead.

66. JESUS ASKS PETER IF HE LOVES HIM
AND COMMANDS HIM TO FEED
AND SHEPHERD JESUS' SHEEP

JOHN 21

15. Therefore, when they had finished eating, Jesus said to Simon Peter, "Simon, *son* of Jonas, do you love Me more than these?" *And* he said to

Him, "Yes, Lord. You know that I love You." He said to him, "Feed My lambs."

16. He said to him again a second time, "Simon, *son* of Jonas, do you love Me?" *And* he said to Him, "Yes, Lord. You know that I love You." He said to him, "Shepherd My sheep."

17. He said to him the third time, "Simon, *son* of Jonas, do you love Me?" Peter was grieved because He said to him the third time, "Do you love Me?" And he said to Him, "Lord, You know all things. You know that I love You." Jesus said to him, "Feed My sheep.

18. Truly, truly I say to you, since you were young, you have dressed yourself and walked wherever you have desired; but when you are old, you shall stretch out your hands, and another shall dress you and bring *you* where you do not desire *to go*."

19. Now He said this to signify by what death he would glorify God. And after saying this, He said to him, "Follow Me."

20. But when Peter turned, he saw the disciple whom Jesus loved following, who also had sat at the supper and *leaned* on His chest, and had said, "Lord, who is it that is betraying You?"

21. Seeing him, Peter said to Jesus, "Lord, what *shall happen* to this one?"

22. Jesus said to him, "If I desire that he remain alive until I come, what *is it* to you? You follow Me."

23. Then this saying went out among the brethren, that that disciple would not die. However, Jesus did not say to him that he would not die; but, "If I desire that he remain alive until I come, what *is it* to you?"

24. This is the disciple who testifies concerning these things and *who* wrote these things; and we know that his testimony is true.

67. JESUS CHRIST'S COMMISSION TO THE APOSTLES BEFORE HIS FINAL ASCENSION TO HEAVEN

MATTHEW 28

18. And Jesus came *and* spoke to them, saying, "All authority in heaven and on earth has been given to Me.

19. Therefore, go *and* make disciples in all nations, baptizing them into the name of the Father, and of the Son, and of the Holy Spirit;

20. Teaching them to observe all things that I have commanded you. And lo, I am with you always, *even* until the completion of the age." Amen.

68. JESUS ASCENDS TO HEAVEN THE SECOND AND FINAL TIME

ACTS 1:1-11

1. The first account I indeed have written, O Theophilus, concerning all things that Jesus began both to do and to teach,

2. Until the day in which He was taken up, after giving command by *the* Holy Spirit to the apostles whom He had chosen;

3. To whom also, by many infallible proofs, He presented Himself alive after He had suffered, being seen by them for forty days, and speaking the things concerning the kingdom of God.

4. And while *they* were assembled with *Him*, He commanded them not to depart from Jerusalem but to "await the promise of the Father, which," *He said*, "you have heard of Me.

5. For John indeed baptized with water, but you shall be baptized with *the* Holy Spirit after not many days."

6. So then, when they were assembled together, they asked Him, saying, "Lord, will You restore the kingdom to Israel at this time?"

7. And He said to them, "It is not for you to know *the* times or *the* seasons, which the Father has placed in His own authority;

8. But you yourselves shall receive power when the Holy Spirit has come upon you, and you shall be My witnesses, both in Jerusalem and in all Judea and Samaria, and unto *the* ends of the earth."

9. And after saying these things, *as* they were looking at *Him*, He was taken up, and a cloud received Him out of their sight.

10. Now while they were gazing intently up into heaven as He was going up, two men in white apparel suddenly stood by them,

11. Who also said, "You men of Galilee, why do you stand *here* looking up into heaven? This *same* Jesus, Who was taken up from you into heaven, shall come in exactly the same manner as you have seen Him go into heaven."

69. JESUS CHRIST DID FAR MORE THAN IS RECORDED

JOHN 21

25. But there are also many other things that Jesus did, which if they were written one by one, I do not suppose that even the world itself could contain the books that would be written. Amen.

Love of God

"For God so loved the world that He gave His only begotten Son, so that everyone who believes in Him may not perish, but may have everlasting life." John 3:16

"In this *way* the love of God was manifested toward us: that God sent His only begotten Son into the world, so that we might live through Him. In this *act* is the love—not that we loved God; rather, that He loved us and sent His Son *to be the* propitiation for our sins." I John 4:9-10

"And we have known and have believed the love that God has toward us. God is love, and the one who dwells in love is dwelling in God, and God in him. By this *spiritual indwelling*, the love *of God* is perfected within us ... There is no fear in the love *of God*; rather, perfect love casts out fear because fear has torment. And the one who fears has not been made perfect in the love *of God*. We love Him because He loved us first." I John 4:16-19

"By this *standard* we know that we love the children of God: when we love God and keep His commandments. For this is the love of God: that we keep His commandments; and His commandments are not burdensome ... And this is the love *of God*: that we walk according to His commandments. This is the commandment, exactly as you heard from *the* beginning, that you might walk in it." I John 5:2-3; II John 6

"If you love Me, keep the commandments—namely, My commandments." John 14:15

"The one who has My commandments and is keeping them, that is the one who loves Me; and the one who loves Me shall be loved by My Father, and I will love him and will manifest Myself to him ... If anyone loves Me, he will keep My word; and My Father will love him, and We will come to him and make Our abode with him. The one who does not love Me does not keep My words; and the word that you hear is not Mine, but the Father's, Who sent Me." John 14:21, 23-24

"As the Father has loved Me, I also have loved you; live in My love. If you keep My commandments, you shall live in My love; just as I have kept My Father's commandments and live in His love ... the Father Himself loves you." John 15:9-10; 16:27

" 'You shall love *the* Lord your God with all your heart, and with all your soul, and with all your mind.' This is *the* first and greatest commandment; and *the* second *one is* like it: 'You shall love your neighbor as yourself.' On these two commandments hang all the Law and the Prophets." Matt. 22:37-40

"A new commandment I give to you: that you love one another in the same way that I have loved you, that *is how* you are to love one another." John 13:34

CHAPTER EIGHT

The Meaning of the Footwashing

The Gospel of John shows that the observance of the Christian Passover includes the ordinance of footwashing. Jesus Christ instituted the footwashing before instituting the bread and the wine as the symbols of His body and His blood. As Jesus commands us to partake of the bread and the wine, so He commands us to participate in the footwashing. The footwashing ceremony is essential to understanding our relationship with Jesus Christ and with one another as Christians under the New Covenant. We can learn many lessons from this simple but profound ceremony.

In the days before Jesus' last Passover, the spirit of competition and self-exaltation was stirred up among the disciples, causing strife over who would be the greatest. The mother of John and James put herself into the very middle of this argument. She personally petitioned Jesus to grant her sons the seats at His right and left hand in His kingdom (Matt. 20:20-23). After reproving James and John for seeking to exalt themselves over their brethren, Jesus taught His disciples a vital lesson in humility:

"And after hearing *this*, the ten were indignant against the two brothers. But Jesus called them to *Him and* said, 'You know that the rulers of the nations exercise lordship over them, and the great ones exercise authority over them. However, it shall not be this way among you; but whoever would become great among you, let him be your servant; and whoever would be first among you, let him be your slave; just as the Son of man did not come to be served, but to serve, and to give His life *as* a ransom for many' "(Matt. 20:24-28).

At His last Passover, Jesus taught this lesson of humility and service by assuming one of the lowest duties of a slave and washing His disciples' feet. This lowly act of service revealed the love and humility of God Himself. Because this service was customarily performed by servants, Peter protested when Jesus began to wash his feet and boldly declared that he would never allow it. "Jesus answered him, 'If I do not wash you, you have no part with Me.' Simon Peter said to Him, 'Lord, not my feet only, but also *my* hands and *my* head.' Jesus said to him, 'The one who has been washed does not need to wash *anything other* than the feet, but is completely clean; and you are clean, but not all.' For He knew the one who was betraying Him; this was the reason He said, 'Not all of you are clean' " (John 13:8-11).

The next words that Jesus spoke clearly reveal His will concerning the footwashing: "Therefore, when He had washed their feet, and had taken his garments *and* had sat down again, He said to them, '**Do you know what**

I have done to you? You call Me the Teacher and the Lord, and you speak rightly, because I am. Therefore, **if I, the Lord and the Teacher, have washed your feet, you also are duty-bound to wash one another's feet; For I have given you an example,** *to show* **that you also should do exactly as I have done to you.**

"Truly, truly I tell you, a servant is not greater than his lord, nor a messenger greater than he who sent him. If you know these things, blessed are you if you do them' " (verses 12-17).

Jesus commanded all who profess Him as their Lord to participate in the footwashing ceremony of the Christian Passover. The words that He spoke to Peter show that our participation is essential to the New Covenant relationship.

What Does It Mean To Have a Part With Jesus Christ?

Jesus told Peter, "Unless I wash you, you have no part with Me." These words have a profound meaning for every Christian. The English word "part" is translated from the Greek word *meros,* which means "a part of something—as a component, a matter, a standing, a share, a place with someone" (Arndt and Gingrich, *A Greek-English Lexicon of the New Testament*).

Having a part with Jesus Christ means partaking of the blessings of the New Covenant, which offers fellowship with Jesus Christ and God the Father in this life and the promise of eternal life in the Kingdom of God. During His last Passover, Jesus promised His disciples a specific reward in the Kingdom of God: "Now you are the ones who have continued with Me in My temptations. And I appoint to you, as My Father has appointed to Me, a kingdom; so that you may eat and drink at My table in My kingdom, and may sit on thrones judging the twelve tribes of Israel" (Luke 22:28-30).

The disciples understood that having a part with Jesus meant ruling with Him in the Kingdom of God. They also knew that Jesus had called them to have a part in the ministry of preaching the gospel during the present age. As His apostles, they would be sent to the twelve tribes of Israel, which were scattered abroad (Jas. 1:1), and to all nations in the world (Matt. 24:14). When Judas Iscariot proved unfaithful to his calling, the eleven remaining disciples were inspired by the Holy Spirit to select a replacement for Judas in order to have twelve founding apostles. The selection of Matthias by lot completed the number (Acts 1:15-26). It is clear from the book of Acts that Matthias received a part in the ministry of the apostles: "And they prayed, saying, 'You, Lord, *the* Knower of the hearts of all, show which one of these two You have personally chosen to receive the part of this ministry and apostleship...'" (verses 24-25).

This record in the book of Acts clarifies the meaning of Jesus' words to Peter during the footwashing. When Jesus told Peter that He must wash his feet or Peter would have no part with Him, Peter understood that he was in danger of losing his apostleship. No wonder Peter responded by saying,

"Lord, not my feet only, but also *my* hands and *my* head." Peter may have been referring to the priestly requirements for washing and bathing before serving at the tabernacle (Ex. 30:17-21; Lev. 16:1-4).

After becoming an apostle, Peter rebuked Simon Magus, a sorcerer at Samaria who was revered as a religious leader, for attempting to buy an apostleship. Peter's condemnation of Simon shows that his evil and covetous heart disqualified him not only from an apostleship but from any part in the ministry of Jesus Christ: "May your money be destroyed with you because you thought that the gift of God might be purchased with money. You have neither part nor lot in this matter, for your heart is not right before God" (Acts 8:20-21).

Having a part with Jesus Christ does not refer exclusively to serving in the ministry. The New Testament teaches that everyone who belongs to Jesus Christ has a part with Him. All who have a part with Jesus Christ now will also have a part in the first resurrection, which will take place at His return. They will be raised to immortality and will reign with Christ during the millennium: "Blessed and holy is the one who has part in the first resurrection; over these the second death has no power. But they shall be priests of God and of Christ, and shall reign with Him a thousand years" (Rev. 20:6).

The resurrection to immortality at the return of Jesus Christ is the hope and goal of every true Christian. Having a part in that resurrection is symbolized by the act of water baptism. The apostle Paul shows how the symbolic burial and resurrection of baptism leads to a part in the first resurrection: "Therefore, if you have been raised [out of the watery grave of baptism] together with Christ, seek the things that are above [your part with Christ], where Christ is sitting at *the* right hand of God. Set your affection on the things that are above, and not on the things that are on the earth. For you have died [to the old nature, as symbolized by baptism], and your life has been hid together with Christ in God. When Christ, *Who is* our life, is manifested, then you also shall be manifested with Him in glory [your eternal part with Christ]" (Col. 3:1-4).

To have a part with Jesus Christ and share His likeness for eternity, we must learn to be like Him in this life. If we share in the sufferings that He experienced, striving to overcome the fleshly nature of sin, we will also be glorified as the sons of God: "...To the one who thirsts, I will give freely of the fountain of the water of life. The one who overcomes shall inherit all things; and I will be his God, and he shall be My son" (Rev. 21:6-7). What a glorious destiny! Those who overcome sin in the flesh will receive eternal life as the glorified sons and daughters of God.

In order to be glorified as the children of God, we must love God with all our hearts and be keeping His commandments. Those who make a practice of breaking the commandments are showing that they do not love Jesus Christ and God the Father (John 14:15, 23-24; I John 5:3). Their disobedience will lead to a part in the lake of fire: "But *the* cowardly, and unbelieving, and abominable, and murderers, and fornicators, and sorcerers, and idolaters, and all liars, shall have their part in the lake that burns with fire and brimstone; which is *the* second death" (Rev. 21:8).

Jesus Himself shows who will have a part in His kingdom: " 'And behold, I am coming quickly and My reward is with Me, to render to each one according as his work shall be. I am Alpha and Omega, *the* Beginning and *the* End, the First and the Last.' Blessed *are* those who keep His commandments, that they may have the right to *eat of* the tree of life, and may enter by the gates into the city. But excluded *are* dogs, and sorcerers, and fornicators, and murderers, and idolaters, and everyone who loves and devises a lie....For I jointly testify to everyone who hears the words of the prophecy of this book, *that* if anyone adds to these things, God shall add to him the plagues that are written in this book. And if anyone takes away from the words of *the* book of this prophecy, God shall take away his part from *the* book of life, and from the holy city, and from the things that are written in this book" (Rev. 22:12-15, 18-19).

Having a part with Jesus Christ requires total and complete obedience—with no variations or exceptions. That is why Jesus required Peter to participate in the footwashing. That is also why Jesus did not wash Peter's hands or his head, as Peter requested. Jesus washed only his feet.

As Peter learned to submit to Jesus Christ, so must we. We must learn to follow Him, conforming our lives to His teaching and His way, in order to have a part with Him. We cannot add to or take from what Jesus commanded. Jesus' command to wash one another's feet during the Christian Passover is no exception. Even if we consider it the least of His commands, we are required to obey His words and to follow His example.

Footwashing and Baptism

When we examine the words that Jesus spoke concerning the footwashing, we find a direct reference to the spiritual cleansing that takes place when repentant believers are baptized. Jesus said to Peter: "The one who has been washed does not need to wash *anything other* than the feet" (John 13:10). The phrase "has been washed" is translated from the Greek word *louoo,* which means "to wash, as a rule the whole body; to bathe, of religious washings...with the allusion to the cleansing of the whole body in baptism" (Arndt and Gingrich, *A Greek-English Lexicon of the New Testament*). Other uses of the word *louoo* in the New Testament show that Jesus was not referring to washing as in a bath, but to the washing of baptism. This same word is used by the apostle Paul in Hebrews 10: "Let us approach *God* with a true heart, with full conviction of faith, our hearts having been purified [sanctified by the blood of Christ] from a wicked conscience, and our bodies having been washed [*louoo*] with pure water" (Heb. 10:22). Paul's words to Titus leave no doubt that he is referring to the washing of baptism, which brings spiritual cleansing: "...according to His mercy He saved us, through *the* washing [*louoo*] of regeneration and *the* renewing of *the* Holy

Spirit" (Titus 3:5).

The apostle Peter shows that baptism in the name of Jesus Christ is a requirement for receiving the gift of the Holy Spirit. On the day of Pentecost, Peter was inspired to proclaim, "Repent and be baptized each one of you in the name of Jesus Christ for *the* remission of sins, and you yourselves shall receive the gift of the Holy Spirit" (Acts 2:38).

The twelve apostles, who had repented and been baptized in the days of Jesus' ministry, were the first to receive the Holy Spirit on the Day of Pentecost (Acts 2:1-4). Their inspired preaching led many others to believe and to be baptized (verses 41-42). These all received the gift of the Holy Spirit by the laying on of hands, as did other believers who were added in the following months (Acts 8:15-17). The conversion of Saul, who became the apostle Paul, took place during this time (Acts 9:1-6). In testifying of his conversion before the unbelieving Jews, Paul repeated the words of Ananias, who had laid hands on him: "The God of our fathers has personally chosen you to know His will, and to see the Just One, and to hear *the* voice of His mouth; for you shall be a witness for Him to all men of what you have seen and heard. And now why do you delay? Arise and **be baptized, and wash [*louoo*] away your sins**, calling on the name of the Lord" (Acts 22:14-16).

The word "baptize" is translated from the Greek *baptizoo,* which means "dip, immerse, plunge, sink, drench, overwhelm" (Arndt and Gingrich, *A Greek-English Lexicon of the New Testament*). Baptism requires complete immersion in water because it symbolizes the burial of the old, sinful nature. Because baptism represents the burial of the old, sinful self in a watery grave, it can be compared to the burial of a dead person. A dead person is not buried by sprinkling a little dirt on the corpse. The dead are placed in graves and are completely covered with earth. In the same manner as a dead person is placed in the grave and completely covered with earth, the one who is baptized must be completely covered with water by immersion.

The believer who desires to be cleansed from sin is baptized into the death of Jesus Christ, symbolically dying to the old nature of sin, and rising from the watery grave to walk in newness of life, as Paul explains: "Or are you ignorant that we, as many as were baptized into Christ Jesus, were baptized into His death? Therefore, we were **buried** with Him by **baptism** into **death** [dying to the old nature]; so that, just as Christ was raised from *the* dead by the glory of the Father, in the same way, we also should **walk in newness of life**" (Rom. 6:3-4).

Jesus Christ paid the penalty for the sins of every human being, and His death is accepted by God the Father in the stead of each repentant sinner who is baptized. Baptism is the outward manifestation of the sinner's repentance and faith in the sacrifice of Jesus Christ for the forgiveness of sins and cleansing of the heart. The spiritual cleansing that takes place at baptism frees each one from the penalty for sin, which is death, and enables him or her to receive the gift of eternal life from God the Father (verse 23).

When a believer is co-joined in the death of Jesus Christ at baptism, he or she is pledging to faithfully keep the commandments of Jesus Christ and God the Father, which are the words of the New Covenant. Each one who remains faithful unto death will be resurrected to eternal life and glory.

To be resurrected to immortality, we must continue to walk in the new way of life that begins at baptism. This newness of life is symbolized by the footwashing ceremony of the Christian Passover. As we participate in the footwashing each year, we are renewing our pledge to walk in the new way of life that God has ordained for us (Eph. 2:10). Since we have already been wholly washed by the waters of baptism, we need only to wash our feet as a renewal of our pledge.

When we wash one another's feet as Jesus commanded, we are re-dedicating ourselves to walk in God's way of life. As we seek to walk in His way, we will be led by the Holy Spirit to resist the sinful desires of the flesh (Gal. 5:16). The Holy Spirit will impart the love of God and will motivate us to keep His commandments: "And this is the love *of God*: that we **walk according to His commandments**..." (II John 6). We will be learning to live by every word of God, which is truth: "For I rejoiced exceedingly at the coming of *the* brethren *who* testified of you in the truth, even how you are **walking in truth**. I do not have any greater joy than these *testimonies* that I am hearing—that my children are **walking in truth**" (III John 3-4). As we walk in the light of God's Word, the blood of Jesus Christ will cleanse us from every sin (I John 1:7).

This spiritual cleansing, which we receive through the blood of the New Covenant, is symbolized by the footwashing ceremony of the Christian Passover. By participating in the footwashing, we confirm our desire to remain under the New Covenant, and we renew our pledge to keep the commandments of God and walk in His Truth.

Footwashing and True Humility

As we follow the example of Jesus Christ by washing one another's feet, we are also learning **the lesson of humility that Jesus taught His disciples**: "The Son of man did not come to be served, but to serve, and to give His life *as* a ransom for many" (Matt. 20:28). Jesus spoke these words a few days before His last Passover. On the night of the Passover, before He was betrayed, He instituted the ceremony of footwashing. By washing His disciples' feet, He demonstrated the attitude of service and humility that He requires of all who profess to follow Him. When He had finished washing the disciples' feet, He told them, "You call Me the Teacher and the Lord, and you speak rightly, because I am.... Truly, truly I tell you, a servant is not greater than his lord, nor a messenger greater than he who sent him" (John 13:13, 16).

This vital lesson in humility applies to every servant of Jesus Christ. No one who is serving Jesus Christ, as a messenger bringing the Word of

God, is ever to be exalted above the brethren.

The apostle Paul did not exalt himself above the brethren. Rather, he followed the example of Jesus Christ and taught others to practice the same humility. Paul wrote, "*Let* nothing *be* done through [motivated by] contention or vainglory, but **in humility** each esteeming the others above himself. Let each one look not *only* after his own things, but *let* each one also *consider* the things of others. Let this mind be in you, which *was* also in Christ Jesus, Who, although He existed [pre-existed] in *the* form of God, did not consider it robbery to be equal with God; but **emptied Himself** [giving up His glory as God], *and* was made in *the* likeness of men, and took the form of a servant; and being found in *the* manner of man, **HE HUMBLED HIM-SELF**, *and* became obedient unto death, even *the* death of *the* cross" (Phil. 2:3-8).

The apostle John also wrote of the pre-existence of Jesus Christ as God (John 1:1-3, 14). John knew that Jesus had given up His power, His glory and His immortality to become a man, made in the likeness of human flesh, for the purpose of becoming the perfect sacrifice of God the Father for the forgiveness of sins—our sins and those of the entire world (I John 2:2). There can be no greater act of humility and service than this!

CHAPTER NINE

The Meaning of the Body of Jesus the Christ

God has manifested His great love to the world by sending His Son Jesus Christ to redeem mankind from sin. The fullness of God's love is revealed in the sacrifice of His only begotten Son, Who willingly gave Himself for the salvation of every human being. "For God so loved the world that He gave His only begotten Son, so that **everyone who believes in Him** may not perish, but **may have everlasting life**" (John 3:16).

The magnitude of His suffering was foretold by Jesus Christ Himself at His last Passover. After breaking the unleavened bread, He said, "Take, eat; this is My body, which *is* being broken for you. This do in the remembrance of Me" (I Cor. 11:24).

Why did Jesus Christ, the Son of God, have to offer Himself for the sins of mankind? Was there no other way to bring salvation to the world? How could His one death atone for the sins of multiple millions of human beings and redeem every one of them from the sentence of death? In order to answer these questions, we must start at the beginning with God's creation of man.

Freedom of Choice

The creation of Adam and Eve is described in detail in Genesis 2. As the account shows, Adam was the first to receive life: "Then the LORD God [*Jehovah Elohim*] formed man of the dust of the ground, and breathed into his nostrils the breath of life; and man became a living soul" (Gen. 2:7, The Holy Scriptures—Jewish Publication Society of America, 1917, herein after referred to as *JPSA*). Adam's wife, Eve, was created from one of his ribs (verses 18, 21-23).

After God had created them, Adam and Eve walked and talked with Him. Since their minds were innocent, they were not ashamed of being naked in God's presence: "And they were both naked, the man and his wife, and were not ashamed" (Gen. 2:25, *KJV*).

God created within Adam's mind a fully functioning language and the capacity to choose (Gen. 2:16-17). Like Adam, Eve was also created with a fully functioning language and the capacity to choose. This capacity is manifested in the account of God's instruction and warning to them in the Garden of Eden: "And the LORD God took the man, and put him into the garden of Eden to dress it and to keep it. And the LORD God commanded the man, saying: 'Of every tree of the garden thou mayest freely eat; but of

the tree of the knowledge of good and evil, thou shalt not eat of it; for in the day that thou eatest thereof thou shalt surely die' " (Gen. 2:15-17, *JPSA*).

Man Chooses the Way of Sin

The book of Genesis records that Adam and Eve received God's instructions before the serpent, Satan the devil, was allowed to test them as to which way they would choose—the way that leads to eternal life or the way that leads to sin and death (Gen. 2:16-17).

"Now the serpent was more subtle than any beast of the field which the LORD God had made. And he said unto the woman, 'Yea, hath God said, Ye shall not eat of every tree of the garden?' And the woman said unto the serpent, 'We may eat of the fruit of the trees of the garden: but of the fruit of the tree which is in the midst of the garden, God hath said, Ye shall not eat of it, neither shall ye touch it, lest ye die.' And the serpent said unto the woman, 'Ye shall not surely die: for God doth know that in the day ye eat thereof, then your eyes shall be opened, and ye shall be as gods, knowing good and evil' " (Gen. 3:1-5, *KJV*).

Instead of obeying God, Eve took some of the fruit, ate it, and gave some to her husband Adam: "And when the woman saw that the tree *was* good for food, and that it *was* pleasant to the eyes, and a tree to be desired to make *one* wise, she took of the fruit thereof, and did eat, and gave also unto her husband with her; and he did eat" (verse 6, *KJV*).

The account of the temptation of Adam and Eve shows that their eating the fruit of the tree of the knowledge of good and evil was not due to ignorance or to misunderstanding but was a willful choice.

From that time on, every human being has been given a choice whether or not to love and obey God. As Creator and Lawgiver, God has decreed that the penalty for disobedience to His commands is death, but through faith, love and obedience, God grants the gift of eternal life (Rom. 6:23). This is the choice that God set before Adam and Eve, as portrayed in the description of the two trees—the tree of life, and the tree of the knowledge of good and evil.

The Consequences of Adam and Eve's Sin

As a result of Adam and Eve's sin of disobedience to God, they were no longer innocent: "**And the eyes of them both were opened** [to know good and evil]**, and they knew that they were naked**; and they sewed fig leaves together, and made themselves aprons. And they heard the voice of the LORD God walking in the garden in the cool of the day: and Adam and his wife hid themselves from the presence of the LORD God amongst the trees of the garden. And the LORD God called unto Adam, and said unto him, Where *art* thou? And he said, I heard thy voice in the garden, and I was afraid, because I *was* naked; and I hid myself. And he said, Who told thee that thou *wast* naked? Hast thou eaten of the tree, whereof I commanded thee that thou shouldest not eat?" (Gen. 3: 7-11, *KJV*.)

The sin of Adam and Eve had profound consequences for all humanity. "Unto the woman he said, I will greatly multiply thy sorrow and thy conception; in sorrow thou shalt bring forth children; and thy desire *shall be* to thy husband, and he shall rule over thee. And unto Adam he said, Because thou hast hearkened unto the voice of thy wife, and hast eaten of the tree, of which I commanded thee, saying, Thou shalt not eat of it: cursed *is* the ground for thy sake; in sorrow shalt thou eat *of* it all the days of thy life; thorns also and thistles shall it bring forth to thee; and thou shalt eat the herb of the field; in the sweat of thy face shalt thou eat bread, till thou return unto the ground; for out of it wast thou taken: **for dust thou *art*, and unto dust shalt thou return**" (verses 16-19, *KJV*).

God's judgment included the sentence of death. Moreover, Adam and Eve were exiled from the Garden of Eden, cutting them off from the tree of life and from access to the Holy Spirit of God, which imparts the power to live forever (Gen. 3:24). The sentence of death passed to all their descendants, who were also cut off from access to the Holy Spirit. Without the Holy Spirit of God, mankind was powerless to resist the temptations of the flesh and the influence of Satan and could not be freed from "the law of sin and death" (Rom. 8:2).

The apostle Paul confirms that the sentence of death came to all mankind as a result of the first human sin: "Therefore, as by one man [Adam] sin entered into the world, and by means of sin *came* death; and in this way, death passed into all mankind; *and it is* for this reason that all have sinned" (Rom. 5:12).

However, when God pronounced His judgment on Adam and Eve, He also gave the first prophecy of the coming Messiah, Who would redeem humanity from the curse of Adam's sin (Gen. 3:15).

The Nature of Man's Sin

The law of sin and death is within every human being and generates the evil desires that the Bible refers to as "fleshly lusts" or "the lust of the flesh" (Eph. 2:3, I Pet. 2:1, II Pet. 2:18). It is these fleshly lusts that lead human beings to commit sin (Jas. 1:14-15).

The fleshly nature of sin within man is further described in Romans 8:7-8: "Because **the carnal mind** [mind of the flesh] *is* **enmity against God**, for it is not subject to the law of God; neither indeed can it *be*. But those who are in *the* flesh cannot please God." Every human being is by nature an enemy of God because of these wicked works, which originate in the mind (Col. 1:21).

The apostle Paul wrote that the sinful nature of the flesh has alienated all human beings from God: "For we have already charged both Jews and Gentiles—ALL—*with* being under sin, exactly as it is written: 'For there is not a righteous one—not even one! There is not one who understands; there is not one who seeks after God. They have all gone out of the way; together they have *all* become depraved. There is not *even* one who is practicing kindness. No, there is not so much as one! Their throats *are* like an open grave; with their tongues they have used deceit; *the* venom of asps *is* under their lips; whose mouths are full of cursing and bitterness; their feet *are* swift to shed blood; destruction and misery *are* in their ways; and *the* way of peace they have not known. There is no fear of God before their eyes.' Now then, we know that whatever the law says, it speaks to those who are under the law, so that every mouth may be stopped, and all the world may become guilty before God" (Rom. 3:9-19).

In Romans 8:2, Paul defines the sinful nature as "the law of sin and death." This law of sin and death is in every human being. God has provided reconciliation for all mankind through the sacrifice of His only begotten Son: "And there is no [Greek *ouk*, the impossibility of] salvation in any other, for neither is there another name under heaven which has been given among men, by which we must [Greek *dei*, mandatory, obligatory] be saved" (Acts 4:12).

The sinful nature makes all human beings vulnerable to the deception of Satan, who is the god of this world (II Cor. 4:4, Rev. 12:9). Together with his fallen angels, he is the ruler over the spiritual darkness and wickedness of this world (Eph. 6:11-12). Satan's evil influence works with human nature to lead all people in the way of disobedience to God—the way of sin and death. The far-reaching effect of Satan's influence is described in Paul's epistle to the Ephesians: "Now you were dead in trespasses and sins, in which you walked in times past according to the course [society and times] of this world, according to the prince of the power of the air [Satan the devil], the spirit that is now working within **the children of disobedience; among whom also we all once had our conduct in the lusts of our flesh**, doing the things willed by the flesh and by the mind, and were [before God's calling] by nature *the* children of wrath, even as the rest *of the world*" (Eph. 2:1-3).

The Nature of God

God is both the Lawgiver and the Judge of all who break His laws. He is also the Savior and the Redeemer of those who repent of their transgressions of His laws. These two aspects of God's nature are clearly revealed in the words that He spoke when Moses was allowed to see His glory: " 'Thou canst not see My face, for man shall not see Me and live. ...Behold, there is a place by Me, and thou shalt stand upon the rock. And it shall come to pass, while My glory passeth by, that I will put thee in a cleft of the rock, and will cover thee with My hand until I have passed by. And I will take away My hand, and thou shalt see My back; but My face shall not be seen' ...And the LORD [*Jehovah*, the covenant name] descended in the cloud, and stood with him there, and proclaimed the name of the LORD. And the LORD passed by before him, and proclaimed: 'The LORD, the LORD, God [*Elohim*, the Creator], merciful [Psa. 103:8-18; 119:64; 136] and gracious [Psa. 86:15; 111:4; 112:4; 116:5, I Pet. 2:3] long-suffering [Rom. 2:4, I Tim. 1:16], and abundant in goodness [Psa. 31:19; 33:5; 107:8, 15, 21, 31, Rom. 2:4] and truth [Deut. 32:4, Psa. 31:5; 33:4, Jer. 4:2, John 14:6]; keeping mercy unto the thousandth generation, forgiving iniquity and transgression and sin [Psa. 103:1-4, Acts 2:38; 3:19, Rom. 3:23-25]; and that will by no means clear the guilty; visiting the iniquity of the fathers upon the children ... unto the fourth generation' " (Ex. 33:20-23; 34:5-7, *JPSA*).

Because God is merciful and gracious, He is ready to forgive the sins of the one who repents (Psa. 86:1-5), and because God is holy and righteous, He cannot allow the unrepentant to escape judgment.

In warning the wicked of his ultimate judgment, God shows that He takes no pleasure in executing it: "As I live, saith the Lord GOD, **I have no pleasure in the death of the wicked, but that the wicked turn from his way and live**; turn ye, turn ye from your evil ways; **for why will ye die, O house of Israel?"** (Ezek. 33:11, *JPSA*.)

Because God is love, He does not delight in the death of the wicked. It is God's desire that every sinner would repent and be saved: "... He is long-suffering toward us, not desiring that any should perish, but that all should come to repentance" (II Pet. 3:9).

The love of God is His greatest attribute and characteristic: "GOD IS LOVE" (I John 4:8, 16). Everything that God does flows from His love!

The magnitude of God's love is revealed in the creation of man. All human beings bear the image and likeness of God: " '**Let us** make man **in our image, after our likeness**, and let them have dominion over the fish of the sea, and over the fowl of the air, and over the cattle, and over all the earth'. ...And God created man **in His own image, in the image of God** created He him; male and female created He them" (Gen. 1:26-27, *JPSA*).

Two Elohim

The Scriptures reveal that there are two who are *Elohim*. This truth is verified by the apostle John:

"In *the* beginning was the Word, and **the Word was with God**, and **the Word was God.** He was in *the* beginning with God. All things came into being through Him, and not even one *thing* that was created came into being without Him. In Him was life, and the life was the light of men ... And the **Word became flesh**, and tabernacled [temporarily dwelt] among us (and we ourselves beheld His glory, *the* glory as of *the* only **begotten with *the* Father**), full of grace and truth" (John 1:1-4, 14). Thus Jesus Christ was with God and was God before He became flesh.

The God of the Old Testament Who walked and talked with Adam and Eve was not the Father. The God Who delivered the Ten Commandments to Moses was not the Father. The God Who appeared to the prophets in visions was not the Father. The God Who appeared to the patriarchs and Who led the children of Israel out of Egypt was the One who became Jesus Christ (Ex. 3:6-8, I Cor. 10:4). Jesus was the *Elohim* of the Old Testament Who became God manifested in the flesh. He was sent to earth by the Father, the other *Elohim* of the Old Testament.

The God Who became the Father never revealed Himself to man in Old Testament times. God the Father was not revealed until the coming of Jesus Christ: "**No one has seen God at any time**; the only begotten Son, Who is in the bosom of the Father, He has proclaimed *Him*" (John 1:18). Jesus Himself said, "And the Father Himself Who sent Me has borne witness of Me. **You have neither heard His voice nor seen His form at any time**" (John 5:37).

It is vital to understand that the Lord God of the Old Testament was made flesh and became Jesus Christ, the Son of God. To become God in the flesh, He emptied Himself of His power and glory. As Jehovah Elohim, He had formed man from the dust of the ground. As Jesus Christ, He sacrificed Himself to redeem mankind from sin and the penalty of eternal death. This sacrifice was essential to the fulfillment of God's purpose for man.

A Little Lower Than God

God has given mankind other attributes which are like His. David was inspired to write, "O Lord, our Lord, how majestic is Your name in all the earth ... When I consider Your heavens, the work of Your fingers, the moon and the stars, which You have ordained; **what is man**, that You do take thought of him? Yet, **You have made him a little lower than God** [Hebrew *elohim*]…" (Psa. 8:1-5, *NASB*).

Many translations of the Bible, including the King James Version, render this verse as "a little lower than the angels." However, the Hebrew word *elohim*, which is used in this verse, refers to deities—not to angels. This word is used countless times in the Hebrew text in reference to both the true God and to false gods. In every other occurrence in the King James Version, *elohim* is correctly translated "God" or "gods." Green's translation conveys the meaning of Psalm 8:5: "For You have made him lack a little from God…" (*The Interlinear Hebrew-Greek-English Bible*).

Of all the creatures that God made to dwell on the earth, only man has been given the attributes of God—including the ability to think and reason, to speak, to write, to plan, to create, to build, to teach, to learn, to judge, and to rule. God gave human beings the capacity to love, to hate, to laugh, to cry, to forgive, to repent, and to experience every type of emotion. All of these qualities are godlike characteristics, which man is privileged to possess. Man is able to experience these godlike attributes because he was given a unique spiritual dimension that God did not give to the rest of His earthly creation. Every human being has been given this quality, which makes each one "a little lower than God." The Bible describes this spiritual quality as the "spirit of man."

The Spirit of Man

The spirit that dwells in man is not another spirit being, such as an angel or demon. Rather, it is a spirit essence that comes from God: "Thus says God, the Lord, who created the heavens and stretched them out, who spread out the earth and its offspring, who gives breath to the people on it, and **spirit** [Hebrew *ruach*] to those who walk in it" (Isa. 42:5, *NASB*).

The spirit of man is different from what the Bible calls the "soul." The word "soul" is translated from the Hebrew *nephesh*, which refers to physical life, whether human or animal. In many occurrences, *nephesh* is translated "creature" or "life" (Gen. 1:20-21, 24, 30; 2:19; 9:4-5, 10, 12, 15-16). When translated "soul," it refers to the physical life and strength of a human being (Gen. 2:7, Ex. 1:5, Lev. 23:30, Deut. 4:29, Josh. 11:11, Ezek. 13:18-19; 18:4, 20). Unlike the soul, which ends with the death of the body, the spirit in man returns to God when a human dies (Eccl. 12:7). The spirit of man is the unique power that gives each person thought and consciousness: "But *there is* a **spirit in man:** and the inspiration of the Almighty giveth them understanding" (Job 32:8, *KJV*). The apostle Paul wrote, "For who among men understands the things of men, except *by* **the spirit of man** which *is* **in him**?" (I Cor. 2:11).

It is the spirit in man that gives him the potential to become a son of God. The Scriptures show that the spirit of man was made to receive and unite with the Holy Spirit of God as a begettal from God the Father: "Everyone who has been begotten by God does not practice sin because His [God the Father's] seed *of begettal* is dwelling within him, and he is not able to *practice* sin because he has been begotten by God" (I John 3:9). This spiritual begettal takes place only after a person has repented and been baptized, and has had the laying on of hands to receive the Holy Spirit. When the Holy Spirit unites with the individual's spirit, he or she is spiritually begotten as a child of God: "...You have received *the* Spirit of sonship, whereby we call out, 'Abba, Father.' The Spirit itself bears witness conjointly with our own spirit, *testifying* that we are *the* children of God" (Rom. 8:15-16).

Because all human beings possess the spirit of man, every individual on earth can receive the Holy Spirit of begettal from God the Father. This is the glorious potential of every human being! In Psalm 8, David expresses his awe at God's purpose in creating man. "...And you did crown him with glory and majesty! **You did make him to rule over the works of Your hands; You have put all things under his feet**, all sheep and oxen, and also the beasts of the field, the birds of the heavens, the fish of the sea, whatever passes through the paths of the seas. O Lord, Lord, how majesty is Your name in all the earth!" (Psa. 8:5-9, *NASB*.) The New Testament shows that this dominion will be granted to all who become the glorified children of God through faith in Jesus Christ (Heb. 2:6-10).

To prepare man for his ultimate destiny, God gave him rulership over the earth: "And God blessed them; and God said unto them: 'Be fruitful, and multiply, and replenish the earth, and subdue it; and have dominion over the fish of the sea, and over the fowl of the air, and over every living thing that creepeth upon the earth' " (Gen. 1:28, *JPSA*). After finishing the creation of the world and of Adam and Eve, "...God saw every thing that He had made, and, behold, it was very good" (verse 31, *JPSA*). Everything that God created on the earth was given to man to be used for his benefit.

Jesus Christ Was God in the Flesh

The Lord God, Who had created man from the dust of the ground, came to earth in the flesh of Jesus Christ: "And undeniably, great is the mystery of godliness: **God was manifested in *the* flesh**..." (I Tim. 3:16). Why did the Lord God of the Old Testament, Jehovah Elohim, become flesh? What kind of flesh did God take upon Himself when He became Jesus Christ? Was His flesh the same as ours, or was He composed of spirit that only appeared to be flesh?

The apostle Paul reveals the answer: "Let this mind be in you, which *was* also in Christ Jesus; Who, although He existed [Greek *huparchoon,* to exist or pre-exist] **in *the* form of God**, did not consider it robbery to be equal with God, but **emptied Himself** [of His power and glory], *and* was **made in *the* likeness** [*homoioma,* the same existence] **of men**, *and* took the form of a servant [*doulos,* a slave]; and being found in *the* manner of man, **He humbled Himself**, *and* became obedient unto death, even *the* death of *the* cross" (Phil. 2:5-8).

These inspired words of Paul confirm that before Jesus Christ became human He was, in fact, Jehovah Elohim. Existing as God, He was composed of ever-living Spirit. It was impossible for Him to die. However, to redeem man from the law of sin and death, it was necessary for Him to die. The only way for God to die was to become human—to be "manifested in the flesh." Thus the God Who had created man in His image and likeness took on the same substance as man.

Paul's words to the Philippians reveal exactly how God did this. The Elohim Who became Jesus Christ "emptied Himself" in order to be made in the likeness of man. In emptying Himself of His glory as God, He placed Himself under the power of God the Father, who reduced Him to only a pinpoint of life. By the power of the Holy Spirit of God the Father, He was impregnated into a human ovum within the virgin Mary's womb.

When the virgin Mary asked the angel Gabriel how it was possible for her to conceive, not having known a man, he answered, "*The* Holy Spirit shall come upon you, and *the* power of *the* Highest shall overshadow you;

and for this reason, the Holy One being begotten [Greek *gennoomenon,* a present tense, passive participle, meaning that the impregnation was taking place at that very moment] in you shall also be called *the* Son of God" (Luke 1:35).

At the instant Jesus was conceived in the womb of the virgin Mary, He became the divinely begotten Son of God, fulfilling the prophecy in Psalm 2: "**I will declare the decree**: the LORD [the Elohim who became the Father] hath said unto me, **Thou *art* my Son; this day have I begotten thee**" (verse 7, *KJV*).

This is also indicated in another prophecy of Jesus' coming in the flesh. In his epistle to the Hebrews, the apostle Paul quotes these words from Psalm 40: "For this reason, when He comes into the world, He says, 'Sacrifice and offering You did not desire, but **You have prepared a body for Me** [Christ's human body of flesh]. You did not delight in burnt offerings and *sacrifices* for sin. Then said I, **Lo, I come** (*as* it is written of Me in *the* scroll of *the* book)**, to do Your will, O God'** " (Heb. 10:5-7).

Jesus revealed that He had authority from God the Father to lay down His life and to receive it back again. "On account of this, the Father loves Me: because I lay down My life, that I may receive it back again. No one takes it from Me, but I lay it down of Myself. **I have authority to lay it down and authority to receive it back again.** This commandment I received from My Father" (John 10:17-18).

Jesus also said of Himself: "I am the living bread, which came down from heaven; if anyone eats of this bread, he shall live forever; and the bread that I will give is even My flesh, which I will give for the life of the world" (John 6:51). In order to give His flesh for the life of the world, Jesus Christ had to be fully human, sharing the same mortal existence that every human being experiences.

Jesus Christ Shared the Human Experience

In writing to the Hebrews, the apostle Paul used many passages in the Old Testament to show that Jesus Christ shared the mortal existence of all human beings. In translating Psalm 8 from the Hebrew into the Greek language, Paul used the middle voice, which expresses God's personal involvement with man: "But in a certain place one fully testified, saying, 'What is man, that You [**Yourself**] are mindful of him, or *the* son of man, that You [**Yourself**] visit him? You did make him a little lower than *the* angels; You did crown him with glory and honor, and You did set him over the works of Your hands; You did put all things in subjection under his feet.' For in subjecting all things to him, He left nothing *that was* not subjected to him. But now we do not yet see all things subjected to him.

"But we see Jesus, Who *was* made a little lower than *the* angels, crowned with glory and honor on account of suffering the death, in order that **by *the* grace of God He Himself might taste [partake of] death for**

everyone; because it was fitting for Him, for Whom all things *were created*, and by Whom all things *exist*, in bringing many sons unto glory, to make the Author of their salvation perfect through sufferings" (Heb. 2:6-10).

Continuing in his letter to the Hebrews, Paul wrote, "Therefore, since the children are partakers of flesh and blood, **in like manner** [Greek *parapleesioos,* or "in exactly the same way"] **He also took part in the same** [flesh and blood], in order that through [His] death He might annul him who has the power of death—that is, the devil; and *that* He might deliver those who were subject to bondage all through their lives by *their* fear of death. For surely, He is not taking upon Himself to help *the* angels; but He is taking upon Himself to help *the* seed of Abraham. **For this reason, it was obligatory** [Greek *opheiloo,* or "owe, be indebted, be obligated"] **for *Him* to be made like *His* brethren** in everything [sharing the same flesh and nature] that He might be a merciful and faithful High Priest *in* things pertaining to God, in order to make propitiation for the sins of the people. For because He Himself has suffered, having been tempted *in like manner*, He is able to help those who are being tempted" (Heb. 2:14-18).

When God entered into covenant with Abraham by taking a maledictory oath, He obligated Himself to die to fulfill the promises of the covenant. Thus, He obligated Himself to take on a mortal body that was subject to death.

Jesus Took on and Overcame Sin in the Flesh

The apostle Paul specifically stated that the flesh of Jesus was sinful: "For what *was* impossible for the law to do, in that it was weak through the flesh, God, having sent His own Son in *the* likeness of sinful flesh, and for sin, condemned sin in the flesh" (Rom. 8:3). A literal translation of the Greek text is **"in *the* likeness of flesh, of sin…"**

Paul's statement that Jesus was made in the likeness of sinful flesh shows that "the law of sin and death" was passed on to Jesus from His mother Mary. Because Jesus had inherited the law of sin and death, He had the potential to sin at any time during His human life. If, as some claim, Jesus was incapable of sin, it would have been impossible for Him to be tempted. Yet, He was tempted by the devil in the wilderness, as the Scriptures record (Matt. 4:1-11, Mark 1:12-13, Luke 4:1-13).

Jesus was fully aware of the consequences of giving in to temptation. **If He had sinned even once, He would have died for His own sins and would never have returned to His glory with the Father.** The apostle Paul shows how earnestly and agonizingly Jesus prayed for strength to resist the temptations of the flesh: "Who, in the days of His flesh, offered up both prayers and supplications with strong crying and tears to Him Who was able TO SAVE HIM FROM DEATH, and was heard because *He* feared [was reverent and submissive to God the Father] *God*. Although He was a Son, *yet* He learned obedience from the things that He suffered; and having been perfected, He became *the* Author of eternal salvation to all those who obey Him" (Heb. 5:7-9).

Thus while Jesus was in the flesh, He experienced exactly the same temptations that we do because He was made "in the likeness of sinful flesh." "For we do not have a high priest who cannot empathize with our weaknesses, but **one Who was tempted in all things** [in every way] **according to *the* likeness of *our own temptations*** [Greek *kath omoioteeta,* or "in every way just as we are"]; **yet *He was* without sin.** Therefore, we should come with boldness to the throne of grace, so that we may receive mercy and find grace to help in time of need" (Heb. 4:15-16).

Jesus was made in the likeness of sinful flesh so that as our High Priest He could sympathize with our weaknesses. Because he has shared the same sinful nature, He can have compassion when we weaken and commit sins. He mercifully intercedes for us with the Father, obtaining His forgiveness for our sins. Through Jesus' ongoing intercession in our behalf, God the Father's mercy and grace can continually be imparted to each one of us.

The gift of grace is possible only through Jesus Christ, Who offered His own sinless body as the substitute sacrifice for our sins: "...Christ also suffered for us, leaving us an example, that you should follow in His footsteps **Who committed no sin; neither was guile found in His mouth ... Who Himself bore** [carried] **our sins within** [Greek *en,* within] **His own body** on the tree..." (I Pet. 2:21-24).

Jesus Gave His Body to Redeem Mankind

From the beginning of the world, it was ordained that Jesus Christ would suffer and die to atone for the sins of mankind: "But we see Jesus, Who *was* made a little lower than *the* angels, crowned with glory and honor on account of suffering the death, in order that **by *the* grace of God He Himself might taste death for everyone**; because it was fitting for Him, for Whom all things *were created*, and by Whom all things *exist*, in bringing many sons unto glory, to make the Author of their salvation perfect through sufferings" (Heb. 2:9-10).

Because He was sinless, Jesus was able to offer His own life for the sins of others as Paul wrote, "For He [God the Father] made Him [Jesus Christ] Who knew [Greek *ginooskoo,* to know by self-experience] no sin *to be* sin for us..." (II Cor. 5:21).

The Creator died for His creation! In so doing, He demonstrated His eternal love for mankind.

"For even when we were without strength, at the appointed time Christ died for *the* ungodly. For rarely will anyone die for a righteous man, although perhaps someone might have the courage even to die for a good man. **But God commends His own love to us because, when we were still sinners, Christ died for us...**" (Rom. 5:6-8).

Each one who repents of sin and accepts the sacrifice of Jesus Christ can be reconciled to God the Father: "For you *were* once alienated and enemies in *your* minds by wicked works; but now He has reconciled *you* in the body of His flesh through the death…" (Col. 1:21-22).

The apostle Paul was inspired and overwhelmed by the greatness of God's plan of salvation for man: "O *the* depth of *the* riches of both *the* wisdom and *the* knowledge of God! How unfathomable *are* His judgments and unsearchable *are* His ways! For who did know *the* mind of *the* Lord, or who became His counselor? Or who first gave to Him, and it shall be recompensed to him again? For from Him, and through Him, and unto Him *are* all things; to Him *be* the glory into the ages of eternity" (Rom. 11:33-36).

Blessings Through Partaking of the Body of Christ

When we accept the body of Jesus Christ for our salvation, we receive not only forgiveness of sin but also the promise of physical healing. As our sin offering, Jesus took upon His own body both our sentence of death and our physical sufferings so that He might be both our Savior and our Healer. Jesus was wounded for our sins and transgressions, and by His stripes we are healed of our sicknesses and diseases (Isa. 53:4-12, Matt. 8:17, Jas. 5:14-16, I Pet. 2:24).

When we understand the significance of the body of Jesus Christ, we can begin to grasp the importance of obeying His command to partake of the unleavened bread of the Christian Passover: "Take, eat; this is My body, which *is* being broken for you. This do in the remembrance of Me" (I Cor. 11:24).

True Christians will be manifesting their acceptance of the body of Jesus Christ for their forgiveness and healing by partaking of the unleavened bread each year at the Christian Passover. By partaking of this symbol of His body, they will be showing that they as individuals have a part in the blessings that are offered through His sacrifice for sins (I Cor. 11:26).

CHAPTER TEN

The Meaning of the Blood
Of Jesus the Christ

The New Covenant was sealed with the blood of Jesus Christ, "...the Lamb of God, Who takes away the sin of the world" (John 1:29). His shed blood is symbolized by the wine that every true Christian partakes of during the Christian Passover ceremony. When Jesus instituted this ceremony, He "took the cup, and after giving thanks, He gave *it* to them, saying, 'All of you drink of it; **for this is My blood, the *blood* of the New Covenant, which is poured out for many for *the* remission of sin*s*' "** (Matt. 26:27-28).

By offering His own blood, Jesus purchased remission of sin for all time: "...Without *the* shedding of blood there is no remission ... But now, once and for all, in *the* consummation of the ages, He has been manifested for *the* purpose of removing sin through His sacrifice *of Himself*" (Heb. 9:22, 26). The blood of Jesus Christ was poured out to remove the sins of all mankind. But Jesus Christ is a personal Savior, which means that His blood must be individually imputed to each one who repents of sin and believes in Him: "...This cup *is* the New Covenant in My blood, **which is poured out for you"** (Luke 22:20).

Each Christian who partakes of the small cup of wine during the Christian Passover service is symbolizing his or her acceptance of the shed blood of Jesus Christ for the forgiveness of sins and deliverance from the penalty of death. By partaking of the wine and the unleavened bread, each one is acknowledging his or her personal faith in the shed blood and the broken body of Jesus Christ, which alone can bring eternal life. Jesus Himself said, "...**Unless you eat the flesh of the Son of man, and drink His blood, you do not have life in yourselves"** (John 6:53).

The blood of Jesus Christ works in many powerful ways to bring eternal life to those who accept His sacrifice. This work began with the establishment of the New Covenant and will continue to the return of Jesus Christ.

The Multi-Faceted Meaning of the Blood of Jesus Christ

Let us examine the many ways in which the blood of Jesus Christ is fulfilling the promise of salvation and eternal life:

1) Jesus Christ ratified the New Covenant with His blood. At the institution of the Christian Passover, Jesus said, "This cup *is* the New Covenant in My blood, which is poured out for you" (Luke 22:20).

No covenant can be established without a blood sacrifice. When God established His covenant with Abraham, He ratified it by passing between the halves of the sacrificial animals (Gen. 15:17-18). This covenant was the foundation for both the Old Covenant with the physical seed of Abraham and the New Covenant with the spiritual seed.

When the Old Covenant was established, the people of Israel agreed to obey all the commandments, laws and statutes of God, which were written in the book of the covenant, known as "the book of the law." The covenant was then ratified with the blood of animals: "And Moses took half of the blood, and put *it* in basins; and half of the blood he sprinkled on the altar. And he took the book of the covenant, and read in the audience of the people: and they said, All that the LORD hath said will we do, and be obedient. And Moses took the blood, and sprinkled it on the people, and said, Behold the blood of the covenant, which the LORD hath made with you concerning all these words" (Ex. 24:6-8, *KJV*). The blood of the sacrificial animals represented the death that would be required of every person who broke the covenant.

The Old Covenant was broken countless times during the history of the people of Israel and Judah. By breaking the covenant, the people forfeited their right to the blessings of God and brought themselves under the curses of the covenant, which included the sentence of death. To redeem them from the curse of death, Jesus Christ, the Lord God of the Old Testament, sacrificed His life. As the God Who had established the covenant, He had the power to end it with His death. Through His death, He established the New Covenant, which offers eternal life.

Like the words of the Old Covenant, the words of the New Covenant are recorded in the New Testament. The books of the New Testament reveal the way to enter the New Covenant and receive the promise of eternal life. This promise was sealed with the blood of Jesus Christ. God Himself, Who cannot lie, guaranteed the promise of salvation with His own blood and is now actively fulfilling that promise by serving as Mediator of the covenant. Every sinner can be reconciled to God the Father by coming to "...Jesus, *the* Mediator of *the* New Covenant, and to **sprinkling of *the* blood of *ratification*,** proclaiming superior things than *that of* Abel" (Heb. 12:24).

2) Jesus Christ redeems sinners and removes sins through His blood. The word "redeem" means to buy back what has been sold. All human beings have been "sold under sin" by transgressing the commandments and laws of God (Rom. 3:23; 7:14, I John 3:4). In becoming the servants of sin, all have earned the penalty of death (Rom. 6:16, 23). The only escape from this death is through Jesus Christ, Who paid the price for the redemption of every human being with His crucifixion and death: "...The Son of man did not come to be served, but to serve, and to give His life *as* a ransom for many" (Matt. 20:28).

Jesus Christ sacrificed His own life as the Passover Lamb of God (I Cor. 5:7). His one perfect sacrifice purchased redemption for sinners throughout all ages: "But Christ Himself has become High Priest of the coming good things, through the greater and more perfect tabernacle, not made by *human* hands (that is, not of this *present physical* creation [the temple in Jerusalem before its destruction]). Not by *the* blood of goats and calves, **but by the means of His own blood**, He entered once for all into the holiest [into the presence of God the Father, as the perfect and complete sin offering], **having *by* Himself secured everlasting redemption *for us*"** (Heb. 9:11-12).

Each one who is redeemed by the blood of Jesus Christ receives forgiveness of sins: "...Wherein He [God the Father] has made us the objects of *His* grace in the Beloved *Son;* in Whom we have redemption through His blood, *even* the remission of sins, according to the riches of His grace" (Eph. 1:6-7). When a person truly repents of his or her sins and accepts the sacrifice of Jesus Christ, God the Father counts every sin the person has committed as paid in full by the blood of His own Son. Each one who is redeemed by the blood of Jesus Christ is freed from the ownership of sin and the penalty of death (Rom. 5:21; 6:1-4). He or she is no longer the property and slave of sin, but has become the property and servant of Jesus Christ and God the Father (Rom. 6:18, 22).

Christians who are walking in the light of God's Word by following the example of Jesus Christ will continue to receive forgiveness through His blood when they stumble and sin: "However, if we walk in the light, as He is in the light, *then* we have fellowship with one another, and **the blood of Jesus Christ, His own Son, cleanses us from all sin.** If we say that we do not have sin, we are deceiving ourselves, and the truth is not in us. **If we confess our own sins, He is faithful and righteous, to forgive us our sins, and to cleanse us from all unrighteousness"** (I John 1:7-9).

3) Jesus Christ justifies and sanctifies sinners through His blood. The gift of justification before God the Father comes through faith in the blood of Jesus Christ: "...having been **justified by faith**....God commends His own love to us because, when we were still sinners, Christ died for us. Much more, therefore, having been justified now by His blood, we shall be saved from wrath through Him" (Rom. 5:1, 8-9). Justification means that a person has been placed in right standing with God and is counted blameless before God the Father. This right standing with God the Father is made possible because the righteousness of Jesus Christ is imputed, or attributed, to the individual.

Justification through the blood of Jesus Christ is granted only to those who repent of their sins and transgressions of God's laws: "Because the hearers of the law *are* not just [justified] before God, but **the doers of the law** [the ones who are keeping the commandments of God] **shall be justified"** (Rom. 2:13).

Every believer who repents of sin and is baptized in the name of Jesus Christ receives complete justification before God: "...But you were **washed**, you were **sanctified**, you were **justified in the name of the Lord Jesus**, and by the Spirit of our God" (I Cor. 6:11). At baptism, the believer not only receives justification, but is also sanctified before God the Father. The blood of Jesus Christ makes this sanctification possible: "For this reason, Jesus, in order that He might sanctify the people by His own blood, also suffered outside the gate" (Heb. 13:12).

To be "sanctified" means to be set aside for a holy use and purpose. The prayer of Jesus on His last Passover night shows that every true believer is being sanctified by the Word of God: "Sanctify them in Your truth; YOUR WORD IS THE TRUTH" (John 17:17). Each one who truly believes in Jesus Christ and is sanctified through His blood is set aside by God's Word and by the Holy Spirit.

4) Jesus Christ purifies the conscience and brings peace with God through His blood. Peace with God the Father is possible only through the blood of Jesus Christ: "For it pleased *the Father* that in Him all the fullness should dwell; and, having made peace through the blood of His cross..." (Col. 1:19-20). The blood of Jesus Christ brings peace with God by removing the enmity that is caused by sin: "For He is our peace...having annulled in His flesh the enmity..." (Eph. 2:14-15).

Jesus removes this enmity by purifying the mind of each one who has repented of sin: "For if the blood of goats and bulls, and *the* ashes of a heifer sprinkled *on* those who are defiled, sanctifies to the purifying of the flesh, to a far greater degree, the blood of Christ, Who through *the* eternal Spirit offered Himself without spot to God, shall purify your conscience from dead works [works leading to death] to serve *the* living God" (Heb. 9:13-14).

Those whose consciences have been purified from the works of the flesh are no longer the enemies of God because they are no longer "alienated ... by wicked works" (Col. 1:21). They have forsaken the way of sin to begin a new life of righteousness, learning to do the good works that God has commanded: "For we are His workmanship, created in Christ Jesus unto *the* good works that God ordained beforehand in order that we might walk in them" (Eph. 2:10). By keeping the commandments of God with a pure conscience, true Christians are manifesting the love that God desires: "Now **the purpose of the commandment is love out of a pure heart, and a good conscience,** and genuine faith" (I Tim. 1:5).

5) Jesus Christ gives direct access to God the Father through His blood. The apostle Paul declares, "But now in Christ Jesus, you who were once far off are made near by the blood of Christ" (Eph. 2:13).

In his epistle to the Hebrews, Paul reveals that those whose consciences have been purified by the blood of Jesus Christ have direct access to God the Father: "Therefore, brethren, having confidence to enter into the *true* holiest [into the presence of God the Father in heaven above] by the blood of Jesus, by a new and living way, which He consecrated for us through the veil (that is, His flesh), and *having* a great High Priest over the house of God, let us approach *God* with a true heart, with full conviction of faith, our hearts having been purified [by the blood of Jesus] from a wicked conscience, and our bodies having been washed with pure water. Let us hold fast without wavering *to* the hope *that* we profess, for He Who promised *is* faithful" (Heb. 10:19-23).

During His ministry, Jesus Himself revealed that His followers would receive direct access to God the Father: "In that day, [after the resurrection of Jesus] you shall ask in My name; and I do not tell you that I will beseech the Father for you, for the Father Himself loves you, because you have loved Me, and have believed that I came forth from God" (John 16:26-27). From the time of Jesus' ascension to heaven, every Christian has been given authority to approach the Father in His name. The only intermediary between Christians and God the Father is Jesus Christ, Who intercedes as High Priest to remove sins with His own blood.

True Christians have no need of a priesthood of men, nor of a temple in which to worship God. Not only do they have direct access to the throne of God the Father in heaven, but He dwells within them through the Holy Spirit: "...For you are a temple of *the* living God, exactly as God said: 'I will dwell in them and walk in *them*; and I will be their God, and they shall be My people....and I shall be a Father to you, and you shall be My sons and daughters,' says *the* Lord Almighty" (II Cor. 6:16, 18).

6) Jesus Christ is building the Church through His blood. Every Christian who has been begotten by the Holy Spirit of God the Father becomes a member of the family of God (Eph. 3:14-15). Each one is a child of God the Father and may call Him, "Abba, Father" (Rom. 8:15). This new relationship with the Father shows the love of God through Jesus Christ, Whose blood makes it possible for human beings to become the children of God: "Behold! What *glorious* love the Father has given to us, that we should be called the children of God!" (I John 3:1).

Every Christian is joined to the body of Jesus Christ at baptism. When a believer is baptized, he or she is baptized into the covenant death of Jesus Christ. In this symbolic covenant death, the believer is united with the body of Jesus Christ, being buried with Him in the baptismal grave and then rising with Him to a new life (Rom. 6:3-4). Upon receiving the Holy Spirit through the laying on of hands, all believers become members of the body of Jesus Christ (I Cor. 12:27). This body is composed of all spiritually begotten Christians and constitutes the true Church (Eph. 1:22-23).

The Church belongs to God the Father, Who has made Jesus Christ its Head, having purchased it with His own blood. Paul told the elders at Ephesus, "Take heed therefore to yourselves and to all the flock, among which the Holy Spirit has made you overseers, to feed the church of God, which He purchased with His own blood" (Acts 20:28).

All members of the true Church of God belong to God the Father. They are no longer the property of sin—nor are they the property of any man or any organization of men. They are the property and the children of God the Father, and Jesus Christ is their Head.

7) Jesus Christ delivers Christians from Satan the devil through His blood. Each Christian who has been redeemed from sin by the blood of Jesus Christ has also been freed from the power of Satan: "Giving thanks to the Father, Who has made us qualified for the share of the inheritance of the saints in the light; Who has personally rescued us from the power of darkness and has transferred *us* into the kingdom of the Son of His love; in Whom we have redemption through His own blood, *even* the remission of sins" (Col. 1:12-14).

Satan is the great evil force, the prince of the power of the air, who captivates the minds and hearts of people and draws them into sin (Eph. 2:1-2). He is, in fact, the god of this world (II Cor. 4:4).

Satan is aided by a host of seducing spirits in his efforts to deceive the people of this world: "And every spirit that does not confess that Jesus Christ has come in the flesh is not from God. And this is the *spirit* of antichrist, which you heard *was* to come, and even now it is already in the world. You are of God, little children, and have overcome them because greater *is* He Who *is* in you [the indwelling of the Holy Spirit of God the Father] than the one who *is* in the world" (I John 4:3-4).

Every Christian who has been begotten by the Holy Spirit of God has been delivered from the power of Satan. But Satan does not give up on those who turn from the way of sin and disobedience. Each Christian must continually be on guard against Satan's deceptions and must use the full power of God and all the spiritual weapons that He provides to resist the devil (Eph. 6:10-18, I Pet. 5:8-9). Christians must draw close to God daily, lest they be drawn into temptation and sin. If they do sin, they must repent and ask God the Father to cleanse them from their sin through the blood of Jesus Christ (I John 1:7-9).

Cleansing by the blood of Jesus Christ is a lifelong process. It is this continued application of the blood of Jesus Christ that gives each Christian the victory over Satan and His devices: "And the great dragon was cast out, the ancient serpent who is called the Devil and Satan, who is deceiving the whole world; he was cast down to the earth, and his angels [evil spirits, or demons] were cast down with him. And I heard a great voice in heaven say, 'Now has come the salvation and the power and the kingdom of our God, and the authority of His Christ because the accuser of our brethren has been cast down, who accuses them day and night before our God.'

"But **they overcame him** [Satan, the devil] **through the blood of the Lamb,** and through the word of their testimony; and they loved not their lives unto death" (Rev. 12:9-11).

8) Jesus Christ is perfecting Christians through His blood. As human beings, with the law of sin and death within our flesh, not one of us is perfect. But in order to enter the Kingdom of God, we must all become spiritually perfect, as God is: "Therefore, you shall be perfect, even as your Father Who *is* in heaven is perfect" (Matt. 5:48).

Nothing we do of and by ourselves can make us perfect before God the Father. The patriarch Job learned this lesson by experience (Job 9:20; 40:9-14; 42:1-6). No amount of human willpower and work can bring spiritual perfection. The only way to attain spiritual perfection is through the blood of Jesus Christ, which enables us to receive the gift of the Holy Spirit from God the Father. The indwelling of the Holy Spirit gives us the power to become like Jesus Christ, Who Himself attained spiritual perfection by overcoming the temptations of the flesh (Heb. 5:8-9).

The very purpose for the coming of Jesus Christ in the flesh was to bring human beings to perfection by reconciling them to God the Father: "And, having made peace through the blood of His cross ... He has reconciled *you* in the body of His flesh through death, **to present you holy and unblamable and unimpeachable before Him** [God the Father]; if indeed you continue in the faith grounded and steadfast, and are not moved away from the hope of the gospel, which you have heard ... *even* the mystery that has been hidden from ages and from generations, but has now been revealed to His saints; to whom God did will to make known what *is* the riches of the glory of this mystery among the Gentiles; which is Christ in you, the hope of glory; Whom we preach, admonishing every man and teaching every man in all wisdom, so **that we may present every man perfect in Christ Jesus**" (Col. 1:20-23, 26-28).

In a vision that the apostle John recorded in the book of Revelation, Jesus Christ appears as the Lamb of God, Who was slain for the sins of the world, and a new song accompanies the prayers of the saints: "Worthy are You to take the book, and to open its seals because You were slain, and did redeem us to God [the Father] BY YOUR OWN BLOOD, out of every tribe and language and people and nation..." (Rev. 5:9).

This is the glorious salvation that Jesus envisioned when He said, **"For this is My blood, the *blood* of the New Covenant, which is poured out for many for *the* remission of sins"** (Matt. 26:28).

CHAPTER ELEVEN

Jesus' One Sacrifice Fulfilled All

Jesus Christ offered Himself as the supreme sacrifice of God the Father for the sins of mankind. Through His one perfect sacrifice, Jesus purchased redemption from sin for all time. The New Testament reveals that His death fulfilled not only the Passover sacrifice but all of the animal sacrifices that were required by the laws that God had given to Moses. All were fulfilled when Jesus died on the Passover day, as the apostle Paul tells us that Jesus "offered ONE SACRIFICE for sins for ever" (Heb. 10:12). That one perfect sacrifice purchased everlasting redemption: "By Whose will we are sanctified through the offering of the body of Jesus Christ ONCE FOR ALL" (Heb. 10:10). And again, "For when He died, He died unto sin ONCE FOR ALL" (Rom. 6:10).

Jesus Was Our Sin Offering

Some of the early Hebrew Christians did not fully understand that the death of Jesus Christ had fulfilled the animal sacrifices that were commanded under the Old Covenant. They were still looking to the Temple sacrifices for sanctification from sin. The apostle Paul wrote his epistle to the Hebrews to explain to them that these sacrifices for sin were no longer required. He explained that the sacrifice of Jesus Christ had fulfilled all the requirements of the Law for the sin offerings that were made at the Temple.

He also explained that, as the Law required, Jesus died outside the gates of the city: "We have an altar from which those who are serving the *present earthly* tabernacle do not have authority to eat; for *pertaining to* those animals whose blood is brought into the holy places by the high priest for *a* **sin** *offering*, the bodies of all these are burned **outside the camp**. For this reason, **Jesus, in order that He might sanctify the people by His own blood, also suffered OUTSIDE THE GATE**" (Heb. 13:10-12).

The fact that Jesus died outside the gates of Jerusalem verifies that His body was a sin offering. The Law of God specifically commanded that all sin offerings were to be burned "outside the camp" (Lev. 4:1-2, 11-12, 21; 16:27). After the blood of the sacrificial animals was sprinkled on the altar, the bodies of the sin offerings were taken across the Kidron Valley to a place high on the Mount of Olives east of the city of Jerusalem, where there was a special altar called the Miphkad Altar. This altar was located near Golgotha, where Jesus was crucified.

"The *Miphkad Altar* and the sin offerings which were sacrificed on it was really a cardinal part of the Temple complex that existed in the time of Christ. This altar was not one with a ramp leading up to a square elevated area, but it is described in the Mishnah as a pit in which the animals could be burnt to ashes (*Parah* 4:2). The *Miphkad Altar* was located *outside* the walls of the Temple (as Ezekiel 43:21 states), but [the bridge across the Kidron Valley and] the roadway leading up to the altar (and including the altar itself) were part of the ritualistic furniture associated with the Temple services....Christ was crucified near the *Miphkad Altar*..." (Ernest L. Martin, *The Secrets of Golgotha*, p. 41).

The location of this altar on the Mount of Olives offered a direct view of the entire Temple area. On the Day of Atonement, those who stood at the site of this special altar could observe the high priest as he was standing near the veil of the Temple, ready to enter the Holy Place. "Even the bullock and the goat which were sacrificed on the day of Atonement (Leviticus 16) had to be killed near the Altar of Burnt Offering within the Temple and then their carcasses were required to be taken out the eastern gate to the Miphkad Altar at the Mount of Olives and there they were burnt to ashes (Leviticus 4)" (Ibid., p. 246).

The ashes of all the animals that were burned on the altar at the Temple were taken to the same place where the sin offerings were burned (Miphkad Altar) and were mingled with the ashes of the sin offerings "and poured out at the base of the Altar (Leviticus 4:12, 21; 6:11) (where the ashes could descend through a conduit system into the Valley of Kidron below)" (Ibid., p. 246). As the supreme sin offering of God the Father, the body of Jesus Christ was offered up when He was crucified on the Mount of Olives, near the altar where the bodies of all sin offerings from the Temple were offered up to God. Thus, Paul wrote: "But He, **after offering one sacrifice for sins for ever,** sat down at *the* right hand of God. Since that time, He is waiting until His enemies are placed *as* a footstool for His feet. For by one offering He has obtained eternal perfection *for* those who are sanctified" (Heb. 10:12-14).

Jesus Was Our Passover Sacrifice

As the Lamb of God, Jesus Christ was sacrificed on the Passover day, Nisan 14/April 5, 30 AD. The apostle Paul affirms that His death fulfilled the sacrifice of the Passover lamb: "For Christ our Passover was sacrificed for us" (I Cor. 5:7).

Jesus Christ was the complete sacrifice of God the Father to fulfill the promises of the New Covenant—the only covenant that offers redemption from sin and the gift of eternal life. The promise of eternal life through the New Covenant was sealed by the beaten, scourged and crucified body of Jesus Christ and the outpouring of His blood. The ceremony that commemorates His supreme sacrifice for the sins of the world was instituted on the night that He was betrayed. That is when His disciples partook of the symbols of His body and His blood, and that is when all His followers are commanded to partake of these symbols. Paul wrote that the instructions of the Lord were to observe it "in that night" when Jesus was betrayed, which was the night of Nisan 14. Christians are to renew the New Covenant every year on that night by participating in the footwashing and by partaking of the broken, unleavened bread and the cup of wine. It is a personal, individual renewal of the New Covenant, "**...This cup is the New Covenant in My blood, which is poured out for you**" (Luke 22:20). Each Christian who takes part in this ceremony is affirming his or her acceptance of the sacrifice of Jesus Christ and is renewing his or her commitment to live by the words of the New Covenant.

By personally renewing the New Covenant, one is able to receive continuing forgiveness and grace from God the Father, Who applies the blood of Jesus Christ to one's sins (I John 1:7-9). Through the grace of God and by repentance, this daily cleansing from sin is accomplished (Matt. 6:12), allowing Christians to remain in fellowship with God the Father and Jesus Christ (I John 1:3). He imparts strength and understanding to each one through His Holy Spirit. Every Christian who is led by the Holy Spirit will be growing in spiritual knowledge and godly character and will ultimately receive the gift of eternal life in the Kingdom of God when Jesus returns (II Pet. 1:4-11).

The Mystery of Godliness

God has revealed in His Word that His desire is to grant eternal life to all who will repent and accept Jesus Christ as personal savior and are baptized for the remission of sins. So marvelous is God's purpose for man that the apostle Paul calls it "**the mystery of godliness.**" This great mystery of God is the very reason for the life, death and resurrection of Jesus Christ: "And undeniably, great is the mystery of godliness: God was manifested in *the* flesh, was justified in *the* Spirit, was seen by angels, was proclaimed among *the* Gentiles, was believed on in *the* world, was received up in glory" (I Tim. 3:16).

It was to raise up sons and daughters for God the Father that Jesus Christ was manifested in the flesh. The mystery of godliness is the knowledge that Jesus Christ was God manifested in the flesh and by the power of the Holy Spirit, Christ dwells within each one whom the Father has called, enabling the believer to overcome the law of sin and death and to receive eternal life at the resurrection: "*Even* **the mystery which has been hidden from the ages and from generations, but now has been revealed to His saints**; to whom God did will to make known what *is* the riches of **the glory of this mystery** among the Gentiles; which is **Christ in you, the hope of glory**" (Col. 1:26-27).

In describing the mystery of godliness, Paul declares that not only was God "manifested in the flesh" but He "was justified in *the* Spirit" (I Tim. 3:16). How was Jesus Christ, as God in the flesh, justified in the Spirit? As the Lord God of the Old Testament, Who had created all things, Jesus emptied Himself of His divine, eternal existence and was made in the likeness of man. He took upon Himself the same sinful flesh that all human beings have, and thus the same judgment that was pronounced upon Adam and Eve and their descendants. Although He was tempted like all other human beings, He overcame the law of sin and death and Satan, the author of sin, through the power of the Holy Spirit. He condemned sin in the flesh by living a perfect life, not once yielding to the pulls of the flesh, but always being led by the Holy Spirit of God the Father. That is how God was justified in the Spirit.

Because Jesus Christ, as God in the flesh, was justified in the Spirit, He has opened the way for all things on earth and in heaven to be reconciled to God the Father: "Giving thanks to the Father, **Who has made us qualified for the share of the inheritance of the saints** in the light; Who has personally **rescued us from the power of darkness** [Satan], and has transferred *us* unto the kingdom of the Son of His love [by giving us the power of His Holy Spirit]; in Whom we have redemption through His own blood, *even* the remission of sins; **Who is *the* image of the invisible God, *the* firstborn of all creation;** because by Him were all things created, the things in heaven and the things on the earth, the visible and the invisible, whether *they be* thrones, or lordships, or principalities, or powers: all things were created by Him and for Him.

"And He is before all, and by Him all things subsist. And He is the Head of the body, the church; Who is *the* **beginning, *the* firstborn from among the dead, so that in all things He Himself might hold the preeminence**. For it pleased *the Father* that in Him all the fullness should dwell; and, having made peace through the blood of His cross, by Him to reconcile all things to Himself; by Him, whether the things on the earth, or the things in heaven" (Col. 1:12-20).

Through Jesus' sacrifice, according to God's great plan of reconciliation, all who repent of their sins, accept Jesus Christ as personal Savior and are baptized receive the gift of salvation, with the promise of eternal life in the Kingdom of God. "But we see Jesus, Who *was* made a little lower than *the* angels, crowned with glory and honor on account of suffering the death, in order that **by *the* grace of God He Himself might taste death for everyone**; because it was fitting for Him, for Whom all things *were created*, and by Whom all things *exist*, **in bringing many sons unto glory**, to make the Author of their salvation perfect through sufferings. **For both He Who is sanctifying and those who are sanctified *are* all of one** [one Father]; **for which cause He is not ashamed to call them brethren**" (Heb. 2:9-11).

Jesus Christ was the first fleshly human being to be resurrected from the dead as a glorified spirit being. At His return, an innumerable number will be granted eternal life as the spirit sons and daughters of God the Father. They will share the same eternal existence and glory as Jesus Christ, as Paul discloses: "The Spirit itself bears witness conjointly with our own spirit, *testifying* that we are *the* children of God. Now if *we are* children, *we are* also heirs—truly, **heirs of God and joint heirs with Christ**—if indeed we suffer together with Him, so that we may also be **glorified together with**

Him. For I reckon that the sufferings of the present time *are* not worthy *to be compared* with the glory that shall be revealed in us" (Rom. 8:16-18).

The apostle John also wrote that the children of God will be like Jesus Christ: "Behold! What *glorious* love the Father has given to us, that we should be called the children of God! For this very reason, the world does not know us because it did not know Him. Beloved, now we are the children of God, and it has not yet been revealed what we shall be; **but we know that when He is manifested, we shall be like Him, because we shall see Him exactly as He is**" (I John 3:1-2).

The hope of being glorified like Jesus Christ and living with Him forever in the Kingdom of God brings true meaning to the observance of the Christian Passover. Every true Christian who shares this hope will be faithfully keeping this solemn ceremony each year on the night that Jesus instituted it. Each one will participate in the footwashing in order to have a part with Jesus Christ in this life and in His kingdom. Each one will partake of the bread and the wine in order to renew the New Covenant and remain under the blood of Jesus Christ throughout the coming year. Each one will determine to live by every word of the New Covenant through the power of the Holy Spirit. This personal renewal of the New Covenant through the Christian Passover ceremony will enable each one to receive the glorious inheritance that awaits the children of God.

CHAPTER TWELVE

A Call to Repentance

Not only is the death of Jesus Christ—God manifested in the flesh—a witness to the world, the nations, the religious leaders and every person, but it is a call to repentance! John the Baptist was sent to prepare the way for Jesus Christ. He preached repentance of sins, instructing the people to believe in Jesus Christ, Who would come after him. After John the Baptist was put in prison, Jesus Christ began His ministry by preaching repentance: "The beginning of the gospel of Jesus Christ, *the* Son of God ... Now after the imprisonment of John, Jesus came into Galilee, proclaiming the gospel of the kingdom of God and saying, 'The time has been fulfilled, and the kingdom of God is near at hand; **repent, and believe in the gospel**' " (Mark 1:1, 14-15).

Jesus made it clear that He came to call sinners to repentance, "I did not come to call *the* righteous [those who think they are righteous], but sinners to repentance" (Mark 2:17); and, He left no doubt that all must repent of their sins: "Now at the same time, *there* were present some who were telling Him about the Galileans, whose blood Pilate had mingled with their sacrifices. And Jesus answered *and* said to them, 'Do you suppose that these Galileans were sinners above all Galileans, because they suffered such things? No, I tell you; **but if you do not repent, you shall all likewise perish**. Or those eighteen on whom the tower in Siloam fell, and killed them, do you suppose that these were debtors above all men who dwelt in Jerusalem? No, I tell you; **but if you do not repent, you shall all likewise perish**' " (Luke 13:1-5).

All Have Sinned

The New Testament defines sin as the transgression of the law (I John 3:4). A literal translation of this verse from the Greek reads: "**Everyone who practices sin is also practicing lawlessness, for sin is lawlessness**."

There is no one in the entire history of the world who has not sinned, except Jesus Christ. That is why He alone can be our Redeemer and our Savior. Every person needs to be saved from his or her sins, because "the wages of sin *is* death, but the gift of God *is* eternal life through Christ Jesus our Lord" (Rom. 6:23).

In his epistle to the Romans, the apostle Paul was inspired to declare emphatically that all have sinned—all have transgressed the laws and commandments of God, and all are sentenced to death. The only escape and salvation is through Jesus Christ: "What then? Are we [Jews] of ourselves better [than the Gentiles]? Not at all! **For we have already charged both Jews and Gentiles—ALL—*with* being under sin**. Exactly as it is written: **'For there is not a righteous one—not even one**! There is not one who understands; there is not one who seeks after God. They have all gone out of the way; together they have *all* become depraved. There is not *even* one who is practicing kindness. No, there is not so much as one! Their throats *are* like an open grave; with their tongues they have used deceit; *the* venom of asps *is* under their lips, whose mouths are full of cursing and bitterness; their feet *are* swift to shed blood; destruction and misery *are* in their ways; and *the* way of peace they have not known. **There is no fear of God before their eyes**.' Now then, we know that whatever the law says, it speaks to those who are under the law, **so that every mouth may be stopped, and all the world may become guilty before God....For all have sinned, and have come short of the glory of God**" (Rom. 3:9-19, 23).

On the day of Pentecost, just fifty-four days after the crucifixion, the apostles began preaching Jesus Christ's gospel of repentance for the remission of sins. On that day, God poured out His Holy Spirit in power, and the apostles spoke in a multitude of languages as a fantastic witness to the Jews from all nations gathered at the temple in Jerusalem for the feast day, who each heard the Gospel in his own language (Acts 2:1-18). When they wondered what this miracle meant, the apostle Peter was inspired to powerfully preach Christ and repentance of sin. His moving witness to the Jews who had gathered at the temple ended with these words: " 'Therefore, let all *the* house of Israel know with full assurance that God has made this *same* Jesus, Whom you crucified, both Lord and Christ.' Now after hearing *this*, they were cut to the heart [convicted of their sins]; and they said to Peter and the other apostles, 'Men *and* brethren, what shall we do?' Then Peter said to them, '**Repent and be baptized each one of you in the name of Jesus Christ for *the* remission of sins, and you yourselves shall receive the gift of the Holy Spirit**'... And with many other words he earnestly testified and exhorted, saying, 'Be saved from this perverse generation.' **Then those who joyfully received his message were baptized**; and about three thousand souls were added that day" (Acts 2:36-40).

The Apostle Paul's Call to Repentance

When the apostle Paul came to Athens, the center of the Greek pagan religions, he preached a powerful message of repentance. As it is recorded in Acts, he exhorted the Athenians to repent of their idolatries and vain religious practices: "Then Paul stood in *the* center of Mars' hill *and* said, 'Men, Athenians, I perceive *that* in all things you are very reverent to deities; for *as* I was passing through and observing the objects of your veneration, I also found an altar on which was inscribed, "To an unknown God." So then, He Whom you worship in ignorance *is* the one *that* I proclaim to you.

"He *is* the God Who made the world and all things that *are* in it. Being *the* Lord of heaven and earth, He does not dwell in temples made by hands; nor is He served by the hands of men, as *though* He needs anything, *for* He gives to all life and breath and all things. **And He made of one blood all the nations of men to dwell upon all the face of the earth, having determined beforehand *their* appointed times and the boundaries of their dwelling, in order that they might seek the Lord, if perhaps they might feel after Him and might find Him; though truly, He is not far from each one of us, for in Him we live and move and have our being**; as some of the poets among you also have said, 'For we are His offspring.'

"Therefore, since we are the offspring of God, we should not think that the Godhead *is* like that which *is made* of gold, or silver, or stone—a graven thing of art *devised by the* imagination of man. For *although* God has indeed overlooked the times of this ignorance, **He now commands all men everywhere to repent,** because He has set a day in which He will judge the world in righteousness by a man Whom He has appointed, having given proof to all *by* raising Him from *the* dead" (Acts 17:22-31). Paul's message of repentance was the same as Jesus Christ's: "If you do not repent, you shall likewise perish."

The Meaning of Repentance

Because of the witness that Jesus Christ has given to the world—all nations, all religions and all people—He commands all men and women to repent and turn to God with all their hearts. Today, God's judgment is at the door. None shall escape unless he or she repents!

What is repentance? There are two kinds of repentance. One is worldly repentance, which is a shallow repentance that leads to death. The other is godly repentance that leads to forgiveness and salvation. The apostle Paul said, "For sorrow unto repentance before God works out salvation not to be repented of; but the sorrow of the world works out death" (II Cor. 7:10).

Godly repentance means a complete abhorrence of one's sins, a complete turning from sin—from the transgression of the laws and commandments of God. Repentance is a complete amendment of life, a turning away from one's own sinful way to the way of love and obedience, keeping the laws and commandments of God and living by every word of God as taught by Jesus Christ.

In the book of Psalms, we find King David's prayer of repentance, uttered when Nathan the prophet came to him after David's affair with Bathsheba and the killing of her husband Uriah. This prayer shows David's complete abhorrence of sin and self as he cried out to God with tears of anguish and sorrow, begging for His mercy and forgiveness. David's repentance was to God, not to any man. He did not confess his sins to a priest.

He did not confess his sins to Nathan the prophet. Just as David did, we are to confess our sins directly to God the Father and Jesus Christ, not to a man. King David's prayer has been preserved for us so that we can understand the attitude of true repentance: "Have mercy upon me, O God, according to thy lovingkindness: according unto the multitude of thy tender mercies blot out my transgressions. **Wash me thoroughly from mine iniquity, and cleanse me from my sin. For I acknowledge my transgressions: and my sin *is* ever before me**.

"**Against thee, thee only, have I sinned, and done *this* evil in thy sight**: that thou mightest be justified when thou speakest, *and* be clear when thou judgest. Behold, **I was shapen in iniquity, and in sin did my mother conceive me**. Behold, thou desirest truth in the inward parts: and in the hidden *part* thou shalt make me to know wisdom. Purge me with hyssop, and I shall be clean: wash me, and I shall be whiter than snow. Make me to hear joy and gladness; *that* the bones *which* thou hast broken may rejoice. **Hide thy face from my sins, and blot out all mine iniquities. Create in me a clean heart, O God; and renew a right spirit within me**. Cast me not away from thy presence; and take not thy holy spirit from me. Restore unto me the joy of thy salvation; and uphold me *with thy* free spirit....**Deliver me from bloodguiltiness, O God, thou God of my salvation**" (Psa. 51:1-14, *KJV*).

Repentance is the first step in the sinner's reconciliation with God the Father and Jesus Christ. God the Father through His Spirit must open a person's mind to understand that he or she is a sinner against Him. As David said, "I have sinned against You and You alone." Then one must believe the gospel of Jesus Christ, that it is because of one's own sins that He had to die. True belief brings repentance and necessitates confessing one's sins to God the Father and asking for forgiveness, remission and pardon of those sins through the blood of Jesus Christ. True, deep, godly repentance will produce a profound change in a person's mind and attitude, which will result in a continuous desire to live by every word of God. The truly repentant person will turn from evil thoughts and ungodly practices and will seek to conform his or her life to the will of God as revealed in the Holy Bible and as led by the Holy Spirit. Repentance and confession of sins is an ongoing process in a Christian's spiritual growth toward perfection in Jesus Christ.

Upon true, heartfelt repentance, God is ready and willing to forgive sin, as shown in another of David's prayers of repentance: "Be merciful unto me, O Lord: for I cry unto thee daily. Rejoice the soul of thy servant: for unto thee, O Lord, do I lift up my soul. **For thou, Lord, *art* good, and ready to forgive; and plenteous in mercy unto all them that call upon thee**. Give ear, O LORD, unto my prayer; and attend to the voice of my supplications. **In the day of my trouble I will call upon thee: for thou wilt answer me**" (Psa. 86:3-7, *KJV*).

God does not require animal sacrifices for the propitiation of sin. He does not require the sinner to perform rote prayers with the aid of a strand of beads. He does not require hundreds of reiterations of "Hail Mary" or "Our Father." God does not require a person to crawl for miles on his or her knees or to perform self-flagellation or ritual bloodletting. God requires only that the sinner have a broken and contrite heart and genuinely repent as it is written: "For thou desirest not sacrifice; else would I give *it*: thou delightest not in burnt offering. **The sacrifices of God *are* a broken spirit: a broken and a contrite heart, O God, thou wilt not despise**" (Psa. 51:16-18, *KJV*).

The apostle John wrote, "If we confess our own sins [directly to God the Father in prayer], He is faithful and righteous, to forgive us our sins, and to cleanse us from all unrighteousness" (I John 1:9). If we repent and confess our sins directly to God the Father and Jesus Christ in heartfelt prayer, God will certainly forgive us. Once our sins are forgiven, we are to quit living in sin as Jesus said, "Sin no more, so that something worse does not happen to you"; and "Go, and sin no more" (John 5:14; 8:11).

The prophet Isaiah wrote: "Wash you, make you clean [through repentance and baptism]; put away the evil of your doings from before mine eyes; **cease to do evil**; **learn to do well**; seek judgment, relieve the oppressed, judge the fatherless, plead for the widow. Come now, and let us reason together, saith the LORD: **though your sins be as scarlet, they shall be as white as snow; though they be red like crimson, they shall be as wool. If ye be willing and obedient, ye shall eat the good of the land: but if ye refuse and rebel, ye shall be devoured with the sword**: for the mouth of the LORD hath spoken *it*" (Isa. 1:16-20, *KJV*).

The Meaning of Water Baptism

After accepting Jesus Christ as one's personal Savior, one must be baptized by complete immersion in water for the remission of sins. Water baptism symbolizes the death and burial of each repentant believer—a spiritual conjoining into the death of Jesus Christ. Through this baptismal death we become a partaker of the crucifixion and death of Jesus Christ, Whose blood is applied as full payment for our sins. Rising up out of the water symbolizes our being conjoined with Jesus Christ in resurrection. When we rise out of the watery grave of baptism, we rise to newness of life. In order to become a new person, we must receive the begettal of the Holy Spirit from God the Father through the laying on of hands. We are then led by the Holy Spirit to walk in loving obedience to God the Father and Jesus Christ.

Paul was most emphatic when he wrote that after baptism we are not to live in sin any longer! "What then shall we say? Shall we continue in sin, so that grace may abound? MAY IT NEVER BE! We who died to sin, how shall we live any longer therein? Or are you ignorant that we, as many as were baptized into Christ Jesus, were baptized into His death? Therefore, we were buried with Him by baptism into death; so that, just as Christ was raised from *the* dead by the glory of the Father, in the same way, we also should walk in newness of life. For if we have been conjoined together in the likeness of His death, so also shall we be *in the likeness* of *His* resurrection. Knowing this, that our old man was co-crucified with *Him* in order that the body of sin might be destroyed, so that we might no longer be enslaved to sin; Because the one who has died *to sin* has been justified from sin. Now if we died together with Christ, we believe that we shall also live with Him" (Rom. 6:1-8).

After true, godly repentance and baptism for the forgiveness of sin, the new believer is justified and put in right standing with God the Father. The apostle Paul explained this operation of God's grace: "Are being justified freely by His grace through the redemption that *is* in Christ Jesus; Whom God has openly manifested *to be* a propitiation through faith in His blood, in order to demonstrate His righteousness, in respect to the remission of the sins that are past....Even the righteousness of God *that is* through *the* faith of Jesus Christ, toward all and upon all those who believe: for there is no difference" (Rom. 3:24-25, 22).

It is Jesus Christ's faith that He had when He willingly gave Himself to be beaten, scourged and crucified that saves us from sins and justifies us to God the Father. Through the power of the Holy Spirit, Jesus imparts His faith to us so that we may live by faith: "I have been crucified [through baptism] with Christ, yet I live. *Indeed,* it is no longer I; but Christ lives in me. For *the life* that I am now living in *the* flesh, I live by faith—that *very faith* of the Son of God, Who loved me and gave Himself for me" (Gal. 2:20).

Salvation by Grace

Once we have been justified, we continually stand in a state of grace before God: "Therefore, having been justified by faith, we have peace with God through our Lord Jesus Christ. Through Whom **we also have access by faith into this grace in which we stand**, and we ourselves boast in *the* hope of the glory of God. And not only *this*, but we also boast in tribulations, realizing that tribulation brings forth endurance, and endurance *brings forth* character, and character *brings forth* hope. **And the hope *of God* never makes us ashamed, because the love of God has been poured out into our hearts through the Holy Spirit, which has been given to us**" (Rom. 5:1-5).

Salvation by grace does not confer a license to sin with impunity. Neither Jesus Christ nor the apostles ever taught such a doctrine. Jesus Himself said, if we love Him, we will keep His commandments: "If you love Me, keep the commandments—namely My commandments.... The one who has My commandments and is keeping them, that is the one who loves Me; and the one who loves Me shall be loved by My Father, and I will love him and will manifest Myself to him.... If anyone loves Me, he will keep My word; and My Father will love him, and We will come to him and make

Our abode with him. The one who does not love Me does not keep My words; and the word that you hear is not Mine, but the Father's, Who sent Me" (John 14:15, 21, 23-24).

In his first epistle, the apostle John shows that we must keep God's commandments. In fact, when we are keeping His commandments, we know that we know Jesus Christ and are being perfected in love: "And by this *standard* we know that we know Him: if we keep His commandments. The one who says, 'I know Him,' and does not keep His commandments, is a liar, and the truth is not in him. On the other hand, ***if* anyone is keeping His Word, truly in this one the love of God is being perfected**. By this *means* we know that we are in Him" (I John 2:3-5).

Many professing Christians claim that they "love the Lord" but then refuse to keep His commandments. To love God is more than an emotion. Our actions must also reflect that love through our obedience. The apostle John wrote: "By this *standard* we know that we love the children of God: when we love God and keep His commandments. **For this is the love of God: that we keep His commandments; and His commandments are not burdensome**" (I John 5:2-3).

The apostle James, a brother of the Lord Jesus Christ, also wrote that we must keep the commandments of God: "For *if* anyone keeps the whole law, but sins in one *aspect*, he becomes guilty of all. For He Who said, 'You shall not commit adultery,' also said, 'You shall not commit murder.' Now if you do not commit adultery, but you commit murder, you have become a transgressor of *the* law. In this manner speak and in this manner behave: as those who are about to be judged by *the* law of freedom" (Jas. 2:10-12).

James further wrote that faith without works is dead—it will lead to death, not to eternal life: "… **faith, if it does not have works, is dead, by itself**. But someone is going to say, 'You have faith, and I have works.' *My answer is:* You prove your faith to me through your works, and I will prove my faith to you through my works. Do you believe that God is one? You do well *to believe this*. Even the demons believe—and tremble *in fear*. But are you willing to understand, O foolish man, that **faith without works is dead**? Was not Abraham our father justified by works when he offered up Isaac, his own son, upon the altar? **Do you not see that faith was working together with his works, and by works *his* faith was perfected**? And the scripture was fulfilled which says, 'Now Abraham believed God, and it was reckoned to him for righteousness'; and he was called a friend of God. You see, then, that **a man is justified by works, and not by faith only**" (Jas. 2:17-24).

Salvation by grace is demonstrated in works—not the humanly devised traditions and works of religion but the good works of loving God and keeping His commandments as Paul notes, "For by grace you have been saved through faith; and this *especially* is not of your own selves; *it is* the gift of God, not of works, so that no one may boast. **For we are His work-**

manship, created in Christ Jesus unto *the* good works that God or-dained beforehand in order that we might walk in them" (Eph. 2:8-10).

When we have received the begettal of the Holy Spirit from God the Father, we are to walk in the way of the Lord and to love God the Father and Jesus Christ with all the heart, and with all the understanding, and with all the soul, and with all the strength (Mark 12:29-34). We are to keep the commandments of God from the heart in the spirit of the law. Finally, we are to grow in grace and knowledge and to be faithful unto death. Then, at the return of Jesus Christ, we will be resurrected to eternal life and glory as a spirit son or daughter of God. To bring many sons and daughters to glory is the reason why Jesus Christ died!

Dear reader, Jesus Christ died for your sins, and He can be your personal Savior. You have a choice either to repent and to believe in the Son of God, accepting His sacrifice for your sins, or to reject Jesus Christ and His words and to receive the judgment of God and eternal death. What will you do? You will be held accountable for your decision. You must choose!

Part Three

**Appendices
And
Bibliography**

APPENDIX A

"The First of the Unleaveneds"

This phrase has caused some confusion. It is certain that this phrase does not refer to the first day of the Feast of Unleavened Bread, because the Feast of Unleavened Bread begins after, not before, the Passover. As recorded in the Gospels, "the first of the unleaveneds" was the day that the lambs were killed. Those who obeyed God's ordinances in Exodus 12 and kept the domestic Passover killed their lambs at the beginning of the 14th of Nisan. Those who followed the traditions of Judaism killed the lambs at the temple on the afternoon of the 14th. The Gospel writers were clearly referring to the 14th, and not to the 15th, as "the first of the unleaveneds." In New Testament times, this term was commonly used for the 14th day of the first month.

"In the first century, it was commonly known that '**the day of the unleaveneds**' in Luke 22:7 was **the 14th Passover day**. G. Amadon, in an article entitled, 'The Crucifixion Calendar,' pointed out the error of those translators who translated this verse to read 'the first day of the festival.' [The following words are cited from this article.] 'But on what authority should the Hebrew translators, as Salkinson and Delitzch, introduce the word *chag* [a Hebrew word for "feast"] into these texts when the corresponding Greek has no word for "feast," and speaks only of the "first of the unleavened bread" —**a common expression for the Jewish 14th with practically all first century writers**' " (*Journal of Biblical Literature*, vol. LXIII, 1944, pp. 188-189, emphasis added).

When we understand the duties that were required to be performed on the Passover day, it becomes clear why that day was called "the first of the unleaveneds" (a literal translation from the Greek). According to Jewish law, all leaven in all residences and properties owned by Jews was to be searched out on Nisan 13. The unleavened bread for the Passover was to be made and ready by 3 p.m. on Nisan 13. The leaven was then gathered and burned by 10 a.m. in the morning on Nisan 14. No one was to eat leaven in any form after 11 a.m. These required practices clearly show why Nisan 14 was referred to as "the first of the unleaveneds": because on that day leaven was removed and burned. Hence, Nisan 14 was the first unleavened day of the year.

APPENDIX B

"Today Is the Third Day Since These Things Took Place"

Those who believe in a Sunday resurrection point to a statement in Luke 24:21 as evidence that Jesus rose from the dead at sunrise on the first day of the week. This statement was made by two of Jesus' disciples: "… today is the third day since these things were done." Because this statement was made on the first day of the week, many have assumed that Jesus rose from the dead early that morning. The King James Version reads:

"And, behold, two of them went that same day to a village called Emmaus, which was from Jerusalem *about* threescore furlongs. And they talked together of all these things which had happened. And it came to pass, that, while they communed *together* and reasoned, Jesus himself drew near, and went with them. But their eyes were holden that they should not know him.

"And he said unto them, 'What manner of communications *are* these that ye have one to another, as ye walk, and are sad?' And the one of them, whose name was Cleopas, answering said unto him, 'Art thou only a stranger in Jerusalem, and hast not known the things which are come to pass there in these days?' And he said unto them, 'What things?'

"And they said unto him, 'Concerning Jesus of Nazareth, which was a prophet mighty in deed and word before God and all the people: and how the chief priests and our rulers delivered him to be condemned to death, and have crucified him. But we trusted that it had been he which should have redeemed Israel: and **beside all this, today is the third day since these things were done**' " (Luke 24:13-21 KJV).

A precise translation of Luke 24:13-21 conveys the true meaning of the Greek text as follows:

"And behold, on the same day, two of them were going to a village called Emmaus, which was about sixty furlongs from Jerusalem. And they were talking with one another about all the things that had taken place.

"And it came to pass, as they were talking and reasoning, that Jesus Himself drew near *and* went with them; but their eyes were restrained, *so that* they did not know Him. And He said to them, 'What *are* these words that you are exchanging with one another as you walk, and *why* are you downcast in countenance?' Then the one named Cleopas answered *and* said to Him, 'Are You only traveling through Jerusalem, and have not known of the things that have happened in these days?'

"And He said to them, 'What things?' And they said to Him, 'The things concerning Jesus the Nazarean, a man Who was a prophet, Who was mighty in deed and word before God and all the people; and how the chief priests and our rulers delivered Him up to *the* judgment of death, and crucified Him. And we were hoping that He was the one Who would redeem Israel. But besides all these things, **as of today, the third day has already passed since these things took place**' "(Luke 24:13-21).

When correctly translated, Luke 24:21 does not support the teaching that Jesus the Christ was raised from the dead on the first day of the week at sunrise. Those who believe that He was resurrected at sunrise on Easter Sunday have been taught a falsehood! This religious myth rejects the sign of Jonah, which was the only sign that Jesus the Christ gave as proof that He was the Messiah. Those who participate in the traditional observance of a Friday crucifixion and an Easter Sunday resurrection are observing traditions of men. Jesus said, "Well did Isaiah prophesy concerning you hypocrites, as it is written, 'This people honors Me with their lips, but their hearts are far away from Me.' But **in vain do they worship Me, teaching *for* doctrine the commandments of men....Full well do you reject the commandment of God, so that you may observe your *own* tradition**" (Mark 7:6-9).

The God of truth cannot be honored by practicing a lie. God the Father rejects that kind of vain worship. Rather, He is seeking those who will worship Him in spirit and in truth, as Jesus said: "But the hour is coming, and now is, when the true worshipers shall worship the Father in spirit and in truth; for the Father is indeed seeking those who worship Him in this manner. God *is* Spirit, and those who worship Him must worship in spirit and in truth" (John 4:23-24).

In order to worship God the Father and Jesus the Christ in spirit and in truth, one must repent of his or her sins, accept the sacrifice of Jesus the Christ for the forgiveness of sins, be baptized by full immersion in water, receive the Holy Spirit through the laying on of hands, and live from that time forward in the love and grace of God by keeping His commandments. These commandments include keeping the seventh-day Sabbath each week, and keeping the Christian Passover and the annual holy days of God at their appointed times each year. Only those who are under His grace, keeping all His commandments and living by His every word, are worshiping Him in spirit and in truth.

Please see "Today is the Third Day Since These Things Took Place" in *A Harmony of the Gospels*, pages 316-321 for a full exegetical study of Luke 24:13-21.

APPENDIX C

"The First Day of the Weeks"

The literal translation of the Greek words μια σαββατων or μια των σαββατων shows that the day which followed the weekly Sabbath was the first day of the seven-week count to Pentecost, thus identifying this day as the Wave Sheaf Day (Lev. 23:10-11, 15-16). The ascension of Jesus Christ on that day fulfilled the offering of the wave sheaf for all time.

APPENDIX D

The Christian Passover Versus The Lord's Supper, Communion, the Eucharist or the Sacrifice of the Mass

Today, Christendom practices "the Lord's Supper," also known as "Communion," "the Eucharist" or within Roman Catholicism, "the Sacrifice of the Mass." Most professing Christians are taught and therefore believe that what they are observing is what Jesus Christ and the apostles also taught and observed. However, the New Testament shows that on the night of His last Passover, Jesus Christ instituted the New Covenant Christian Passover, which the apostolic, primitive Church continued to observe for over 100 years.

After the death of the apostle John in 100 AD, and influenced by pagan Gnostic Hellenistic religious practices emanating out of Rome and Egypt, the early churches were confronted with an intense doctrinal war over the observance of the Christian Passover on the 14th day of the first month. The observance of Easter was eventually adopted in lieu of the Passover. The celebration of the Eucharist (or the sacrifice of the Mass) and other new "Christian" practices—such as a Sunday "Sabbath" instead of the seventh day weekly Sabbath—were also adopted. Yet, the churches of God in Asia Minor steadfastly retained the observance of the weekly seventh day Sabbath, the 14th Passover and all the biblical holy days.

Historian Samuele Bacchiocchi correctly notes that numerous passages show that the apostle Paul, the apostle to the Gentiles, "...still respected and regulated his life by the normative liturgical calendar of the temple" (*From Sabbath to Sunday*, p. 81). There is no doubt that the calendar he is referring to is the sacred calculated Hebrew calendar, which is still used by the true churches of God today. Bacchiocchi further states,

"Moreover we know from the Quartodeciman's sources (i.e. those who kept Passover on Nisan 14 according to the Jewish reckoning), which apparently represented a direct continuation of the custom of the primitive Church, that the paschal feast [the New Covenant Passover] was indeed observed by Christians ... that until A. D. 135 Christians everywhere [meaning Jewish and Gentile congregations] observed the Passover on the Jewish date ..." (Ibid., p. 81, bracketed comments added).

In Asia Minor, in 150 AD, Polycrates, a faithful minister of God, withstood the apostate bishops of Rome and Egypt. He defended the apostolic practice of the observance of the Christian Passover on the 14th day of the first month of the calculated Hebrew calendar. Eusebius records the testimony of Polycrates, the leader of the Asia Minor resistance, who held fast against this invasion of false doctrine: "... but the bishops in Asia were led by Polycrates in persisting that it was necessary to keep the custom which had been handed down to them of old [from Jesus and the apostles]. Polycrates himself in a document which he addressed to Victor and to the church of Rome, expounds the tradition which had come to him as follows: 'Therefore we keep the day undeviatingly, neither adding nor taking away, for in Asia great luminaries sleep, and they will rise on the day of the coming of the Lord, when he shall come with glory from heaven and seek out [literally to raise up] all the saints. Such were Phillip of the twelve apostles, and two of his daughters who grew old as virgins, who sleep in Hierapolis, and another daughter of his, who lived in the Holy Spirit, rests at Ephesus. Moreover, there is also John, who lay on the Lord's breast ... the martyr, and teacher. He sleeps at Ephesus. And there is also Polycarp at Smyrna, both bishop and martyr, who sleeps at Laodicea, and Papirius, too, the blessed, and Melito the eunuch, who lived entirely in the Holy Spirit, who lies in Sardis, waiting for the visitation from heaven when he will rise from the dead. **All these kept the fourteenth day of the Passover according to the gospel, never swerving, but following according to the rule of the faith**. And I also, Polycrates, the least of you all, live according to the tradition of my kinsmen, and some of them have I followed. For seven of my family were bishops and I am the eighth, and my kinsmen ever kept the day when the people put away the leaven. Therefore, brethren, I who have lived sixty-five years in the Lord and conversed with the brethren from every country, and have studied all the holy Scriptures, am not afraid of threats, for they have said who were greater than I, "It is better to obey God rather than men" ' " (Eusebius, *The Ecclesiastical History,* Vol. I, pp. 505-507).

After the death of Polycrates and his fellow Christians in Asia Minor, the churches of God continued to resist the relentless pagan conspiracy against the true faith of Jesus Christ. They not only continued to practice the true teachings of the New Testament, but they preserved the authentic Greek New Testament text, now known as the Byzantine text. Other faithful brethren were in the distant Mesopotamian Valley, the mountainous regions of Europe and the British Isles. The true Christian brethren in these regions faithfully preserved the Christian faith from the ravages of Roman, Orthodox, Jewish Orthodox and Gnostic communities. Opposing all corrupting influences, they preserved the testimony of Jesus Christ and the true Christian Passover.

***The True Christian Passover*:** When we closely examine the New Testament Scriptures, it is most evident that Jesus Christ instituted the New Covenant Passover—the Christian Passover—on the night of the 14th day of the first month of the calculated Hebrew Calendar. The Passover in the Old Testament was originally instituted by God Himself on the 14th day of the first month in 1488 BC (Genesis 15; Exodus 12 and Lev. 23:4-5). It was to be observed once a year on that date and on that date only. There was only one exception for those who were unclean or on a journey outside the country. If one was clean within one month, or back within the borders of Israel within one month, then they could keep the Passover on the 14th day of the second month (Num. 9:9-14).

When Jesus instituted the new ceremony of the Christian Passover, He did not change the day or the frequency of observance. The new ceremony consists of the footwashing, the eating of unleavened bread and the drinking of wine. The Christian Passover was never to be observed more than once a year—and then, only on the night of the 14th day of the first month. (For a complete work on the Passover—Old and New Testaments—order the book *The Christian Passover* by Fred R. Coulter. It is the most detailed book ever written concerning the Christian Passover. It explains in full detail what is summarized in this appendix).

***The Lord's Supper*:** Paul wrote his two epistles to the Corinthian congregation to correct them concerning many things. Most of these wrong practices and heresies were apparently the result of false apostles, whom the brethren had allowed to come into their congregations and teach false doctrines and another Jesus to them: "For indeed, if someone comes preaching another Jesus, whom we did not preach, or you receive a different spirit, which you did not receive, or a different gospel, which you did not accept, you put up with it as *something* good: (II Cor. 11:4). He further warned them that regardless of how they appeared or what they said, they were of Satan the devil and not of God: "For such *are* false apostle—deceitful workers who are transforming themselves into apostles of Christ. And *it is* no marvel, for Satan himself transforms himself into an angel of light. Therefore, *it is* no great thing if his servants also transform themselves as ministers of righteousness—whose end shall be according to their works: (verses 13-15).

One of the practices in question was the so-called "Lord's Supper," noted in I Corinthians 11:20. Some believe that Paul was correcting the Corinthians for inappropriately eating "the Lord's Supper." However, that is not true. Rather, he was correcting a heresy: "Now *in* this *that* I am commanding *you*, I do not praise you, because when you assemble together, it is not for the better but for the worse. For first of all, I hear that there are divisions among you when you are assembled together in the church, and I partly believe *it*. For it is necessary that **heresies be among you**, so that the ones who are approved may become manifest among you" (verses, 17-19).

Paul explained that the teachings concerning the Passover were those that he had personally received from the Lord: "For I received from the Lord that which I also delivered to you, that the Lord Jesus in the night in which He was betrayed took bread" (I Cor. 11:23). The night that Jesus was betrayed was the Passover night: "Now on the first of the unleaveneds, the disciples came to Jesus, saying to Him, 'Where do You desire *that* we prepare for You to **eat the Passover**?' And He said, 'Go into the city to such a man, and say to him, 'The Teacher says, "My time is near; **I will keep the Passover with My disciples** at your *house.*" ' Then the disciples did as Jesus had directed them, and **prepared the Passover**. And after evening had come, He sat down with the twelve" (Matt. 26:17-20). Luke's account reads: "Then they went *and* found *everything* exactly as He had said to them; and **they prepared the Passover**. Now when the hour had come, He sat *down,* and the twelve apostles with Him. And He said to them, 'With *earnest* desire **I have desired to eat this Passover with you** before I suffer. For I tell you that I will not eat of it again until it be fulfilled in the kingdom of God' " (Luke 22:13-16).

The apostle Paul wrote, "… For Christ our Passover was sacrificed for us. For this reason, let us keep the feast, not with old leaven, nor with *the* leaven of malice and wickedness, but with *the* unleavened *bread* of sincerity and truth" (I Cor. 5:7-8).

Whatever meal the Corinthians were eating and calling "the Lord's Supper" was not to be eaten when they assembled. In the strongest negation possible, Paul wrote: "Therefore, when you assemble together in one place, it is **not** to eat *the* Lord's Supper" (verse 20). The Greek word ουκ *ouk*, translated "not," means the impossibility of eating the "the Lord's Supper." Furthermore, Paul specifically wrote that if anyone was hungry, he or she was to eat at home before coming to observe the Christian Passover: "But if anyone is hungry, let him eat at home, so that *there will be* no *cause* for judgment *when* you assemble together. And the other matters I will set in order when I come" (verse 34).

All other references to "the Lord's Supper" and later "the Eucharist" come from the "early church fathers" in Rome and Egypt. Because the Roman Catholic Church has taught it, most people have assumed, believed and accepted as fact that the "early church fathers" were the true successors of the apostles. However, history shows that they were not the true successors to the apostles but were actually the successors of the false apostles as found in the New Testament writings.

***Communion*:** The translators of the King James 1611 Version of the Bible translated the Greek word **κοινωνια** *koinonia* as "communion" to reflect their later interpretation. However, *koinonia* is translated predominately as "fellowship." In the KJV, of the 19 times *koinonia* is used in the

New Testament Greek text, it is translated 12 times as "fellowship"; 4 times as "communion"; 1 time as "contribution"; 1 time as "communicate"; and 1 time as "communication."

In First Corinthians Ten, the word *koinonia* should be more properly translated "fellowship" instead of "communion" in reference to the Christian Passover. A more accurate translation makes it clear: "Therefore, my beloved, flee from idolatry. I speak as to those who are wise; you judge what I say. **The cup of blessing that we bless, is it not** *the* **fellowship of the blood of Christ? The bread that we break, is it not** *the* **fellowship of the body of Christ?** For we, being many, are one body *and* one bread, because we are all partakers of the bread. Consider Israel according to *the* flesh. Are not those who eat the sacrifices partakers of the altar? What then am I saying? That an idol is anything, or that which is sacrificed to an idol is anything? **But that which the Gentiles sacrifice, they sacrifice to demons, and not to God; and I do not wish you to have fellowship with demons. You cannot drink** *the* **cup of** *the* **Lord, and** *the* **cup of demons. You cannot partake of** *the* **table of** *the* **Lord, and** *the* **table of demons**" (I Cor. 10:14-21). From these scriptures, it appears that the Corinthian Christians were still practicing some pagan temple rituals.

After the death of the apostles, the Christianization of pagan practices gained momentum. History shows that through the centuries, the Catholic Church appropriated various pagan festivals and renamed them, putting a "Christian" veneer on them and ascribing a new meaning to their observance. The Most Reverend Louis Laravoire Morrow confirms that this is in accordance with the traditions of the Catholic Church: "*In the history of the Church* we find that she often christened pagan festivals, making use of dates and ceremonies, and endowing them with an entirely new and Christian significance" (*My Catholic Faith*, p. 416).

Ancient Israel also mixed pagan practices in direct violation of the commandments of God although God specifically warned them prior to entering the Promised Land: "Observe and hear all these words which I command thee, that it may go well with thee, and with thy children after thee for ever, when thou doest that which is good and right in the sight of the LORD thy God. When the LORD thy God shall cut off the nations from before thee, whither thou goest to possess them, and thou succeedest them, and dwellest in their land; **take heed to thyself that thou be not snared by following them, after that they be destroyed from before thee; and that thou inquire not after their gods, saying, How did these nations serve their gods? even so will I do likewise. Thou shalt not do so unto the LORD thy God: for every abomination to the LORD, which he hateth, have they done unto their gods; for even their sons and their daughters they have burnt in the fire to their gods.** What thing soever I command you, observe to do it: thou shalt not add thereto, nor diminish from it" (Deut. 12:28-32, *KJV*).

The Eucharist—the Sacrifice of the Mass: Catholics claim that Jesus instituted the "Eucharist," the so-called "Sacrifice of the Mass" on the night of His last supper. That is not correct. Jesus instituted the Christian Passover. He never would have instituted a ceremony derived from rank heathen paganism! (See Alexander Hislop's comprehensive book, *The Two Babylons*, pp. 156-165, for a complete historical/theological dissertation, showing that the Roman Catholic "Eucharist—the Sacrifice of the Mass" was derived from heathen pagan religions, and not from Scripture. The reader may obtain those pages from www.biblicaltruthministries.org; or www.cbcg.org).

Moreover, Catholic doctrine purports that the priest conducting the Mass has the power to call Christ down from heaven and command Him to put the presence of his literal body and blood into the consecrated wafers and wine for the celebration of the Eucharist.

This is heresy. No man can command God to do any thing at any time. If that were so, then man would be God and God would be his slave.

In addition, it is an absolute impossibility for the literal flesh and blood of Jesus Christ to be present—anywhere. Regardless of the claims of the Roman Church and the prayers of the priests, Jesus Christ's flesh is not present in the communion wafer, nor is His blood present in the wine. His blood, shed on the Passover day in 30 AD, was shed **ONCE** for all time for all human sins (Heb. 9:28; 10:10, 12).

Finally, Jesus Christ, Who is seated at the right hand of God the Father in heaven above, is not composed of flesh and blood. His flesh was transformed into spirit when He was resurrected from the dead. As a spirit being, He lives eternally. In a vision, Jesus revealed His full-glorified spirit form to the apostle John. In the beginning of the book of Revelation John wrote:

"Behold, He is coming with the clouds, and every eye shall see Him, and those who pierced Him; and all the tribes of the earth shall wail because of Him. Even so, Amen. 'I am the Alpha and the Omega, *the* Beginning and *the* Ending,' says the Lord, 'Who is, and Who was, and Who *is* to come— the Almighty.' I, John, who *am* also your brother and joint partaker in the tribulation and in the kingdom and endurance of Jesus Christ, was on the island that *is* called Patmos because of the Word of God and the testimony of Jesus Christ. I was in *the* Spirit on the day of the Lord; and I heard a loud voice like a trumpet behind me, saying, 'I am the Alpha and the Omega, the First and the Last'; and, 'What you see, write in a book, and send *it* to the churches that *are* in Asia: to Ephesus, and to Smyrna, and to Pergamos, and to Thyatira, and to Sardis, and to Philadelphia, and to Laodicea.'

"And I turned to see the voice that spoke with me; and when I turned, I saw seven golden lampstands; and in *the* midst of the seven lamp-stands *one* like *the* Son of man, clothed in *a garment* reaching to the feet, and girded about the chest with a golden breastplate. And His head and hair *were* like white wool, white as snow; and His eyes *were* like a flame of fire; and His feet *were* like fine brass, as if *they* glowed in a furnace; and His voice *was* like *the* sound of many waters. And in His right hand He had seven stars, and a sharp two-edged sword went out of His mouth, and His countenance *was* as the sun shining in its *full* power. And when I saw Him, I fell at His feet as if dead; but He laid His right hand upon me, saying to me, 'Do not be afraid; I am the First and the Last, even the one Who is living; for I was dead, and behold, I am alive into the ages of eternity. Amen. And I have the keys of *the* grave and of death" (Rev. 1:7-18).

What Does it Mean to Eat Jesus' Flesh and Drink His Blood? Jesus instituted the New Covenant Christian Passover ceremony on the night of His last Passover. After instituting the footwashing ceremony by washing the apostles' feet, He then instituted the ceremony of eating the broken unleavened bread and of drinking the wine: "Jesus took the bread and blessed *it*; *then He* broke *it* and gave *it* to the disciples, and said, 'Take, eat; this is My body.' And He took the cup; and after giving thanks, He gave *it* to them, saying, 'All of you drink of it; for this is My blood, the *blood* of the New Covenant, which is poured out for many for *the* remission of sins' " (Matt. 26:26-28).

When Jesus instituted the first Christian Passover ceremony, the bread was *symbolic* of His flesh and the wine was *symbolic* of His blood. His literal flesh and blood were not present in the bread and wine at that initial Passover or in any subsequent Passover.

Jesus Himself explained what eating His flesh and drinking His blood meant: "Therefore, Jesus said to them, 'Truly, truly I say to you, unless you eat the flesh of the Son of man, and drink His blood, you do not have life in yourselves. The one who eats My flesh and drinks My blood has eternal life, and I will raise him up in the last day; for My flesh is truly food, and My blood is truly drink. The one who eats My flesh and drinks My blood is dwelling in Me, and I in him. **As the living Father has sent Me, and I live by the Father; so also the one who eats Me shall live by Me**" (John 6:53-57).

In Psalm 34, David prophesied of this when He wrote: "**O taste and see that the LORD is good: blessed is the man that trusteth in him**" (verse 8). The action of "trusting" in the Lord is symbolized by "tasting" the Lord and tasting (or eating) is "living by" the Lord, as Jesus declared. In the same way that David did not mean that one was to literally taste or eat the Lord, Jesus did not mean that one was to literally eat His flesh and drink His blood transubstantiated in the bread and wine. Therefore, when one eats the bread and drinks the wine of the Christian Passover service, he or she is pledging before God the Father that they will live by Jesus Christ—by His every word—as God manifested in the flesh.

We must live by Jesus Christ, for He and He alone is our personal Savior.

APPENDIX E

Scourging and Crucifixion
In Roman Tradition

(William D. Edwards, MD, Department of Pathology, Mayo Clinic, Rochester, MN; Wesley J. Gabel, MDiv, West Bethel United Methodist Church, Bethel, MN.; Floyd E Hosmer, MS, AMI, Dept of Medical Graphics, Mayo Clinic, Rochester, MN; Homestead United Methodist Church, Rochester, MN; review of article and excerpts from *On The Physical Death of Jesus Christ*, <u>JAMA</u>, March 21, 1986 – Vol 255, No. 11).

Scourging Practices

Flogging was a legal preliminary to every Roman execution, and only women and Roman senators or soldiers (except in cases of desertion) were exempt. The usual instrument was a short whip with several single or braided leather thongs of variable lengths, in which small iron balls or sharp pieces of sheep bones were tied at intervals. For scourging, the man was stripped of his clothing, and his hands were tied to an upright post. The back, buttocks, and legs were flogged either by two soldiers (lictors) or by one who alternated positions. The severity of the scourging depended on the disposition of the lictors and was intended to weaken the victim to a state just short of collapse or death. As the Roman soldiers repeatedly struck the victim's back with full force, the iron balls would cause deep contusions, and the leather thongs and sheep bones would cut into the skin and subcutaneous tissues. Then, as the flogging continued, the lacerations would tear into the underlying skeletal muscles and produce quivering ribbons of bleeding flesh. Pain and blood loss generally set the stage for circulatory shock. The extent of blood loss may well have determined how long the victim would survive on the cross. After the scourging, the soldiers often taunted their victim.

Crucifixion Practices

Although the Romans did not invent crucifixion, they perfected it as a form of torture and capital punishment that was designed to produce a slow death with maximum pain and suffering. It was one of the most disgraceful and cruel methods of execution and usually was reserved only for slaves, foreigners, revolutionaries, and the vilest of criminals. Roman law usually protected Roman citizens from crucifixion, except perhaps in the case of desertion by soldiers.

(The cross) was characterized by an upright post and a horizontal crossbar, and it had several variations. It was customary for the condemned man to carry his own cross from the flogging post to the site of crucifixion outside the city walls. He was usually naked, unless this was prohibited by local customs. Since the weight of the entire cross was probably well over 300 lb. (136 kg), only the crossbar was carried. The crossbar, weighing 75 to 125 lb. (34 to 57 kg), was placed across the nape of the victim's neck and balanced along both shoulders. Usually, the outstretched arms then were tied to the crossbar. The processional to the site of crucifixion was led by a complete Roman military guard, headed by a centurion. One of the soldiers carried a sign on which the condemned man's name and crime were displayed. Later, the sign would be attached to the top of the cross. The Roman guard would not leave the victim until they were sure of his death.

Outside the city walls was permanently located the heavy upright wooden post, on which the crossbar would be secured. To prolong the crucifixion process, a horizontal wooden block or plank, serving as a crude seat, often was attached midway down the post.

At the site of execution, by law, the victim was given a bitter drink of wine mixed with myrrh (gall) as a mild analgesic. The criminal was then thrown to the ground on his back, with his arms outstretched along the crossbar. The hands could be nailed or tied to the crossbar, but nailing apparently was preferred by the Romans. The nails were tapered iron spikes approximately 5 to 7 in (13 to 18 cm) long with a square shaft 3/8 in (1 cm) across. The nails commonly were driven through the wrists rather than the palms.

After both arms were fixed to the crossbar, the crossbar and the victim, together, were lifted onto the post. Next, the feet were fixed to the cross, either by nails or ropes. Nailing was the preferred Roman practice. Although the feet could be fixed to the sides of the post or to a wooden footrest, they usually were nailed directly to the front of the post. To accomplish this, flexion of the knees may have been quite prominent, and the bent legs may have been rotated laterally.

When the nailing was completed, the sign was attached to the cross, by nails or cords, just above the victim's head. The soldiers and the civilian crowd often taunted and jeered the condemned man, and the soldiers customarily divided up his clothes among themselves. The length of survival generally ranged from three or four hours to three or four days and appears to have been inversely related to the severity of the scourging. However, even if the scourging had been relatively mild, the Roman soldiers could hasten death by breaking the legs below the knees.

Not uncommonly, insects would light upon or burrow into the open wounds or the eyes, ears, and nose of the dying and helpless victim, and birds of prey would tear at these sites. Moreover, it was customary to leave the corpse on the cross to be devoured by predatory animals. However, by Roman law, the family of the condemned could take the body for burial, after obtaining permission from the Roman judge.

Since no one was intended to survive crucifixion, the body was not released to the family until the soldiers were sure that the victim was dead. By custom, one of the Roman guards would pierce the body with a sword or lance. Traditionally, this had been considered a spear wound to the heart through the right side of the chest—a fatal wound probably taught to most Roman soldiers. Moreover, the standard infantry spear, which was 5 to 6 ft (1.5 to 1.8 m) long could easily have reached the chest of a man crucified on the customary low cross.

Medical Aspects of Crucifixion

With a knowledge of both anatomy and ancient crucifixion practices, one may reconstruct the probable medical aspects of this form of slow execution. Each wound apparently was intended to produce intense agony, and the contributing causes of death were numerous.

The scourging prior to crucifixion served to weaken the condemned man and, if blood loss was considerable, to produce orthostatic hypotension and even hypovolemic shock. When the victim was thrown to the ground on his back, in preparation for transfixion of his hands, his scourging wounds most likely would become torn open again and contaminated with dirt. Furthermore, with each respiration, the painful scourging wounds would be scraped against the rough wood of the post. As a result, blood loss from the back probably would continue throughout the crucifixion ordeal.

It has been shown that the ligaments and bones of the wrist can support the weight of a body hanging from them, but the palms cannot. Accordingly, the iron spikes probably were driven between the radius and the carpals or between the two rows of carpal bones, either proximal to or through the strong bandlike flexor retinaculum and the various intercarpal ligaments. The driven nail would crush or sever the rather large sensorimotor median nerve. The stimulated nerve would produce excruciating bolts of fiery pain in both arms. Although the severed median nerve would result in paralysis of a portion of the hand, ischemic contractures and impalement of various ligaments by the iron spike might produce a clawlike grasp.

It is likely that the deep peroneal nerve and branches of the medial and lateral plantar nerves would have been injured by the nails driven through the feet. Although scourging may have resulted in considerable blood loss, crucifixion per se was a relatively bloodless procedure, since no major arteries, other than perhaps the deep plantar arch, pass through the favored anatomic sites of transfixion.

The major pathophysiologic effect of crucifixion, beyond the excruciating pain, was a marked interference with normal respiration, particularly exhalation. The weight of the body, pulling down on the outstretched arms and shoulders, would tend to fix the intercostal muscles in an inhalation state and thereby hinder passive exhalation. Accordingly, exhalation was primarily diaphragmatic, and breathing was shallow. It is likely that this form of respiration would not suffice and that hypercarbia would soon result. The onset of muscle cramps or tetanic contractions, due to fatigue and hypercarbia, would hinder respiration even further.

Adequate exhalation required lifting the body by pushing up on the feet and by flexing the elbows and adducting the shoulders. However, this maneuver would place the entire weight of the body on the tarsals and would produce searing pain. Furthermore, flexion of the elbows would cause rotation of the wrists about the iron nails and cause fiery pain along the damaged median nerves. Lifting of the body would also painfully scrape the scourged back against the rough wooden post. Muscle cramps and paresthesias of the outstretched and uplifted arms would add to the discomfort. As a result, each respiratory effort would become agonizing and tiring and lead eventually to asphyxia.

The actual cause of death by crucifixion was multifactorial and varied somewhat with each case, but the two most prominent causes probably were hypovolemic shock and exhaustion asphyxia. Other possible contributing factors included dehydration, stress-induced arrhythmias, and congestive heart failure with the rapid accumulation of pericardial and perhaps pleural effusions. Death by crucifixion was, in every sense of the word, excruciating (Latin, excruciatus, or "out of the cross").

Scourging of Jesus

At the Praetorium, Jesus was severely whipped. (Although the severity of the scourging is not discussed in the four Gospel accounts, it is implied in one of the epistles (1 Peter 2:24). A detailed word study of the ancient Greek text for this verse indicates that the scourging of Jesus was particularly harsh.) It is not known whether the number of lashes was limited to 39, in accordance with Jewish law. The Roman soldiers, amused that this weakened man had claimed to be a king, began to mock him by placing a robe on his shoulders, a crown of thorns on his head, and a wooden staff as a scepter in his right hand. Next, they spat on Jesus and struck him on the head with the wooden staff. Moreover, when the soldiers tore the robe from Jesus' back, they probably reopened the scourging wounds.

The severe scourging, with its intense pain and appreciable blood loss, most probably left Jesus in a preshock state. Moreover, hematidrosis had rendered his skin particularly tender. The physical and mental abuse meted out by the Jews and the Romans, as well as the lack of food, water, and sleep, also contributed to his generally weakened state. Therefore, even before the actual crucifixion, Jesus' physical condition was at least serious and possibly critical.

Death of Jesus

Two aspects of Jesus' death have been the source of great controversy, namely, the nature of the wound in his side and the cause of his death after only several hours on the cross.

The gospel of John describes the piercing of Jesus' side and emphasizes the sudden flow of blood and water. Some authors have interpreted the flow of water to be ascites or urine, from an abdominal midline perforation of the bladder. However, the Greek word used by John (pleura) clearly denoted laterality and often implied the ribs. Therefore, it seems probable that the wound was in the thorax and well away from the abdominal midline.

Although the side of the wound was not designated by John, it traditionally has been depicted on the right side. Supporting this tradition is the fact that a large flow of blood would be more likely with a perforation of the distended and thin-walled right atrium or ventricle than the thick-walled and contracted left ventricle. Although the side of the wound may never be established with certainty, the right seems more probable than the left. The water probably represented serous pleural and pericardial fluid, and would have preceded the flow of blood and been smaller in volume than the blood. Perhaps in the setting of hypovolemia and impending acute heart failure, pleural and pericardial effusions may have developed and would have added to the volume of apparent water. The blood, in contrast, may have originated from the right atrium or the right ventricle or perhaps from a hemopericardium.

Jesus' death after only three to six hours on the cross surprised even Pontius Pilate. The fact that Jesus cried out in a loud voice and then bowed his head and died suggests the possibility of a catastrophic terminal event.

The actual cause of Jesus' death, like that of other crucified victims, may have been multifactorial and related primarily to hypovolemic shock, exhaustion asphyxia, and perhaps acute heart failure. A fatal cardiac arrhythmia may have accounted for the apparent catastrophic terminal event.

Clearly, the weight of historical and medical evidence indicates that Jesus was dead before the wound to his side was inflicted and supports the traditional view that the spear, thrust between his right ribs, probably perforated not only the right lung but also the pericardium and heart and thereby ensured his death.*

Editor's Note: From Scripture there is reason to believe that the spear that was thrust into Jesus side was the cause of His death. In the Gospel of John, the parallel account reads: "And so, when Jesus had received the vinegar, He said, 'It is finished.' And bowing His head, He yielded up *His* spirit. The Jews therefore, so that the bodies might not remain on the cross on the Sabbath, because it was a preparation *day* (for that Sabbath was a high day), requested of Pilate that their legs might be broken and *the bodies* be taken away. Then the soldiers came and broke the legs of the first *one*, and *the legs* of the other who was crucified with Him. But when they came to Jesus *and* saw that He was already dead, they did not break His legs; but **one of the soldiers had pierced His side with a spear**, and immediately blood and water had come out" (John 19:30-34).

The Greek verb ενυξεν *enuzen* is an aroist past tense verb of νυσσω *nusso*. Therefore, this aroist verb ενυξεν *enuzen* clearly indicates that the soldier had pierced Jesus' side with the spear in the immediate past, that is just prior to the time that the other soldier came to break Jesus' legs, but found that He was dead already.

When the missing part of Matthew 27:49 is restored, it is clear that the final cause of Jesus' death was from the spear that the soldier had thrust into His side. This full verse reads: "But the rest said, 'Let Him alone! Let us see if Elijah comes to save Him.' *Then another took a spear and thrust it into His side, and out came water and blood.*"

The latter half of this verse, which includes the words *"...Then another took a spear and out came water and blood,"* has been omitted from the King James Version. However, some ancient manuscripts contain this part of the verse. The latter part of the verse is also found in other manuscripts that are designated by letter (L, T, Z) and by number (33, 49, 892 and 1241). Older translations which contain the complete verse are the Moffatt translation and the Fenton translation. Newer translations generally footnote this portion of Matthew 27:49 rather than including it in the text. The weight of evidence indicates that the latter half of the verse is an authentic part of the Greek text and should be included in translations of the New Testament. The veracity of this portion of Matthew 27:49 is substantiated by the records in John 19:34 and 20:27.

BIBLIOGRAPHY

Apostolic Constitutions – Didascalia Apostolorum, Book V.

Arndt and Gingrich. *A Greek-English Lexicon of the New Testament.* The University of Chicago Press: Chicago, 1952.

Berry, George Ricker. *The Interlinear Greek-English New Testament.* Zondervan Publishing House: Grand Rapids, 1979.

Brenton, Sir Lancelot C. L. *The Septuagint With Apocrypha: Greek and English.* Hendrickson Publishers: Peabody, MA, 1999.

Bacchiocchi, Samuele. *From Sabbath to Sunday.* The Pontifical Gregorian University Press, Rome 1977

Chicago Tribune Magazine, 29 August 1993.

Coulter, Fred R. *The New Testament In Its Original Order—A Faithful Version With Commentary.* York Publishing: Hollister, CA 2004

_____, *A Harmony of the Gospels in Modern English—the Life of Jesus Christ,* third edition. York Publishing: Hollister, CA, 2001

_____, *The Christian Passover—What Does It Mean? When Should It Be Observed—the 14th or the 15th?,* second edition York Publishing: Hollister, CA 1999

Dio's Roman History. *Loeb edit. Book LVI: 29-30, Vol. 7.*

Edersheim, Alfred. *The Life and Times of Jesus the Messiah.* Hendrickson Publishers: Peabody, MA, 1989.

Finegan, Jack. *Handbook of Biblical Chronology.* Hendrickson Publishers: Peabody, MA, 1998.

Freedman, David Noel. *The Anchor Bible Dictionary.* Doubleday: New York, 1992.

Hobbs, Edwards. EHOBBS@wellesley.edu, 12 July 1997.

Josephus, Flavius. *The Life and Works of, Seven Dissertations.* Translated by William Whiston, A.M.

Kudler and Mickler. *Solar and Lunar Eclipses of the Ancient Near East.*

Lietzmann, Hans. *A History of the Early Church.* The World Publishing Company: Cleveland, 1963.

Liddell, Scott and Jones. A Greek-English Lexicon. *Clarendon Press: Oxford, 1996.*

Lust, Eynikel, Hauspie. A Greek-English Lexicon of the Septuagint. *Deutsche Bibelgesellschaft, 1996.*

Martin, Dr. Ernest L., Secrets of Golgotha. *Ask Publications*: Portland OR. 1991.

Morrow, S.T.D., Most Reverend Louis Laravoire, My Catholic Faith. Kenosha, WI, 1963

Robertson, A.T. Word Pictures in the New Testament. *Broadman & Holman Publishers: Nashville, TN, 2000.*

Seutonius. Ed. J. C. Rolfe. LCL, Vol. 1.

Tardo. *Sunday Facts and Sabbath Fiction.* Faithful Word Publications: Arabi, LA, 1992.

The Bible. A New Translation by James Moffatt. Harper & Brothers Company: New York, 1950.

The Holy Bible. The Revised Berkeley Version in Modern English. Zondervan Publishing House: Grand Rapids, 1969.

The Holy Scriptures. According to the Masoretic Text—A New Translation. The Jewish Publication Society of America: Philadelphia, 1917, 1955.

Unger's Bible Dictionary. *Moody Press: Chicago, 1963.*

Vincent's Word Studies in the New Testament. *Hendrickson Publishers: Peabody, MA, 1984.*